SINGAPORE-CHINA RELATIONS
50 YEARS

World Scientific Series on Singapore's 50 Years of Nation-Building

Published

50 Years of Social Issues in Singapore
  edited by David Chan

Our Lives to Live: Putting a Woman's Face to Change in Singapore
  edited by Kanwaljit Soin and Margaret Thomas

50 Years of Singapore–Europe Relations: Celebrating Singapore's Connections
  with Europe
  edited by Yeo Lay Hwee and Barnard Turner

50 Years of Singapore and the United Nations
  edited by Tommy Koh, Li Lin Chang and Joanna Koh

50 Years of Environment: Singapore's Journey Towards Environmental Sustainability
  edited by Tan Yong Soon

50 Years of the Chinese Community in Singapore
  edited by Pang Cheng Lian

Singapore–China Relations: 50 Years
  edited by Zheng Yongnian and Lye Liang Fook

For more information about this series, go to http://www.worldscientific.com/page/sg50

World Scientific Series on
Singapore's 50 Years of Nation-Building

SINGAPORE-CHINA RELATIONS

50 YEARS

Editors

Zheng Yongnian
Lye Liang Fook

East Asian Institute
National University of Singapore
Singapore

World Scientific

NEW JERSEY • LONDON • SINGAPORE • BEIJING • SHANGHAI • HONG KONG • TAIPEI • CHENNAI • TOKYO

Published by

World Scientific Publishing Co. Pte. Ltd.

5 Toh Tuck Link, Singapore 596224

USA office: 27 Warren Street, Suite 401-402, Hackensack, NJ 07601

UK office: 57 Shelton Street, Covent Garden, London WC2H 9HE

Library of Congress Cataloging-in-Publication Data
Singapore-China relations : 50 years / edited by Zheng Yongnian and Lye Liang Fook.
    pages cm. -- (World Scientific series on Singapore's 50 years of nation-building)
    Includes bibliographical references and index.
    ISBN 978-9814713559 (alk. paper) -- ISBN 978-9814713856 (alk. paper)
    1. Singapore--Relations--China. 2. China--Relations--Singapore. I. Zheng, Yongnian, editor. II. Lye, Liang
Fook, editor.
    DS610.47.C6S56 2015
    303.48'45957051--dc23
                                2015031783

British Library Cataloguing-in-Publication Data
A catalogue record for this book is available from the British Library.

In-house Editor: Dong Lixi

Typeset by Stallion Press
Email: enquiries@stallionpress.com

Printed in Singapore

Contents

About the Editors and Contributors
(Listing Based on Order of Chapters)

ZHENG Yongnian is professor and director of the East Asian Institute (EAI), National University of Singapore (NUS). He is the editor of the Series on Contemporary China (World Scientific Publishing) and editor of China Policy Series (Routledge). He is also the editor of *China: An International Journal* and the co-editor of *East Asian Policy*. He has studied both China's transformation and its external relations. His papers have appeared in journals such as *Comparative Political Studies, Political Science Quarterly, Third World Quarterly* and *China Quarterly*. He is the author of numerous books, including *The Chinese Communist Party as Organizational Emperor, Technological Empowerment, De Facto Federalism in China, Discovering Chinese Nationalism in China* and *Globalization and State Transformation in China*, and co-editor of dozens of books on China's domestic development and international relations including the latest volumes *China Entering the Xi Era* and *China and International Relations: The Chinese View and the Contribution of Wang Gungwu* (2010). Besides his research work, Professor Zheng has also been an academic activist. He served as a consultant to United Nations Development Programme on China's rural development and democracy. In addition, he has been a columnist for *Xinbao* (Hong Kong) and *Zaobao* (Singapore) for many years, writing numerous commentaries on China's domestic and international affairs. Professor Zheng received his BA and MA degrees from Beijing University and his PhD at Princeton University. He was a recipient of Social Science Research Council-MacArthur Foundation Fellowship (1995–1997) and John D and Catherine T MacArthur Foundation Fellowship (2003–2004).

He was professor and founding research director of the China Policy Institute, the University of Nottingham, United Kingdom (2005–2008). He can be reached at eaizyn@nus.edu.sg.

LYE Liang Fook is assistant director and research fellow at the EAI, NUS. His research interests cover China's central-local relations, political legitimacy, print media, China–ASEAN relations and China–Singapore relations. He was part of a team that completed a study on the Suzhou Industrial Park, a flagship project between China and Singapore. He has also conducted research into the Sino-Singapore Tianjin Eco-city project, the second flagship project between China and Singapore. His publications have appeared in Routledge, *International Relations of the Asia Pacific, Journal of Chinese Political Science*, Eastern Universities Press, Institute of Southeast Asian Studies Publishing, Konrad Adenauer Stiftung Publishing, World Scientific Publishing and *China: An International Journal*. Besides the academia, he manages the Singapore Secretariat of the Network of East Asian Think Tanks (NEAT) and the Network of ASEAN–China Think Tanks (NACT), two Track II bodies that aim to foster ASEAN plus Three cooperation and ASEAN plus One cooperation respectively. He can be reached at eaillf@nus.edu.sg.

John WONG is professorial fellow and academic adviser at the EAI, NUS. Previously, he was research director at EAI and director of the Institute of East Asian Political Economy. Professor Wong also taught at the University of Hong Kong, the National University of Singapore and Florida State University. He had held visiting appointments at Harvard University's Fairbank Centre, Yale's Economic Growth Centre, Oxford's St Antony's College and Stanford's economics department. He also held the ASEAN chair at the University of Toronto. Professor Wong has written and edited 35 books and published more than 500 articles and papers on China and other East Asian economies. He has also circulated over 90 policy-related reports to the Singapore government. He holds a PhD in economics from the University of London. He can be reached at eaiwongj@nus.edu.sg.

LIM Wen Xin is a research assistant at the EAI, NUS. She received her B Soc Science (Hons) in Economics and Chinese Studies from NUS in 2013. Her research interests include economic and political contexts in contemporary China, China's relations with Southeast Asian countries, China's media and East Asian popular culture. She can be reached at eailwx@nus.edu.sg.

Sarah Y TONG graduated from Beijing University of Aeronautics and Astronautics and worked at the Development Research Centre of China's State Council for several years. She obtained her PhD in Economics from the University of California at San Diego. She was assistant professor of the Department of Economics and research fellow of the EAI, both at the NUS. Currently, she is senior research fellow at the EAI. Her research interests concentrate on the recent development and transformation of Chinese economy, including development in trade and foreign investment, development of regions, financial sector reforms, the reforms of state-owned enterprises, and industrial policies and restructuring. Her work appeared in journals such as *Journal of International Economics, Global Economic Review, China: An International Journal, Review of Development Economics, China and the World Economy, Comparative Economic Studies* and *China Economic Review*. In addition to contributing chapters to numerous books on contemporary China, she edited and co-edited three books including *China and Global Economic Crisis* (2010), *Trade, Investment and Economic Integration* (2014) and *China's Evolving Industrial Policies and Economic Restructuring* (2014). She can be reached at eaityt@nus.edu.sg.

CHIANG Min-Hua is visiting research fellow at the EAI, NUS. Her research interests include economic development in East Asia, Asia-Pacific economic regionalism and power relations. She can be reached at eaicmh@nus.edu.sg.

CHEN Gang is research fellow at the EAI, NUS. He has published extensively on China's environmental and energy policies. He is the single author of *China's Climate Policy* (London: Routledge, 2012) and *Politics of China's Environmental Protection: Problems and Progress* (Singapore: World Scientific, 2009). He can be reached at eaicg@nus.edu.sg.

Singbridge leverages Singapore's successful developmental experience to invest in, develop and manage integrated cities and sustainable urban solutions internationally, particularly in China. The company adopts an integrated approach to master-planning and helps develop cities which can sustain economic growth within an ecological environment and support a vibrant and harmonious community. A member of the Ascendas-Singbridge Group, Singbridge projects include the Sino-Singapore Guangzhou Knowledge City; Raffles City Chongqing; the Singapore-Sichuan Hi-tech Innovation Park that integrates industry with urban living; and the Sino-Singapore Jilin Food Zone, a premium foot and mouth disease free zone with an integrated food safety system to ensure the integrity of food supply. Singbridge can be reached at contact@singbridge.sg.

ZHAO Litao is senior research fellow at the EAI, NUS. He obtained his PhD degree in sociology from Stanford University. His research interests include social stratification and mobility, sociology of education, organisational analysis and China's social policy. His research has appeared in *China Quarterly, Research in Social Stratification and Mobility, International Journal of Educational Development, Social Sciences in China, Built Environment, Journal of Social Policy* and so on. He has authored, co-authored, edited or co-edited six books, including *China's Social Development and Policy*, published by Routledge in 2013. He can be reached at eaizlt@nus.edu.sg.

LIM Tai Wei is research fellow adjunct at the EAI, NUS and senior lecturer at UniSIM (SIM University). He teaches history and his research interests are in East Asian History, focusing particularly on China and Japan. He graduated from Cornell University with a PhD and has worked in Singapore, the United States, Japan and Hong Kong. He can be reached at eailimt@nus.edu.sg.

HUANG Yanjie holds a Bachelor of Social Science with Honours (Economics) and a Master of Arts (History) from the NUS. As research assistant at the EAI from November 2008 to July 2015, his research interests covered China's contemporary social and economic development. He is currently pursuing a PhD in Modern Chinese History at the Colombia University in the City of New York. He can be reached at yh2798@columbia.edu.

ZHAO Lingmin holds a Master's Degree in International Relations from Jinan University. She is a columnist and senior journalist at Southern News Group. Her contributions on international issues and China's diplomacy have appeared in prominent Chinese newspapers like *Lianhe Zaobao* and *Xinjingbao* (New Beijing News). She used to be executive chief editor of *Nanfengchuang* (2004–2011) and a visiting research fellow at the EAI (2012–2013). She can be reached at smartzhaolm@126.com.

Acknowledgement

We would like to thank World Scientific Publishing for approaching the East Asian Institute (EAI) of Singapore to consider the idea of a book on Singapore–China relations to commemorate the 25th anniversary of bilateral ties as well as to celebrate Singapore's jubilee year in 2015. This publication is the outcome of this initiative and we look forward to many more fruitful years of collaboration with World Scientific.

Our thanks also extend to the contributors who have put in much time and effort to come up with the chapters in this book. All the chapters are written in the name of individual authors except for the one by Singbridge which is a contribution by a Singapore company with a strong presence in China. We are happy to collaborate with Singbridge as we believe that knowledge is best shared and can benefit a bigger audience when an open and cross-sectoral approach is adopted.

We further wish to convey our gratitude to our editors at EAI, Jessica Loon and Ho Wei Ling, who have gone through numerous versions of drafts to produce what you see in this publication. Without their conscientious and meticulous efforts, we would not have come this far.

Introduction

ZHENG Yongnian and LYE Liang Fook

When World Scientific Publishing approached us to write a book to commemorate the anniversary of relations between Singapore and China, we were initially daunted. It is no easy task as the book would have to be of considerable length to give a proper account of the breadth and depth of bilateral relations. We were also working within a tight time frame as the anniversary was in October.

After careful consideration, we decided to embark on this project as we are honoured to be able to play a role, albeit a small one, to commemorate the 25th anniversary of the establishment of diplomatic relations between Singapore and China in 2015 as well as the 50th anniversary of Singapore's independence. Instead of going for length, we decided that the best way to review the ties between the two countries is to identify several hallmarks or distinguishing features of this relationship. Although these features are captured or embedded in the various chapters that follow, we think it is important to highlight them here for readers to better appreciate the intricacies of bilateral ties and how far they have progressed from the initial years. We also understand that readers have a penchant to only selectively read those chapters that are of interest to them and it is our 'ardent' hope that the introduction would be one of them.

One of the most distinguishing features of the Singapore–China relationship is the distinct shift away from acrimony, or some may even argue confrontation, to cooperation in various fields and at many levels. In the 1950s and 1960s, and to some extent the 1970s, Singapore and China were at opposing ends of the political and ideological spectrum. At that time, China lent support to overseas communist elements that sought to disrupt the ability of the newly formed governments in Southeast Asia to govern including Singapore which won self-government in 1959 and independence in 1965. Singapore was also lambasted in the Chinese media for being 'running dogs of the American imperialists'.[1]

It is worth noting that even in those tumultuous years, Singapore, unlike other Southeast Asian countries such as Indonesia, the Philippines and Thailand, never completely broke off ties with China. It maintained trade ties with China and kept the Bank of China branch in Singapore open in spite of strong pressure from the federal government in Kuala Lumpur for it to be closed.[2]

Today, Singapore–China ties have moved well beyond the early tumultuous years. The two countries now enjoy cooperation in many fields such as economics, business, arts, culture, education and the environment. They also interact at many levels ranging from government-to-government ties involving top leaders, ministers and officials to people-to-people exchanges of tourists, students and cultural troupes. The breadth and depth of the relationship show how far ties have progressed beyond its initial years. Another indicator of how far relations have progressed is China's recognition of Singapore as an independent and sovereign nation. This may sound like common sense but it was not too long ago that there was a strong perception that Singapore was a Chinese society or Chinese nation on account of its large Chinese majority. Inherent in such a perception is the belief that Singapore ought to be able to empathise with China more or even assume a position that is supportive of China. Over the years, such a perception has waned considerably.

On its part, Singapore has always been careful not to be seen as a third China especially in the eyes of its immediate neighbours with large Malay majorities. Over time, Singapore's concern has lost its saliency due to the success of its immediate neighbours in nation-building and their interest in developing closer ties with China. A Singapore–China relationship that is based on mutual respect and mutual benefit irrespective of size or the ethnic make-up of the domestic population is a development that deserves to be welcomed and reinforced.

---

[1] Lee Kuan Yew, *From Third World to First: The Singapore Story, 1965–2000*, New York, HarperCollins Publishers Inc., 2000, p. 602.

[2] The Bank of China branch celebrated the 80th anniversary of its establishment in Singapore in April 2015 by organising an exhibition showcasing the history of the branch in Singapore. See "BOC Singapore Branch Launches 80th Anniversary Exhibition", *Xinhuanet*, 17 April 2015 available at <http://news.xinhuanet.com/english/2015-04/17/c_134160830.htm> (accessed 20 April 2015).

From the perspective of a small country, this affords Singapore room to manoeuvre vis-à-vis China as a major power. For a big country like China, such a relationship would reaffirm China's oft repeated claim that its development is peaceful and brings myriad opportunities for growth to other countries.

A second distinguishing feature of the Singapore–China relationship is the strong foundation laid by the former leaders of the two countries, in particular, the late Chinese paramount leader Deng Xiaoping and the late Lee Kuan Yew. In the 1970s, as individual ASEAN countries like Malaysia, the Philippines and Thailand started to normalise relations with China, Singapore also went ahead to improve relations with China though it decided to establish formal ties only after all the other ASEAN countries had done so.[3] Singapore made this decision, as mentioned earlier, to assuage the concerns of its immediate neighbours. Even then, a milestone in ties was reached when Lee embarked on his first visit to China as Singapore's prime minister in 1976, on the basis of the groundwork laid by Singapore's Foreign Minister S Rajaratnam in 1975.

Two years later, in 1978, Deng (then vice premier) visited Singapore where he was struck by the country's rapid development since independence in 1965.[4] Singapore leaders believed that what Deng saw in Singapore helped to strengthen his resolve to carry out China's open door and reform policy in the same year of 1978. Deng and Lee kept up the momentum of their relationship in the 1980s by meeting in 1980, 1985 and 1988. Deng was to further single out Singapore as a model for China's reforms during his Southern Tour in 1992. His remarks not only sparked 'Singapore fever' in China (with hundreds of Chinese delegations coming to Singapore in that year alone) but also provided the political window for the two countries to explore deeper cooperation. The result was the Suzhou Industrial Park where Lee played an instrumental role in conceiving and driving this project on the Singapore side.

The high regard China has for Lee can be gleaned from its response to his passing in March 2015. In his condolence message, Chinese President Xi Jinping stated that Lee 'is an old friend of the Chinese people, and a founder, pioneer and impeller of China–Singapore relations'. Xi further noted that Lee 'together with the older generations of the Chinese leadership, charted the course for China–Singapore relations, and made great contributions to the

---

[3] Malaysia was the first ASEAN country to normalise ties with China on 31 May 1974, followed by the Philippines on 9 June 1975 and Thailand on 1 July 1975. Indonesia, which had severed ties with China in April 1967, only normalised relations with China on 8 August 1990. Shortly after, Singapore followed suit to establish ties with China on 3 October 1990.

[4] Deng Xiaoping was the first senior Chinese leader to visit Singapore.

enhancement of friendship between the two peoples and the expansion of bilateral cooperation'.[5] Separately, Chinese Premier Li Keqiang noted that Lee's 'contributions to China–Singapore relations and China's reform and opening-up will surely be written into the annals of history'. Li added that China 'stands ready to work together with Singapore to carry forward the friendly tradition co-initiated and carefully nurtured by several generations of leaderships of the two countries and to continuously advance the China–Singapore friendly cooperative relations'.[6] The Chairman of the Standing Committee of China's National People's Congress Zhang Dejiang, China's Vice Premier Zhang Gaoli and China's Foreign Minister Wang Yi also sent separate condolence messages to their Singapore counterparts.[7]

A third distinguishing feature of the Singapore–China relationship is the presence of a number of high level institutional mechanisms to drive cooperation between the two countries. Foremost among them is the Joint Council for Bilateral Cooperation (JCBC) headed by Singapore's Deputy Prime Minister (DPM) Teo Chee Hean and China's Vice Premier Zhang Gaoli, who is also a member of the Political Bureau Standing Committee, China's highest decision-making body. The JCBC is the highest level institutional mechanism that oversees bilateral cooperation including the Suzhou Industrial Park and the Sino-Singapore Tianjin Eco-city, the two flagship projects of the two countries. DPM Teo co-chairs the leadership forum and the social management forum with his Chinese counterparts. Furthermore, Singapore has established cooperation platforms with seven other provinces in China at the ministerial or vice-ministerial levels.

---

[5] In the same message, President Xi Jinping noted that Lee was the 'founder of the Republic of Singapore and also a strategist and statesman widely respected by the international community'. See "President Xi Jinping Sends Message of Condolences to President Tony Tan Keng Yam of Singapore over the Death of Lee Kuan Yew", Chinese Embassy in Singapore website, 23 March 2015, available at <http://www.chinaembassy.org.sg/eng/sgsd/t1248466.htm> (accessed 20 April 2015).

[6] "Premier Li Keqiang Sends Message of Condolences to Prime Minister Lee Hsien Loong of Singapore over the Death of Lee Kuan Yew", Chinese Embassy in Singapore website, 23 March 2015, available at <http://www.chinaembassy.org.sg/eng/sgsd/t1248464.htm> (accessed 20 April 2015).

[7] Zhang Dejiang's Singapore counterpart is Speaker of Parliament Halimah Yacob. Vice Premier Zhang Gaoli's Singapore counterpart is Deputy Prime Minister Teo Chee Hean. Wang Yi's Singapore counterpart is Foreign Minister K Shanmugam.

It is extremely rare for a small country like Singapore to have several high-level institutional mechanisms with a big country like China. For Singapore, these mechanisms are invaluable to providing its leaders, ministers, officials and even businessmen with a number of avenues to interact and build ties with their Chinese counterparts. They also provide convenient platforms for both sides to meet regularly to review existing areas of cooperation and explore new ones.

These platforms indicate a Singapore that is constantly striving and determined to stay relevant to developments in China. As a small country, Singapore is unable to dictate the course of world events or set trends. The best that it can do is to anticipate future scenarios or trends and position itself accordingly. By staying alert, nimble and pro-active, Singapore can continue to ride on the opportunities that China's growth offers.

For China, these platforms are an indication that it sees value in continuing to adapt the Singapore experience. There is a view that the rapid socio-economic progress that China has made over the past decades has diminished the relevance of Singapore's experience to China. Without a doubt, the pace of China's progress has been breathtaking and unprecedented. Yet Singapore has not remained static all this while but has also made progress, albeit at a less rapid pace given its higher starting point. Despite this asymmetry in development, China continues to engage Singapore in areas such as leadership and governance, rule of law, community building, social and religious harmony, and environmental protection.

Among the newly industrialised economies (NIEs), Singapore's attractiveness to China has arguably increased. Comparatively, Hong's Kong's attractiveness to China as a model has declined significantly. In the past, when China was relatively unplugged from the world economy, Hong Kong was referred to as an important gateway for China to reach the world and for the world to come to China through Hong Kong. There is now very little of such talk. Moreover, the relationship between Hong Kong and China is experiencing a high state of flux and would require a period of adjustment before a new equilibrium is attained. As for Taiwan, China considers it a renegade province to be eventually brought under its full administration. It is also politically incorrect for China to refer to Taiwan as a model for development.

A fourth distinguishing feature of the Singapore–China relationship is the prevalence of key projects closely associated with the government of the two countries. Foremost among them are the two flagship projects, i.e. the Suzhou Industrial Park (that broke ground in 1994) and the Sino-Singapore Tianjin Eco-city (that broke ground in 2008). These two projects are government-to-government projects where the governments of the two countries are actively involved in reviewing their progress and coming up with initiatives and measures to drive these two projects forward. In fact, these two projects come under the purview of the JCBC. However, in terms of implementation, these two projects are commercially run to ensure their long-term sustainability.

There is another group of projects that is also closely associated with the two countries but where the private sector plays a leading role in their development. These include the Sino-Singapore Guangzhou Knowledge City, the Sino-Singapore Jilin Food Zone, the Singapore-Sichuan Hi-tech Innovation Park and the Singapore-Nanjing Eco Hi-tech Island. In these projects, though the private sector is the primary driver, the governments of the two countries play a supporting role by creating a conducive environment for the private sector to operate.

When Singapore's Prime Minister Lee Hsien Loong visited the Sino-Singapore Guangzhou Knowledge City in September 2014, he acknowledged the success of such a project model led by the private sector. In his response to the media, he reportedly said that the way both governments took a backseat through 'supporting the project with training, with advice, with guidance' has worked and that he was happy with the results.[8] In other words, such a model of development is a viable one that leverages on the resources and expertise of the private sector.

To be realistic, it is not possible for the governments of the two countries to be involved in too many flagship projects given their resource constraints. This is especially so for Singapore given its very limited resources. An equally important reason, if not more so, is the high political risks involved. In particular, by lending their names or reputation to these projects, the two governments have a primary and heavy responsibility to ensure that the projects are successful. A successful project will in turn have a positive impact on bilateral relations. Conversely, if they are not successful, the projects will produce an unintended opposite effect which can become a liability in the bilateral relationship.

It is therefore important for the governments of the two countries to weigh carefully and make a considered decision on embarking on additional government-to-government projects. Indeed, that is the approach taken by the two governments. Both sides have outlined important criteria for a possible third flagship project involving the two countries. Prime Minister Lee Hsien Loong reportedly said that the project must have a balance between policy and

---

[8] "PM: S'pore-Guangzhou Venture Raises Bar for Govt-to-Govt Projects", *The Straits Times*, 13 September 2014.

commercial goals. According to him, 'To start a third government-to-government project, there has to be a clear understanding of what the objective is, the economic policy and, at the same time, how can we package it so that it's a commercially cogent and viable project'. He added that '[t]hen also, (we) have to decide where we're going to do this. These are things we're studying and discussing with the Chinese side and we hope to come to a conclusion soon'.[9] Other important factors would include the project fitting in with China's priorities and be fully supported by the local authorities.[10]

When President Tony Tan met with his Chinese counterpart President Xi Jinping during his state visit to China in July 2015, the two leaders noted the 'good progress' made on the exploration of a third flagship project in western China. It was also noted that 'this will be a new, innovative and high-quality flagship project for bilateral cooperation, building on the success of the China–Singapore Suzhou Industrial Park and the Sino-Singapore Tianjin Eco-city'. President Xi further stressed that the third flagship project would be a 'priority and serve as a demonstrative project for China's "One Belt One Road" initiative, the Western Region Development and the Yangtze River Economic Belt strategies'.[11]

Both the flagship projects and those private-led ones that are closely associated with the two governments represent different viable models of economic cooperation. Together, they lend substance to bilateral ties. More specifically, they serve as concrete manifestations of how the strong relationship between the two countries has been translated into viable projects on the ground that produce mutual benefits for the two countries and their citizens involved.

These four distinguishing features make the Singapore–China relationship stand out from China's relations with other countries. While China's ties with other countries may share similarities with some of these features, very few of them share all of the features. The Singapore–China relationship is even more 'special' considering Singapore's small size and its large Chinese majority. These two factors, in a realpolitik sense, work against Singapore in the conduct of its relations with big countries especially one like China with a large Chinese majority. The fact that these two factors have not seriously hobbled

[9] "S'pore Seriously Considering Third China Park Project", *Business Times*, 12 September 2014.
[10] "PM Shares Views on 3rd Govt-to-Govt Project with China", *The Straits Times*, 16 September 2014.
[11] "President Tony Tan Keng Yam's State Visit to the People's Republic of China", MFA's Press Statement, 3 July 2015, available at <http://www.mfa.gov.sg/content/mfa/media_centre/press_room/pr/2015/20150511/press_201507030.html> (accessed 5 July 2015).

the development of a substantive relationship is a big achievement. One may even argue that Singapore's early stress and China's recognition (at least at the official level) that Singapore is not a Chinese society or Chinese nation has laid a solid and 'healthy' foundation for relations to grow and prosper.

We hope that this book can add to the many important contributions by numerous other authors and publications that have dwelt on Singapore–China relations or particular aspects of this relationship. They are too numerous and we can only attempt to provide a brief overview here. Prominent themes in the literature are on the political and security dimensions of the relationship in addition to their economic/commercial ties. One of the more recent publications focuses on economic relations, covering topics such as the political economy of Singapore's unique relations with China,[12] investment and trade, the Suzhou Industrial Park, the Sino-Singapore Tianjin Eco-city, tourism and educational collaboration.[13] The book attempts to show that even in the specific area of economic ties, the relationship has become much more comprehensive and intertwined, a development that has brought about immense benefit to the two countries.

Since 2012, the College of ASEAN Studies at the Guangxi University for Nationalities (in Guangxi province that hosts the annual China–ASEAN Expo) has published, on an annual basis, a Yellow Book (*huangpishu*) on developments in each of the 10 ASEAN countries and the state of China's relations with each of these countries. In the 2014 issue, there is a chapter on China–Singapore relations that emphasises the need for an 'upgraded version' of ties in view of the existing broad-based relationship.[14] Such a theme echoes the official position of the Chinese government which has called for China and Singapore to work together to upgrade their relations.[15]

---

[12] The word 'unique' refers to the role played by the leaders of the two countries in laying the foundation for ties to grow. In particular, Deng Xiaoping referred to Singapore in his Southern Tour in 1992 that provided the opening for the two countries to broaden and deepen their relationship further. 'Unique' also refers to the high-level JCBC that oversees all aspects of cooperation between the two countries.

[13] Saw Swee-Hock and John Wong (eds.), *Advancing Singapore–China Economic Relations*, Singapore, Institute of Southeast Asian Studies Publishing, 2014.

[14] Gao Xianju, "Zhongguo yu Xinjiapo: Dazao Guanxi 'Shengjiban' (China and Singapore: Forge an Upgraded Version of Relations)" in *Annual Report of ASEAN's Development*, Beijing, Shehui wenxian chubanshe, 2014.

[15] In May 2013, when China's Foreign Minister Wang Yi visited Singapore and called on Prime Minister Lee Hsien Loong, Wang said that the Chinese government is willing to work with the Singapore government to forge an 'upgraded version' of China–Singapore relations. See

Other academics have looked at Deng Xiaoping's ASEAN tour of 1978 (when he visited Thailand, Malaysia and Singapore),[16] the challenges and strategies of doing business in China,[17] the contributions of chambers of commerce and associations,[18] ancestral ties,[19] hedging policy,[20] and specific flagship projects like the Suzhou Industrial Park[21] and Sino-Singapore Tianjin Eco-city.[22] In several instances, Singapore–China relations are examined from the perspective of China's relations with ASEAN as a whole and in the economic, political and security dimensions.[23] At times, the authors have examined softer aspects of the relationship covering issues like *guanxi* (relationship based on

---

"Singapore's Prime Minister Lee Hsien Loong Meets with Wang Yi", China's Foreign Ministry website, 8 May 2013, available at <http://www.fmprc.gov.cn/ce/cenp/eng/zgwj/t1038491.htm> (accessed 22 April 2015).

[16] Lee Lai To, "Deng Xiaoping's ASEAN Tour: A Perspective on Sino-Southeast Asian Relations", *Contemporary Southeast Asia*, vol. 3, no. 1, June 1981, pp. 58–75.

[17] Eric W K Tsang, "Internationalisation as a Learning Process: Singapore MNCs in China", *The Academy of Management Executive*, vol. 13, no. 1, *Global Competitiveness*, Part II, February 1999, pp. 91–101; Patrick Lambe and Edgar Tan, *Challenges of Doing Business in China: Case Studies for Singapore SMEs*, Singapore, Singapore Institute of Management, 2003; Heidi Dahles, "Venturing across Borders: Investment Strategies of Singapore–Chinese Entrepreneurs in Mainland China", *Asian Journal of Social Science*, vol. 32, no. 1, 2004, pp. 19–41; and Sree Kumar, Sharon Siddique and Yuwa Hedrick-Wong, *Mind the Gaps: Singapore Business in China*, Singapore: Institute of Southeast Asian Studies Publications, 2005.

[18] Sikko Visscher, *The Business of Politics and Ethnicity: A History of the Singapore Chinese Chamber of Commerce and Industry*, Singapore: National University of Singapore Press, 2007.

[19] Yow Cheun Hoe, "Weakening Ties with the Ancestral Homeland in China: The Case Studies of Contemporary Singapore and Malaysian Chinese", *Modern Asian Studies*, vol. 39, no. 3, July 2005, pp. 559–597.

[20] Kuik Cheng-Chwee, "The Essence of Hedging: Malaysia and Singapore's Response to a Rising China", *Contemporary Southeast Asia*, vol. 30, no. 2, August 2008, pp. 159–185.

[21] Pan Yungong, Zhou Zhifang and Zhao Dasheng, *Jiejian yu shijian: Suzhou gongye yuanqu jiejian Xinjiapo jingyan xutan* (*Adaptation and Practices: Further Exploring Singapore Experience Transfer in SIP*), Shanghai, Shanghai shehui kexue chubanshe, 2000; Wang Pien and Andrew C. Inkpen, "China–Singapore Industrial Park", Research Paper Series, Singapore, Faculty of Business Administration, 2002; Alexius A. Pereira, *State Collaboration and Development Strategies in China: the Case of the China–Singapore Suzhou Industrial Park, 1992–2002*, New York, RoutledgeCurzon, 2003.

[22] Wilhelm Hofmeister, Patrick Rueppel and Lye Liang Fook (eds), *Eco-cities: Sharing European and Asian Best Practices and Experiences*, Singapore, Select Books Pte Ltd, 2014.

[23] Denny Roy, "Southeast Asia and China: Balancing or Bandwagoning?", *Contemporary Southeast Asia*, vol. 27, no. 2, August 2005, pp. 305–322; Shamsul Khaha and Lei Yub, "Evolving China-ASEAN Relations and CAFTA: Chinese Perspectives on China's Initiatives in

networking)[24] and religion. There was an interesting study that looked at the visits made by Venerable Hong Choon (who was president of the Singapore Buddhist Federation and abbot of Kong Meng San Phor Kark See) to China between 1982 and 1990, before diplomatic ties were established. The study argues that through his travels to China, Venerable Hong Choon played the role of an 'unofficial and non-political diplomat', using religion as an instrument to bridge and foster friendly ties between the two countries.[25]

At the governmental level, the late Lee Kuan Yew had shared his invaluable insights and perspectives on Singapore–China relations and on China in a number of publications.[26] Equally important was Deng Xiaoping's 1992 Southern Tour speech when he said that 'Guangdong should catch up with Asia's four dragons (Hong Kong, Singapore, South Korea and Taiwan) in 20 years, not only in economics but also in social order and social climate. China should do better than these countries in these matters'.[27] He added that 'Singapore enjoys good social order. They govern the place with discipline. We should tap their experience and learn how to manage better than them (新加坡的社会秩序算是好的,他们管得严,我们应该借鉴他们的经验,而且比他们管得更好)'.[28] As mentioned earlier, Deng's speech set the stage for relations to move to a higher plane. Other scholars have highlighted the high regard Lee Kuan Yew and Deng Xiaoping had of each other that translated into significantly improved relations between the two countries.[29] In addition to these two leaders, there are publications on the contributions made by former

---

Relation to ASEAN Plus 1", *European Journal of East Asian Studies*, vol. 12, no. 1, 2013, pp. 81–107.

[24] Bian Yanjie and Soon Ang, "Guanxi Networks and Job Mobility in China and Singapore", *Social Forces*, vol. 75, no. 3, March 1997, pp. 981–1005.

[25] Jack Meng Tat Chia, "Buddhism in Singapore–China Relations: Venerable Hong Choon and his Visits, 1982-1990", *The China Quarterly*, no. 196, December 2008, pp. 864–883.

[26] Lee Kuan Yew, *From Third World to First: The Singapore Story, 1965–2000*, pp. 573–660; Lee Kuan Yew, *One Man's View of the World*, Singapore, Straits Times Press Pte Ltd, 2013, pp. 12–67; *Lee Kuan Yew: The Grand Master's Insights on China, the United States, and the World*, Interviews and Selections by Graham Allison and Robert D. Blackwell, with Ali Wyne, Cambridge, Massachusetts, The MIT Press, 2013, pp. 1–18 and pp. 37–50.

[27] Lee Kuan Yew, *From Third World to First: The Singapore Story, 1965–2000*, p. 714.

[28] Shenzhen Propaganda Department (ed.), *Deng Xiaoping yu Shenzhen: 1992 Chun* (Deng Xiaoping and Shenzhen: Spring 1992), Shenzhen, Haitian chubanshe, 1992, p. 9.

[29] Ezra F Vogel, *Deng Xiaoping and the Transformation of China*, Cambridge, Massachusetts: The Belknap Press of Harvard University Press, 2011, pp. 287–291.

Singapore Foreign Minister S Rajaratnam and former Deputy Prime Minister Goh Keng Swee who was economic adviser to China's State Council from 1985 to 1990.[30]

Furthermore, the National Archives of Singapore, with the support of the Ministry of Information, Communications and the Arts (today known as the Ministry of Communications and Information), has come up with a pictorial publication on the milestones in bilateral ties over a 45-year period from 1965 to 2010. In the initial years after Singapore's independence, the pictorial draws readers' attention to the fact that before diplomatic relations were established in October 1990, the two countries had unofficial contacts through sports exchanges. Most notably, China's table tennis team visited Singapore in 1972[31] and played exhibition matches at the Gay World Stadium.[32] This was followed by visits of China's national badminton team and national football team in the same year of 1974.[33] Towards the later part of the 1970s, with the end of the Cultural Revolution in China, the Singapore National Theatre Trust arranged for a number of cultural troupes from China to perform in Singapore.[34] As this pictorial was also intended to

---

[30] Kwa Chong Guan, *S Rajaratnam on Singapore: From Ideas to Reality*, Singapore, World Scientific Publishing, 2006 and Zheng Yongnian and John Wong, *Goh Keng Swee on China: Selected Essays*, Singapore, World Scientific Publishing, 2013.

[31] It was not just a one-way street. On its part, the Singapore Table Tennis Association (established in 1931) sent a 14-member team to participate in the First Afro-Asian Table Tennis Invitational Tournament in Beijing in November 1971. This inaugural event marked Beijing's return to the world table tennis scene after the hiatus brought about by the Cultural Revolution that began in 1966.

[32] Gay World Stadium, one of three amusement parks built in Singapore before World War II (established in 1936), was a popular and affordable entertainment site for Singaporeans. The other two were New World and Great World City. It had cabarets, operas, movies, gaming, stunt performances, shopping outlets and sports matches. For more details, please see "Gay World (Happy World)", Singapore's National Library Board, available at <http://eresources. nlb.gov.sg/infopedia/articles/SIP_1044_2006-06-01.html> (accessed 21 April 2015).

[33] "Milestones of the China–Singapore Connection: Friendship and Cooperation, Growing from Strength to Strength, 1965–2010", Pictorial Publication by the National Archives of Singapore, pp. 9–10. The publication complements an exhibition on 'Milestones of the China–Singapore Connection: Friendship and Cooperation, Growing from Strength to Strength' that was jointly organised by the National Archives of Singapore and State Archives Administration of China to mark the 20th anniversary of diplomatic ties between the two countries in 2010.

[34] "Milestones of the China–Singapore Connection: Friendship and Cooperation, Growing from Strength to Strength, 1965–2010", pp. 23–25.

mark the 20th anniversary of diplomatic relations, there was much coverage on the visit by Chinese Vice President Xi Jinping to Singapore in November 2010.[35] Among the highlights of the visit was Vice President Xi's unveiling of Deng Xiaoping's marker at the Asian Civilisation Museum Green (with Minister Mentor Lee Kuan Yew) and his presiding over the ground breaking of the China Cultural Centre at Queen Street (with Senior Minister Goh Chok Tong).[36]

At the community or semi-official level, the Singa Sino Friendship Association of Singapore and China–Singapore Friendship Association of China came up with a commemorative souvenir in 2000 on the occasion of the 10th anniversary of diplomatic relations. The commemorative souvenir is a collection of short articles written by ambassadors from Singapore and China as well as academics, businessmen, leaders of associations and cultural and sports institutions who were involved in one way or another in the promotion of ties between the two countries.[37] At the corporate levels, there were publications on specific topics like Singaporean enterprises in China,[38] Chinese enterprises in Singapore[39] and the Suzhou Industrial Park (SIP).[40] On the SIP, the Chinese authorities in Suzhou had also published a three-part series detailing the developments of the SIP over an 11-year period from 1994 to 2005. The first part focuses on the basic attributes of Suzhou and the conception of the SIP. The second part examines the process of building the SIP while the third

---

[35] Chinese Vice President Xi Jinping's visit to Singapore in November 2010 was to commemorate the 20th anniversary of diplomatic relations.

[36] "Milestones of the China–Singapore Connection: Friendship and Cooperation, Growing from Strength to Strength, 1965–2010", pp. 141–152. Among other things, Deng Xiaoping's marker highlights Deng's role in promoting China–Singapore relations.

[37] "Xin Zhong jianjiao shizhounian (Singapore China 10th Anniversary of Diplomatic Relations)", jointly published by Singa Singapore Friendship Association of Singapore and China–Singapore Friendship Association of China, Singapore: World Scientific Publishing Co. Pte Ltd, 2000.

[38] *Touzi wanli xing: Xinjiapo danlian gongsi zai Zhongguo* (*Singapore Enterprises: 14 Success Stories on Temasek-linked Companies in China*), jointly published by International Enterprise Singapore, *Lianhe Zaobao* and Lingzhi Media Pte Ltd, 2004.

[39] Weng Donghui, *Zhongzi qiye zai Xinjiapo de chenggong jingyan* (Chinese enterprises successful experience in Singapore), Singapore: Candidcreation, 2004.

[40] *Bold Vision, Vibrant Chords: Sino-Singapore Suzhou Industrial Park*, published in Singapore by Keppel Corporation Ltd, 2009.

part highlights the economic and non-economic achievements of the SIP till end 2005.[41] The publication of such a detailed chronicle on the SIP shows the commitment of the Suzhou authorities to the success of the SIP.

On the basis of the brief literature review, this book seeks to provide readers with not only an overview of Singapore–China relations but also an in-depth look at specific aspects of the relationship. Before delving into each of the chapter, an explanation of the term '50 Years' in the title of this book is in order.

The '50 Years' refers to the period from Singapore's independence in 1965 to 2015. The point we would like to highlight is that exchanges between the two countries did not just start from 1990 when diplomatic ties were established but extend way back to the period before Singapore's independence in 1965 or even before the People's Republic of China was founded in 1949. In this sense, the '50 Years' should not be literally taken as a precise time period but should be regarded as a reminder to readers to think back in terms of a longer time frame. At the same time, the term '50 Years' is broad enough to include the 25th anniversary of diplomatic relations from 1990 to 2015 which is also what this book seeks to commemorate. This book thus offers a timely review of the state of relations. It builds on the work of previous publications, in particular, those that were done to commemorate the 10th and 20th anniversaries of diplomatic relations as mentioned earlier. The '50 years' also refers to the 50th anniversary of Singapore's independence.

Following on from this introduction, John Wong and Lye Liang Fook provide an overview of relations between Singapore and China in Chapter 1. They observe that way before the founding of the People's Republic of China, China's relations with Southeast Asia, traditionally called *Nanyang* or South Sea (which Singapore is a part of) were extensive and deep-rooted on account of history, geography and migration. Today, the two countries interact in many fields and at many levels. They highlight the people-to-people exchanges such as China's active involvement in Singapore's annual Chingay Parade, River Hongbao and Huayi festival. Singapore is also among the handful of countries in the world to receive a pair of pandas from China. It has also embarked on nascent military

---

[41] Suzhou gongye yuanqu difang zhi bianzuan weiyuan huibian (Suzhou Industrial Park Compilation Committee ed.), Suzhou gongye yuanqu zhi, 1994–2005, I, II and III (Local Chronicles of Suzhou Industrial Park, 1994–2005, Parts I, II and III), Nanjing, Jiangsu renmin chubanshe, 2012.

cooperation with China. Furthermore, there is the high level JCBC and other bilateral mechanisms to oversee cooperation between the two countries. The authors are of the view that such mechanisms are likely to become more important with the passing of the older generation of leaders on both sides.

In Chapter 2, Zheng Yongnian and Lim Wen Xin examine the instrumental role Lee Kuan Yew played in Singapore–China relations. They argue that Lee succeeded in building a special relationship with China because he and Singapore had been an important part of China's dual transformation, i.e. from being one of the poorest economies to becoming the world's No. 2 and from being isolated to become plugged into the international community. Lee was also China's interlocutor to the world, by helping the West and China understand each other better. They note that Lee had engaged China before Deng rose to power in China in 1978, though real change in bilateral ties only took place after Deng assumed power. The two got along well together as they shared a high level of mutual respect and trust. They were also on the same plane in that both had a strong mission in developing their respective countries and were driven by pragmatism and their country's national interest. In the post-Deng era, Singapore has built on the foundations laid by Deng and Lee through continuously positioning itself to be relevant to China's growth.

On the economic front, Sarah Tong in Chapter 3 observes that bilateral trade between Singapore and China has displayed resilience during difficult times and grown strongly since relations were normalised. When ideological differences and Cold War hostility were prevalent from 1965 to the late 1970s, two-way trading activities continued unabated, albeit at a low level. From 1990 to 2001, total bilateral trade grew by 14% a year on average, which was slightly lower than the period from 1978 to 1990. This was in part due to the impact of the Asian financial crisis in 1997 and 1998. With China's ascension to the World Trade Organisation in 2001 and the implementation of the China-ASEAN Free Trade Agreement in 2005, total bilateral trade surged 26% a year on average from 2001 to 2007. Since 2008, the growth in total bilateral trade has showed down. The nature of Singapore's exports to and imports from China has also changed markedly over the years reflecting changes in their domestic economic structure. Apart from trade in goods, the two countries have enhanced their trade in services. Capital flows between the two countries have also expanded rapidly. Since 1997, China has become Singapore's largest investment destination.

In Chapter 4, Chiang Min-Hua observes the rapid rise of China as a source market for tourists to Singapore. By 2003, 13 years after diplomatic ties were established, China rose to become Singapore's second largest tourism source market after Indonesia. This development has boosted the development of Singapore's tourism sector due to the large size of Chinese tourists and their propensity to spend a bigger proportion of their expenditure on shopping. Chiang notes that even though the number of Singapore's tourists to China at close to one million in 2013 was small as a proportion of total visitors to China, this figure is higher than that of other ASEAN countries with a much bigger population. Furthermore, Singapore is one of the most important foreign investors in China and a large proportion of this investment goes into the service sector of which tourism is an integral part of. In addition, several policy initiatives such as the China–Singapore Free Trade Agreement have helped to promote investment in tourism services between the two countries.

In Chapter 5, Lye Liang Fook argues that the SIP has laid a good foundation for the development of bilateral ties. To support his argument, he examines four key aspects: (i) the highly unusual origin of the SIP where the seeds of early cooperation could be traced to Deng Xiaoping's visit to Singapore in 1978; (ii) the defining feature of the SIP which involved the transfer of Singapore's economic management and public administration experience. This experience was then known as Singapore's 'software' which was essentially embodied in its laws, rules, regulations, together with its work processes and systems and, most important of all, in the values and problem-solving attitudes of its experienced officers. Today, the success of the SIP can be attributed to the foundation laid in the early years in addition to the significant contributions by the Chinese side; (iii) the continued success of the SIP based on economic and non-economic indicators. Today, what sets the SIP apart from other industrial parks is this software (tied to the Singapore brand name) that it can offer to investors and residents alike; and, (iv) the setting up of an overarching bilateral mechanism to initially oversee the development of the SIP but which has since been upgraded to cover other aspects of cooperation.

On the basis of the SIP, Singapore and China have developed a second flagship project. In Chapter 6, Chen Gang regards the Sino-Singapore Tianjin Eco-city as the most well-known and successful among the numerous eco-city projects in China. The Eco-city marries Singapore's expertise and experience in urban green living with China's pressing need to manage the growth of its cities in a sustainable manner. It is positioned not as a place for the well-heeled and influential but as a location where residents from all walks of life can live, work and play. A key challenge in making the Eco-city stand out from other eco-projects is to have the right 'software' in place such as the mind-set of officials in terms of their values and problem-solving attitudes. Another challenge is to develop the right 'heartware'. This refers to the eco-consciousness of residents living in the Eco-city such as whether they are green at heart, whether they actively pursue practices like recycling and whether they actively protect the environment. In other words, residents themselves have to become champions of green living for the Eco-city to be a success.

In Chapter 7, Singbridge shares a private-sector perspective on what it has been doing in two key projects among several of its projects in China. The two projects are the Sino-Singapore Guangzhou Knowledge City (SSGKC) and Sino-Singapore Jilin Food Zone (SSJFZ). Unlike the SIP and the Tianjin Eco-city which are government-to-government projects, SSGKC and SSJFZ are driven by the private sector with strong government support. They represent a different but equally important model of cooperation between Singapore and China. They are a further demonstration of Singapore's continuing efforts to stay relevant to China's growth and to derive mutual benefits by collaborating in areas of mutual interest. While there are challenges in the course of implementation, they ought to be seen as affording opportunities for both the Singapore and Chinese parties to work together to build even stronger ties. In many ways, the success of the two projects will help to strengthen the presence of Singaporean companies in China and this will in turn reinforce the bilateral relationship.

Zhao Litao in Chapter 8 traces the development of educational exchanges from merely providing language training to much broader and deeper levels of collaboration involving primary, secondary and tertiary levels. Although Singapore offered language training to China before diplomatic ties were established, the pace of collaboration was only stepped up with the signing of a memorandum of understanding in 1999 that institutionalised educational exchanges. According to one study, Chinese students make up nearly 56% of international students in Singapore. Apart from student exchange programmes, there are also leadership training programmes between the two countries. The Head of China's Central Organisation Department Li Yuanchao once remarked in 2010 that among the destinations China sends its leading officials for training, Singapore is the 'top choice'. The growing educational links between Singapore and China are driven by factors such as China's growing importance, the language and cultural affinity between the two countries, and their broadening and deepening political and economic ties.

On the cultural side, Lim Tai Wei looks at the 'soft' contributions made by the Chinese community in Singapore in Chapter 9. The Chinese community refers in general to Chinese Singaporeans whose forefathers were migrants. Lim gives an overview of successive waves of Chinese migrants into Singapore, with each arrival adding a layer of richness and complexity to the make-up of the local Chinese community, much like an interwoven piece of fabric that is difficult to separate. He highlights the contributions made by the Chinese community in the five main areas of education, economy, arts and culture, after-life traditions and food culture (with relevant photographs that provide an attractive visual appeal). On the anti-migrant feelings palpable in recent years, he is of the view that such feelings are held by a minority. The mainstream view remains that migrants have made important contributions to Singapore and are an integral part of Singapore's social fabric.

How Singapore is portrayed in the official and popular media in China is the focus of Chapter 10 by Huang Yanjie and Zhao Lingmin. They note a dichotomy in how these two types of media look at Singapore. The official media tends to focus on aspects of Singapore which are of policy interest to the Chinese government such as its political system, clean government, public housing and social management. In these areas, the views of the official media have been relatively stable. Even during hiccups in relations such as Deputy Prime Minister Lee Hsien Loong's visit to Taiwan in July 2004, while most Chinese printed media were critical of the visit, the criticisms were mild and restrained compared to the harsh views of netizens in online media. In contrast, the popular media tend to show greater variation in their portrayal of Singapore. In the 1980s and early 1990s, there was a perception of Singapore as a distant cultural relative, a romanticised image shaped by Singapore TV dramas, movies and songs that were shown in China. Since then, a more realistic view of Singapore has prevailed due to the opening up of more avenues of interaction and information between the two countries. For one, there are more accounts of Singapore from Chinese travellers and migrants.

Last but not least, in Chapter 11, John Wong and Lim Tai Wei look at Chinese studies in Singapore at two levels. At one level, it can be viewed in terms of its evolution as an academic subject in Singapore. Here, the authors note that Chinese studies was shaped by factors such as the domestic political considerations in Singapore in its earlier years that did not result in a conducive intellectual climate for scholars to engage in Chinese studies; the bilingual policy and de-sinification of Singapore society; and the different quality of immigrant stock that came to Singapore compared to those that went to Hong Kong and Taiwan. At the second level, Chinese studies can be looked at as a think tank research subject in Singapore. Here, the authors provide insights into the evolution of the Institute of East Asian Philosophy, to the Institute of East Asian Political Economy and finally to the present name of East Asian Institute. With each name change, the focus of the institute shifted from the early days of 'China watching' to the present state of watching China and studying China.

Chapter 1

China–Singapore Relations: Looking Back and Looking Forward

JOHN Wong and LYE Liang Fook

Well before formal ties were established, Singapore and China already had extensive interactions as part of China's relations with Southeast Asia. During the height of Beijing's difficult relations with Southeast Asia in the 1950s and 1960s, Singapore maintained its economic ties with China. Today, the two countries enjoy a broad-based, substantive and rapidly expanding relationship. Chinese leader Deng Xiaoping's mention of Singapore in 1992 as a reference for China's reform laid the basis for further cooperation. Apart from the rapport among the leaders, institutional mechanisms like the Joint Council for Bilateral Cooperation have become more important in driving bilateral ties.

Pragmatism and pragmatism

China's relations with Southeast Asia, traditionally called *Nanyang* ("South Sea") by the Chinese, are extensive and deep-rooted on account of history, geography and migration. After the formation of the People's Republic of China (PRC) in 1949, the relations assumed new dimensions, with complex ideological and geo-political forces coming into play, giving rise to more than two decades of Cold War relations. It was not till the early 1970s, with the advent of international détente, that individual Southeast Asian countries began to normalise relations with China.

As part of Southeast Asia and the post-World War II order established by the United States, Singapore is not free from the influence of geostrategic political and economic forces that have generally shaped China's overall relations with the Southeast Asian region. When China's relations with some Southeast Asian countries became very tense during the Cold War period, it also adversely affected Singapore's relations with China.

On the other hand, Singapore's relations with China have also been guided by a high sense of pragmatism. In separating trade from politics, pragmatism had enabled China–Singapore relations to survive the Cold War period. In the 1950s and 1960s when China's trade with Indonesia, the Philippines and Thailand was either seriously disrupted or banned altogether, China's trade with Singapore continued uninterrupted.[1] In fact, for four decades from 1950 to 1990, China–Singapore trade was conducted in the absence of a formal diplomatic framework.

After 1979, with the start of economic reform and open door policy under the leadership of Chinese leader Deng Xiaoping, China's approach to foreign relations was also characterised by pragmatism. This led to further growth of the two-way relations between China and Southeast Asia (or ASEAN) in general and between China and Singapore in particular. Singapore rose to the occasion and seized the opportunity to expand its economic ties with China, especially after Deng's tour of South China in early 1992. Accordingly, in 2014, Singapore was China's top foreign investor for the second consecutive year (since 2013) with investments amounting to US$5.8 billion in over 700 projects and China was Singapore's largest trading partner in 2014 with bilateral trade in goods increasing by 5.4% to S$121.5 billion. In the first half of 2014, Singapore was China's third largest foreign trading partner for trade in services, after the United States and Japan.[2]

On her part, China's economy is also slowly 'looking south'. In a speech he gave in 2011, then Minister Mentor Lee Kuan Yew said that there were more than 3,500 Chinese companies in Singapore, including 156 listed on the Singapore

---

[1] Indonesia broke off diplomatic ties with China in April 1967 when President Sukarno came into power. Ties were only resumed in August 1990. The Philippines suspended trade ties with China in 1949 after the PRC was formed and established diplomatic relations with China in June 1975. Similarly, Thailand joined the Philippines (and the United States) in suspending trade ties with China during the Cold War. It only established diplomatic ties with China in July 1975. Malaysia normalised relations with China in May 1974, becoming the first ASEAN country to do so. Singapore was the last among the ASEAN countries to establish diplomatic ties with China on 3 October 1990.

[2] Speech by Lim Hng Kiang (minister for trade and industry) at the Singcham-Singapore Business Federation Chinese New Year Networking Reception, Park Royal Hotel, Singapore's Ministry of Trade and Industry website, 21 February 2015, available at <http://www.mti.gov.sg/NewsRoom/Pages/Mr-Lim-Hng-Kiang-at-the-Singcham-Singapore-Business-Federation-(SBF)-Chinese-New-Year-Networking-Reception.aspx> (accessed 28 April 2015). In 2013, China was Singapore's top trading partner, with total trade amounting to S$115.2 billion.

Exchange.[3] Today, there are more than 6,000 Chinese companies in Singapore.[4] More Chinese firms are expected to venture abroad in search of brands, talents and technology, and Singapore, with its strong economic fundamentals and credit rating, is well-positioned to benefit from this trend. With growing afflu-ence, the Chinese are also making more trips overseas and Singapore, on account of its unique image as a clean and safe garden city, has become a prime destination. China was Singapore's second largest source of visitor arrivals at 2.3 million in 2013, an increase of more than four times from 0.57 million in 2003.

At the political level, China and Singapore have generally maintained a warm relationship since the beginning of international détente in the 1970s, in part because there are no outstanding issues and no areas of open conflict between them. Following Deng Xiaoping's remark in his *Nanxun* speech in early 1992, which singled out Singapore as a country that had achieved success-ful economic development along with a high degree of social order, China had organised numerous official 'observation tours' to Singapore to study Singapore's development experiences.

Over the years, many Chinese political and Party leaders, including its Political Bureau members, senior members of the National People's Congress (NPC) and the Chinese People's Political Consultative Conference (CPPCC), have visited Singapore. Singapore's leaders, cabinet ministers and senior civil servants have also visited China to exchange views and renew ties. In fact, Lee Kuan Yew, Singapore's founding father and first prime minister, had stated that since his first visit to China in 1976, he had made it a point to visit the country regularly — once a year if possible. Over the years, he had met each of the top leaders, namely, Mao Zedong, Hua Guofeng, Deng Xiaoping, Jiang Zemin, Hu Jintao and Xi Jinping.[5]

In July 1999, on the eve of making a trip to Beijing to celebrate the 25th anniversary of Sino-Malaysian diplomatic ties,[6] the characteristically outspoken

---

[3] Speech by Minister Mentor Lee Kuan Yew at the 25th Anniversary Dinner of the Singapore Federation of Chinese Clan Associations at Raffles City Convention Centre, Singapore's Prime Minister's Office website, 18 January 2011, available at <http://www.pmo.gov.sg/mediacentre/ speech-minister-mentor-lee-kuan-yew-25th-anniversary-dinner-singapore-federation-chinese> (accessed 2 March 2015).

[4] "S'pore 'Must Work Hard to Stay Relevant to China'" *The Straits Times*, 5 July 2015, available at <http://www.straitstimes.com/asia/spore-must-work-hard-to-stay-relevant-to-china> (accessed 8 July 2015).

[5] Lee Kuan Yew, *One Man's View of the World*, Singapore: Singapore Press Holdings, 2013, p. 29.

[6] Dr Mahathir led a 205-strong business delegation (comprising 193 ethnic Chinese Malaysians) to Beijing in August 1999.

Malaysian Prime Minister Mahathir Mohammed made a blunt statement to debunk the so-called 'China threat' theory. He said that the world must accept that China, with its 1.3 billion very hardworking and intelligent people cannot help but be a powerful country in due course:

> We have to live with this eventually. If we can live with the US as the sole superpower, there is no reason why we cannot live with China as a world power. China has practically no history of conquering and colonising neighbours. European powers have.[7]

Such similar sentiment on the importance of living and working with China is generally shared by many other countries including Singapore. In fact, Singapore leaders and ministers have on numerous occasions expressed their confidence that China will succeed in making progress in various fields of its development and take its rightful place in the community of nations; Singapore thus recognises the importance of staying relevant to and riding on the opportunities presented by China's growth. Singapore leaders and ministers have further stressed the importance of the US–China relationship which will have far-reaching implications for the peace, stability and growth of countries in the Asia-Pacific region.

In his keynote address at the Shangri-la Dialogue 2015 (which is also the year marking the 25th anniversary of Singapore–China ties) Singapore's Prime Minister Lee Hsien Loong observed that:

> So far, China's rise has been peaceful, within the established international order, and the key to this peaceful rise continuing is the US–China relationship....All Asian countries hope that US–China relations will be positive. No country wants to choose sides between the US and China. And we are glad that successive US administrations and successive Chinese leaderships have engaged, worked together and managed the problems which have come up between them, despite nationalistic pressures on both sides and inevitable tensions from time to time.[8]

---

[7] "Dr. Mahathir's World Analysis: Japanese Economic Recovery Tied to Asian Prosperity", *New Straits Times*, 6 July 1999.

[8] Keynote Address by Lee Hsien Loong, Prime Minister of Singapore", Shangri-la Dialogue 2015, 29 May 2015, available at <https://www.iiss.org/en/events/shangri%20la%20dialogue/archive/shangri-la-dialogue-2015-862b/opening-remarks-and-keynote-address-6729/keynote-address-a51f> (accessed 2 June 2015). Prime Minister Lee's remarks were made against the backdrop of China stepping up its land reclamation and construction activities in the South

At the strategic level, it is important for the United States and China to get their relationship on a right footing. On its part, Singapore has opted for realistic and pragmatic cooperation with China on the basis of mutual respect and mutual benefit. To analyse China–Singapore relations, in the past and in the future, this chapter will be divided into three main sections. The first section will provide an overview of Singapore's ties with China when it was part of Pan-Malaya and through the Cold War years. The purpose is to show that the ties between Singapore and China extend way back before the formal establishment of diplomatic ties. Ties had a natural dynamics of their own, driven largely by factors such as history, geography and migration. During the Cold War period, when China's relations with other ASEAN states were either banned or disrupted, Singapore's trade ties with China continued unabated. This showed the high level of pragmatism that prevailed in the bilateral relationship that has continued to this day.

The second section of the chapter will bring readers to the present state of broad-based relations between Singapore and China. While the economic relationship remains a key anchor, the ties between the two countries have broadened and deepened in many other areas. Emphasis will be placed on highlighting areas not mentioned in the other chapters including cultural exchanges, China's loan of a pair of pandas to Singapore and even nascent military cooperation. An overview of these selected areas is not intended to be comprehensive in scope but rather to provide readers with a sense of how far relations have developed.

The third section of the paper will look at how relations between the two countries have become more institutionalised. This trend of greater institutionalisation has and will continue to benefit Singapore in a number of ways. For one, they provide Singapore with several platforms to pursue cooperation with China at the not only national level but also sub-national level. The trend of greater institutionalisation has also enabled Singapore to better augment the personal ties that exist between the leaders of the two countries. In this sense, institutionalisation and personal rapport complement each other very well.

In the past, relations can be described as driven more by strong personalities such as Deng Xiaoping and Lee Kuan Yew who held each other in high regard and got along well with each other. At the present moment and in the future, it appears that strong personalities may not necessarily prevail on both sides. In such

China Sea (SCS) and the United States sending of its naval and air assets to the same area in an apparent effort to register its unhappiness with China's latest actions in the SCS.

a situation, the important role of institutions may become more apparent as they provide convenient platforms for both sides to constantly review existing cooperation and explore new ones.

Looking back

Singapore has geographically and historically been an integral part of Southeast Asia. Its interactions with China, in the past and presently, can be viewed not only within a bilateral context but also as part of a wider region. In fact, Singapore–China relations go back a long way, well before the establishment of diplomatic relations in October 1990.

Even before the founding of the PRC in 1949, China's relations with Southeast Asia, traditionally called *Nanyang* or South Sea by the Chinese (and of which Singapore is a part of), are extensive and deep-rooted on account of history, geography and migration.

Geographically, Singapore was part of the 'Pan-Malayan lands'. Historically, the trade between China and Pan-Malaya dated back to the early centuries. A fair amount of trade was recorded as early as the Tang Dynasty (618–907). Early trade activities were often mixed with tribute-bearing missions, a peculiar Chinese way of conducting diplomacy with the smaller states in *Nanyang*. However regular and steady growth in trade started only after the second part of the 19th century, with an increased influx of Chinese immigrant labour into British Malaya.

In fact, the Chinese had frequented Malayan lands long before the Portuguese conquered Malacca in 1511. In 1349, Wang Dayuan, a Chinese trader from Quanzhou (Fujian province) gave an account of life in Temasek, the name of old Singapore.[9] In 1409, Admiral Zheng He led an expedition to Malacca and made it one of China's tributary states. However, it was not until 1819 when the English East India Company established a settlement in Singapore that sizeable Chinese communities began to grow. In 1826, Penang, Malacca and Singapore were administratively brought together to form the Straits Settlements under the rule of the British colonial government of Bengal. With this administrative centralisation, the economies of the Straits Settlements started to grow rapidly.

---

[9] In his overseas travels during the Yuan dynasty, Wang provided the first foreign eyewitness account of Temasek as well as other localities (that stretched from China to Maluku to east Africa in an account called Dao Yi Zhi Lue [岛夷志略] in 1349). See John N Miksic, *Singapore and The Silk Road of the Sea, 1300–1800*, Singapore: NUS Press, 2013, pp. 169–181.

After 1842 when Hong Kong became a British colony, Singapore linked up with it to become an entrepot centre for the expanding trade between China and Southeast Asia. This in turn drew many Chinese immigrants, mainly from Fujian and Guangdong, to the Straits Settlements. In 1860, ethnic Chinese constituted 60% of Singapore's total population of 82,000, 15% of Malacca's 67,000 and nearly 30% of Penang's 67,000. Most Chinese migrated to Malaya under the contract-labour system. They soon became traders and craftsmen, and eventually dominated the economic life of the Straits Settlements.

To a large extent, the growth of Singapore was historically due to the continuing waves of migration from China. These waves of migration not only helped to augment Singapore's population size but also gave rise to cultural affinity between Singapore and China especially in terms of the shared values, language, customs, beliefs and religious practices. More importantly, they provided an important source of labour for Singapore's economic growth.[10]

In contrast to some Southeast Asian countries, Sino-Pan-Malayan trade had not been terminated following the birth of the New China in 1949.[11] In fact, China was buying a lot of Malayan rubber during the Korean War, until the imposition of an UN embargo on China in 1951. Following the embargo, Malaya did not export a single ton of rubber to China in 1952 compared with 22,700 tons in 1951.[12] Even though exports from Singapore to China were almost halted in 1952, Singapore continued to import from China that same year. Thus, trade between Singapore and China was not disrupted completely.[13]

In fact, following its success at industrialisation under the first Five-Year Plan (1953–1957), China started to produce a wide range of manufactured products for export to the industrially less sophisticated markets. Thus Southeast Asia became the natural destination of China's first major export drive, with Singapore playing a sort of spearhead on account of her strategic location and entrepot status. In February 1956, the Singapore branch of the Bank of China (China's de facto embassy in the absence of diplomatic relations)

---

[10] Today, Singapore continues to welcome Chinese immigrants, especially skilled and talented ones, to settle down in Singapore.

[11] The Philippines suspended trade with China after the PRC was formed in 1949. Apart from the Philippines, China's trade with Indonesia and Thailand were either seriously disrupted or banned in the 1950s and 1960s.

[12] "Rubber Exports Drop Last Year", *The Straits Times*, 11 January 1953, p. 3.

[13] John Wong, "The Role of China in Singapore and Southeast Asian Trade", *Southeast Asian Journal of Social Science*, vol. 3, no. 1, 1975, p. 51.

staged a 'China Products Exhibition' at its showroom at Battery Road in Singapore. This was reportedly the first exhibition of its kind to be organised in Malaya by a communist country. On show were more than 1,000 different items including bicycles, sewing machines, electrical appliances, textiles, porcelain, silk, tea, medicine, food products and products of some cottage industries. Looking to boost sales, Chinese dealers of these products in Singapore claimed that the prices of most commodities were reasonable and competitive.[14]

Apart from the opening of this exhibition at the Bank of China, other 'China Products Exhibitions' were subsequently held at other venues such as the Great World Amusement Park.[15] In one such exhibition held there in August 1956, it was reported that 'Hamid melons' (a type of muskmelon that originated from Hami, Xinjiang) were brought into Singapore for the first time.[16]

With the lifting of the UN embargo in June 1956, Chinese buyers returned to the Singapore rubber market.[17] Not long after, in September 1956, the first Singapore trade mission (albeit an unofficial one) led by Yap Pheng Geck visited Beijing to explore the expansion of business ties between the two countries. Yap was an English-educated Chinese who was a prominent banker and a committee member of the Singapore Chinese Chamber of Commerce at that time.[18] During that trip, he reportedly led a big delegation of over 60 personnel

---

[14] "Peking Woos Overseas Chinese through Trade", *The Straits Times*, 3 February 1956, p. 8 and "Peking Eyes on Our Market: Singapore Exhibition Soon", *The Singapore Free Press*, 9 January 1956, p. 1.

[15] The Great World Amusement Park or Great World was a popular location in Singapore in the 1950s and 1960s, and even the 1970s. It was a place where residents were known to head for to enjoy various opera and revue shows, carnival rides and good food. For further details, please see 'Great World Amusement Park', Singapore National Library Board, available at <http://eresources.nlb.gov.sg/infopedia/articles/SIP_1046_2006-06-09.html> (accessed 30 January 2015).

[16] "The First Hamid Melons Arrive — the Verdict is 'Delicious' ", *The Straits Times*, 15 August 1956, p. 5.

[17] John Wong, "The Role of China in Singapore and Southeast Asian Trade", p. 51.

[18] Yap Pheng Geck was born in Johore in 1901. He was educated at the Anglo-Chinese School in Singapore and obtained a degree from the University of Hong Kong. He started his working career as a teacher until 1931. He served as a volunteer in the Straits Settlement Volunteer Corps (SSVF), a military reserve force under the British, from 1925. In 1932, he was commissioned as an officer and commanded the 'E' Chinese Company of the Second Battalion of the SSVF until the fall of Singapore. After the war, he joined the Sze Hai Tong Banking and Insurance Company (that merged with the Overseas Banking Chinese Corporation in 1998)

made up largely of Chinese representatives from the Chinese Chamber of Commerce and businesses related to rubber, timber, shipping, textiles, foodstuffs, sundry goods, copra, wine and spirits, spray painting, paper and Chinese drugs. In a deliberate effort to show that this was not a trade delegation made up entirely of Chinese representatives, Yap reportedly included in his delegation some Indian, European and even Malay business representatives.[19]

Trade relations between Singapore and China were not all that smooth sailing in the 1950s. China's successful industrialisation led to a large influx of labour-intensive manufactured goods (particularly cotton textiles) into Pan-Malaya, which resulted in a serious trade dispute between the two sides and prompted the Kuala Lumpur government to impose a partial trade ban on imports from China. The formation of Malaysia in 1963 (through a merger of Singapore, Malaya, Sabah and Sarawak) caused a further deterioration in Sino-Malaysian relations as China supported Indonesia's confrontation against Malaysia. Sino-Malaysian relations reached its lowest ebb when Kuala Lumpur took measures to close the Penang and Singapore branches of the Bank of China in the 'Bank of China incident'. In reality, the closure order on the Singapore branch of the Bank of China was never implemented, as Singapore repealed it immediately after its separation from Malaysia in August 1965.

After independence, Singapore was able to pursue a more open trade policy with China that was relatively free from political and ideological hangovers. One instance of this was Singapore's first 19-member trade mission to China in October 1971 led by the president of the Singapore Chinese Chamber of Commerce Wee Cho Yaw.[20] The purpose of the mission was to further strengthen trade between the two countries and to study China's industrial development.[21] Another purpose of the trade mission was to request China to

---

as manager and became chairman of the Central Board of Pineapple Packers of Malaya. See "Leaders of Business in Malaya", *The Straits Times*, 23 January 1953, p. 10. See also Yap Pheng Geck, *Scholar, Banker, Gentleman Soldier*, Singapore, Institute of Southeast Asian Studies, 1982.

[19] "Singapore Plans to Outbid Hong Kong in Business Talks with China", *The Straits Times*, 12 July 1956, p. 6.

[20] Accompanying the 19-member mission were three journalists, i.e. Leslie Fong of *The Straits Times*, Pang Cheng Lian of the *New Nation* and William Lee of *Sin Chew Jit Poh*.

[21] At that time, Wee Cho Yaw reportedly said that the quality of Chinese goods was 'excellent' and the prices were 'cheap' and that they were 'especially suited to the needs of Singaporeans'. He also commended China for not only being able to 'meet the needs of its 700 million people but also to earn foreign exchange by exporting its goods'. See "Two Targets of the Mission to China", *The Straits Times*, 8 October 1971, p. 18.

consider providing a few ships to ply between Singapore and Europe to help break the near monopoly of shipping lines by the Far East Freight Conference (FEFC). Before the trade mission, Singapore shippers, especially those in the rubber and timber business, were extremely unhappy with the FEFC for announcing an impending increase in freight charges in January 1972 on top of an earlier increase in February 1971.[22] In their view, the substantial increase in freight charges would seriously affect their business as they were already hit by falling prices of the commodities they supplied. In the event, the trade mission managed to secure China's in-principle agreement to help Singapore break away from the contract system operated by the FEFC.[23]

In the 1970s, as individual ASEAN countries started to normalise relations with China, Singapore also went ahead to improve ties with China; it however decided to establish formal ties only after all the other ASEAN states had done so with Beijing. Singapore–China relations improved with the first ever visit by Singapore's Foreign Minister Rajaratnam to China in March 1975. Among the highlights of the visit was a meeting with Chinese Premier Zhou Enlai.[24] This paved the way for the visit by Singapore Prime Minister Lee Kuan Yew to China in May 1976 where Lee met Chairman Mao Zedong.[25] Although the meeting with Chairman Mao did not amount to a 'substantive conversation' given the latter's ailing health, Lee was of the view that the Chinese side had extended a courtesy to the Singapore delegation through such a meeting to signal that they considered Singapore important enough.[26]

---

[22] At that time, the FEFC had a near monopoly on shipping lines in and out of Singapore. It had announced an increase of freight charges by 10% in February 1971 and made a further announcement in September 1971 (a month before the first trade mission led by Wee Cho Yaw to China) to raise freight charges by another 20% in January 1972.

[23] "China's Aid Package", *The Straits Times*, 21 October 1971, p. 1.

[24] On this trip, Rajaratnam was accompanied by Senior Minister of State of Foreign Affairs Lee Khoon Choy, three officials (Joseph Koh, foreign ministry desk officer and secretary of the delegation; Howe Yoon Chong, Port of Singapore Authority and Development Bank of Singapore chairman; and, I F Tang, Economic Development Board deputy chairman) and five Singapore newsmen. At that time, there were no direct flights to Beijing. The Singapore delegation had to make a one-night stop-over in Hong Kong before travelling to Canton (today's Guangzhou) and then onward to Beijing. See "Raja Sees the Sights in Canton after Train Journey", *The Straits Times*, 13 March 1975 and "It All Began at a Dinner in New York...", *The Straits Times*, 14 March 1975, p. 1.

[25] Lee Kuan Yew did not meet Zhou Enlai during his visit in May 1976 as the latter had passed away in January 1976.

[26] "Lee Kuan Yew, *From Third World to First: The Singapore Story, 1965 – 2000*, New York, HarperCollins Publishers Inc., 2000, p. 582.

On the basis of these political milestones, the two countries took further steps to establish more formal trade ties. In December 1979, Singapore and China signed a trade agreement that provided a broad framework for increased trade and economic cooperation.[27] This was followed a few months later in June 1980 with a bilateral agreement to set up commercial representative offices in each other's country.[28] Singapore went on to set up a Trade Office in Beijing in September 1981; China opened a similar office in Singapore in the same month.[29] However, Singapore waited until October 1990 to formalise diplomatic ties with China, a few months after Indonesia did so in that same year. This move sent an unequivocal message to its immediate neighbours that Singapore was an independent and sovereign actor on the international stage and was not acting at the behest of another state on account of its large Chinese population. On hindsight, this approach laid a good foundation for the bilateral relationship to grow and prosper to what it is today.

A broad-based relationship

Singapore–China relations have moved beyond their strong economic ties into many other areas of cooperation. Today, the two countries enjoy a broad-based relationship that spans the realm of trade and investment, finance, politics, socio-cultural exchanges to the environment and even military cooperation. As a number of these areas are mentioned in the other chapters of this book, this section will only highlight three other particular areas of cooperation, namely, cultural exchange, panda diplomacy and military cooperation.[30]

---

[27] This trade accord was signed by Singapore's Finance Minister Hon Sui Sen and Chinese Foreign Trade Minister Li Qiang in a ceremony attended by Senior Vice Premier Deng Xiaoping. See "Hon Signs Trade Accord with Beijing", *The Sunday Times*, 30 December 1979, p. 1.

[28] This agreement was signed between Chinese Vice Minister for Foreign Trade Wang Runsheng and Permanent Secretary of Singapore's Ministry of Trade and Industry Ngiam Tong Dow. See "Boost in Trade Ties with China", *The Business Times*, 16 June 1980, p. 1.

[29] The first Singapore Trade Representative to China was Tan Song Chuan, then deputy trade director of Trade Development.

[30] The other chapters of this book will look at the economic relationship, tourism and educational exchanges, Chinese cultural traditions and practices in Singapore, China Studies in Singapore and bilateral projects like the Suzhou Industrial Park and the Sino-Singapore Tianjin Eco-city Project.

(i) *Cultural exchanges*

Many in Singapore look forward to the Chingay Parade held every year during the first weekend of the Lunar New Year.[31] Since its first street parade in 1973, the nature of the parade has shifted from depicting aspects of Chinese culture (such as dragon and lion dances, martial arts performances and street opera) to a national event with multicultural and international flavours (with performances by other ethnic races and participation by foreign groups). Apart from providing entertainment during the festive occasion, the parade provides a platform for Singapore residents regardless of their age, language and creed to come together as one to celebrate their diversity as well as better appreciate the cultures of other countries.

Although not the first foreign group to participate in Singapore's Chingay Parade, China's dance troupes and bands have been a regular feature at this national event.[32] In 1994, it was reported that China, together with Japan, the Philippines, New Zealand and Taiwan, sent dance troupes and bands to perform at the 22nd Chingay Parade along Orchard Road.[33] Since then, China has been actively participating at this national event by sending groups from various parts of China.

Most notably, Chingay Parade 2015 became a commemorative event to celebrate the 25th anniversary of diplomatic relations between Singapore and China.[34] China sent contingents from four localities, namely, Gansu, Suzhou, Tianjin and Xinjiang. Among the 20 floats on display during the parade, two of them were from Suzhou and Tianjin, underscoring the close ties between these two cities and Singapore.[35] These two cities host the two flagship bilateral projects between Singapore and China, i.e. the Suzhou Industrial Park (SIP) and Sino-Singapore Tianjin Eco-city.

Another event that showcases the close cultural collaboration between Singapore and China is the annual River Hongbao, held back-to-back with the

---

[31] The word Chingay is equivalent to the Mandarin words *zhuang yi* (妆艺), which means 'the art of costume and masquerade' in the Hokkien dialect.

[32] The first foreign group to participate in Singapore's Chingay Parade was four Japanese pop singers who came in 1987. See Chingay 2015 website at <https://chingay.org.sg/about-chingay> (accessed 4 March 2015).

[33] "Chingay: Crowds Lap Up International Flavour", *The Straits Times*, 20 February 1994.

[34] Besides China, Chingay 2015 was also an event to commemorate Singapore's 50 years of diplomatic ties with India and Thailand and 40 years with South Korea.

[35] See "The Most Popular Float", Chingay 2015 website at <https://chingay.org.sg/chingay2015/most-popular-float> (accessed 4 March 2015).

Chingay Parade. The River Hongbao festive celebrations started in 1987 along the banks of the Singapore River (hence its name). It was the outcome of a joint effort by the Singapore government and the Chinese community in Singapore to stimulate the interest of Singaporeans, especially the younger ones, in their Chinese heritage and culture. It was then felt that the Lunar New Year was becoming a 'very quiet affair' with more and more people leaving the country on holidays instead of staying home to celebrate the festival with their families. Hence, the idea of a River Hongbao with various celebratory activities to promote Chinese culture and traditions during the Lunar New Year period was conceived.

At virtually every River Hongbao, the organising committee[36] would try to partner with a different province from China to showcase unique features of Chinese culture and traditions from that particular province. Invariably, these would normally include performances by cultural troupes and bands, handicraft demonstrations, culinary delights, and display of iconic items and products.

Before diplomatic relations were established, it was reported that among the highlights of River Hongbao 1990 (that began in the month of January) was a Chinese dance performance by a 70-strong troupe from Beijing as well as folk and pop songs by local and foreign artistes.[37] It was also reported that Peng Liyuan, wife of current Chinese President Xi Jinping who was then a mid-ranked official in Fujian province, had performed at this same event.[38]

During River Hongbao 2010, the Lantern Festival Office of Chengdu was responsible for putting up 88 giant lanterns meticulously made from ceramic utensils and white sugar syrup. Thirty artisans were involved in this gargantuan effort. They spent a month in Chengdu to prepare the ceramic materials before they were shipped to Singapore in early January 2010. Another month was spent on assembling these items in Singapore in time for the River Hongbao.[39] For River Hongbao 2015, apart from the dazzling lantern displays, a major

---

[36] When the River Hongbao was launched in 1987, it was lead-managed by the Singapore Press Holdings (SPH). The organisation of the event was done by the staff of SPH's Chinese newspaper, *Lianhe Zaobao*, with the support of four other co-organisers, i.e. the Singapore Federation of Chinese Clan Associations, Singapore Chinese Chamber of Commerce and Industry, Singapore Tourist Promotion Board and People's Association. In 1990, the Singapore Federation of Clan Association was asked to lead-manage the event from 1991. Since 2009, a group of Singapore's Members of Parliament have led the organisation of this event with the continuing support of the five original institutions.

[37] "Traditional Goodies for Hongbao Special", *The Straits Times*, 14 January 1990.

[38] "Peony Fairy Makes Entry as 'First Lady'", *The Straits Times*, 23 March 2013.

[39] "Bigger, better river show", *The Straits Times*, 23 January 2010.

highlight was a tightrope performance 20 metres off the ground by an acrobatic troupe from Xinjiang.[40] There were also performances by singers and dancers from the music institute of Xinjiang Normal University and the dance department of the National Taiwan University of Physical Education and Sport.[41]

Apart from the River Hongbao and Chingay Parade, various artists from China have also performed at the annual Huayi or Chinese Festival of Arts. An anchor event under the Singapore Esplanade, Huayi seeks to showcase the works of different genres of Chinese artists (in Singapore and around the world) to an international audience in Singapore. When it was launched in 2003, Huayi featured the famous Kun opera, 'Peony Pavilion', directed by Chen Shizheng and performed by a cast of 20 from China. [42] In that same year, there were also performances by Chinese pianist Li Yundi and Beijing Modern Dance Company's Rearlight.[43] Since 2003, Chinese artists have been a regular feature at the Huayi.

The active participation of China in local national events in Singapore such as the Chingay Parade, River Hongbao and Huayi shows how far relations have moved beyond the turbulent period of the 1950s, 1960s and even 1970s. At that time, Singapore was extremely wary about how the cultural dimension of its large Chinese majority population might play into the hands of China and how it could incur the suspicions of its immediate neighbours. Such concerns are now a thing of the past. Today, China's participation has not only raised the appeal of these local national events but also enhanced the vibrancy of Singapore's cultural landscape. It may even be argued that China's participation has indirectly helped to promote the nation-building efforts of Singapore when its citizens come together as one to celebrate these events.

---

[40] The two tightrope walkers were Adili Wuxor and Abulaiti-Maijun who are Guinness World Record holders of numerous tightrope-related stunts.

[41] The tightrope walking took place from 19 to 22 February 2015. See "Year of the Goat Starts on a High with River Hongbao Carnival and Chinatown Celebrations", *The Straits Times*, 19 February 2015, available at <http://www.straitstimes.com/news/singapore/more-singapore-stories/story/year-the-goat-starts-high-river-hongbao-carnival-and-chi#sthash.JQFRzyjB.dpuf> (accessed 4 March 2015).

[42] The archaic Kun opera is regarded as the precursor to modern Chinese opera forms. With a history of some 400 years or more, it stands out for its distinctive poetic lyrics, elegant melodies and subdued dance steps. See "Pavilion Gets Second Cycle", *The Straits Times*, 24 January 2003.

[43] "Pavilion Gets Second Cycle", *The Straits Times*, 24 January 2003. There was also a concert by famous Taiwanese singer Tsai Chin.

(ii) *China cultural centre*

To foster exchange and cooperation in the fields of arts and culture, Singapore and China have signed a memorandum of understanding (MOU) to build a China Cultural Centre in Singapore. The MOU was signed during the state visit of Chinese President Hu Jintao to Singapore in November 2009. A year later, in November 2010, on the occasion of the 20th anniversary of bilateral ties, the two countries held a ground-breaking ceremony for the China Cultural Centre at Queen Street which is a part of Singapore's Arts and Heritage District. The ceremony was witnessed by Senior Minister Goh Chok Tong and visiting Chinese Vice President Xi Jinping (see picture).

Senior Minister Goh Chok Tong and Vice President Xi Jinping Officiating at the Ground-breaking Ceremony of the China Cultural Centre

Source: China's government website, available at <http://www.gov.cn/english/2010-11/15/content_1745942.htm> (accessed 5 March 2015).

The China Cultural Centre is the first such centre in the world to be designed by a local architect.[44] In terms of its functions, the centre aims to promote closer cultural ties between the two countries by providing collaborative opportunities

---

[44] The local architect is the renowned Dr Liu Thai Ker of RSP Architects, Planners and Engineers.

for Singapore and Chinese artists and arts groups, as well as presenting performances, exhibitions, lectures and workshops to the general public. It will also offer classes in areas such as Mandarin, calligraphy and wushu, and house a library of books on China. There are plans for exhibitions of Chinese and Singapore art, film screenings as well as lectures on various aspects of Chinese culture. The functions of the centre are likely to evolve over time to include other cultural areas relevant to both countries.[45] The centre is expected to be ready in 2015 to commemorate the 25th anniversary of the establishment of diplomatic relations between the two countries.

Concurrently, Singapore is also building a Chinese Cultural Centre in Shenton Way which is expected to be ready in 2016.[46] Going beyond promoting Chinese arts, culture, traditions and customs, the centre seeks to strengthen Singapore's multicultural identity. It will therefore include in its activities collaborations with non-Chinese cultural and arts groups. It will also serve as a venue for community activities and interactions. The purpose is to promote a more inclusive and harmonious society.

It appears that the Chinese Cultural Centre (by Singapore) and China Cultural Centre (by China) have a different focus. While the latter is focused on promoting China's soft power in overseas host countries through its arts and culture, the former is more concerned with strengthening the bonds not only among the Chinese community but also between the Chinese and non-Chinese communities in Singapore. In this sense, there is clear demarcation in the roles and functions of these two cultural institutions. They are therefore likely to complement rather than be in competition with each other.

(iii) *Panda diplomacy*

The cultural exchange between Singapore and China is not confined to the people-to-people level. An integral part of cultural exchange includes the sending overseas of a country's national treasure or icon. In this regard, Singapore was

---

[45] "Groundbreaking Ceremony of the China Cultural Centre in Singapore", Singapore's Ministry of Information, Communications and the Arts website, 15 November 2010, available at <http://www.mci.gov.sg/mobile/news/media/groundbreaking-ceremony--of-the-china-cultural-centre-in-singapore> (accessed 4 March 2015).

[46] The ground-breaking ceremony of the Chinese Cultural Centre took place in September 2014. Sited next to the Singapore Conference Hall, it will include an art gallery, a 150-seat recital hall, a multi-purpose hall and a 530-seat auditorium. See "PM Lee Attends Groundbreaking Ceremony for New Singapore Chinese Cultural Centre", *The Straits Times*, 29 September 2014.

among a handful of countries to have the rare opportunity to receive Giant Pandas, an endangered species and a national treasure, from China in 2012. It is an indication of the importance China attaches to its relations with Singapore.

This is not the first time that Singapore is hosting Giant Pandas from China. In September 1990, two male pandas An An and Xin Xing arrived in Singapore for a 100-day exhibition to celebrate the establishment of diplomatic relations between the two countries in October 1990. The two pandas left Singapore on 4 January 1991.[47]

This time round, the announcement that Singapore would receive a pair of pandas was made during Chinese President Hu Jintao's visit to Singapore in November 2009. The pandas would be on loan to Singapore for a period of 10 years. At the time of the announcement, Singapore was reportedly the seventh country — after the United States, Japan, Spain, Austria, Australia and Thailand — handpicked to house overseas pandas.[48]

Singapore made meticulous and extensive preparations to receive its two special Chinese VIPs (Very Important Pandas). For instance, spare land around the Singapore Zoo was set aside to plant four particular species of bamboo as food for the pandas. A climate-controlled enclosure of 1,500 square metres was built at a cost of S$8.5 million. A dedicated team of Singapore veterinarians and keepers were trained to handle the pandas. A naming contest was also held and a panel of judges eventually decided on the names of Kai Kai (meaning victorious) and Jia Jia (meaning beautiful and fine) for the pandas.[49]

When Singapore's Prime Minister Lee Hsien Loong met Liu Qibao, party secretary of Sichuan, on 2 September 2012 while on an official visit there, he made it a point to convey to Liu that Kai Kai and Jia Jia can expect a 'royal welcome' in Singapore. He further informed Liu that he had visited the Singapore Zoo on the same morning of his flight to Chengdu. The zoo authorities had told him that 'everything is ready and they are just waiting for the pandas to arrive'.[50]

A few days thereafter, on 6 September, Kai Kai and Jia Jia touched down in Singapore on a chartered Singapore Airlines flight. Before they departed from their home base in Ya'an (Sichuan), they were accorded a ceremonial send-off reception. Among the Singapore guests present were Senior Minister of State

---

[47] "It's Panda Mania All over Again", *The Straits Times*, 22 November 2009.
[48] "Animal Diplomacy", *The Straits Times*, 14 November 2009.
[49] The panel of judges comprised representatives from the Singapore Tourism Board, Chinese Embassy, Wildlife Reserves Singapore and the sponsor, CapitaLand.
[50] "All Ready for Pandas, Says PM Lee", *The Straits Times*, 2 September 2012.

for Trade and Industry Lee Yi Shyan and Chairman of Wildlife Reserves Singapore Clarie Chang. When they arrived in Singapore, the Singapore guests present included Minister of State for Trade and Industry Teo Ser Luck, former President S R Nathan and Clarie Chang.[51] Minister in the Prime Minister's Office S Iswaran officiated at the opening of the panda enclosure in November 2012.

Kai Kai and Jia Jia appear to have settled down well at the Singapore Zoo. In an effort to go one step further, the zoo authorities are trying to get the pair to breed. In 2014, Wildlife Reserves Singapore Chief Sciences Officer Cheng Wen-Haur noticed slight changes in the behaviour of the two in that Kai Kai appears to be more interested in Jia Jia compared to a year ago when he was more engrossed in his food.[52] Apparently, squat training has also been conducted for Kai Kai in an effort to strengthen his hind limbs so that he can maintain the standing position during mating.[53]

If Kai Kai and Jia Jia can reproduce, their cubs will be Singapore's gift to China. This will be an outcome of great political symbolism. In fact, the best indicator that Singapore is taking good care of Kai Kai and Jia Jia is to get them to breed. Singapore will then be returning China a favour by helping it to increase the number of pandas in its possession while contributing to the worldwide conservation of this endangered species.[54]

(iv) *Military cooperation*

Defence ties between Singapore and China have also grown over the years. In January 2008, Singapore and China signed the Agreement on Defence Exchanges and Security Cooperation, the first such defence agreement between the two countries. The agreement also marks a natural progression from the two countries' deepening of bilateral economic and political ties.[55]

---

[51] "S'pore Welcomes its First Resident Pandas", *The Straits Times*, 7 September 2012.

[52] "Kai Kai Steals Glances at Jia Jia, Raising Hopes for a Panda Cub", *The Straits Times*, 1 September 2014.

[53] "'Fertile' Kai Kai Lifts Hope of Baby Panda", *The Straits Times*, 4 April 2014.

[54] Based on the agreement struck between Wildlife Reserves Singapore and China Wildlife Conservation Association, any panda cubs will be sent back to China when they are two years old.

[55] The agreement was signed between Permanent Secretary of Defence Chiang Chie Foo and People's Liberation Army Deputy Chief of Staff Lieutenant General Ma Xiaotian on behalf of their respective ministries. See "Factsheet: Agreement on Defence Exchanges and Security Cooperation between China and Singapore", Singapore's Ministry of Defence website,

The defence agreement formalises on-going activities between Singapore's Ministry of Defence and the People's Liberation Army (PLA) that include exchanges of visits, attendance at courses and seminars, and port calls. It also includes new areas of cooperation such as Humanitarian Assistance and Disaster Relief.[56]

On the basis of this agreement, the two sides have pursued practical and mutually beneficial cooperation at a pace that both sides are comfortable with. In June 2009, the Singapore Armed Forces (SAF) and PLA conducted their first bilateral training exercise on counter-terrorism in Guilin, China. The exercise, involving around 60 participating troops each from the SAF and PLA, focused on the conduct of security operations for major events and consequence management concepts related to chemical, biological, radiological and explosive threats.[57]

Alternating between locations, the two sides conducted their second joint counter-terrorism training exercise in Singapore in November 2010. Although the number of troops from each side remained at around 60, the number of agencies that participated in the exercise appeared to have increased.

On the Singapore side, apart from the 2nd People's Defence Force and SAF Chemical, Biological, Radiological and Explosives Defence Group that took part in the 2009 inaugural exercise, there were personnel from Headquarters 1st Singapore Infantry Brigade, the Medical Response Force and SAF Military Police Command. On the Chinese side, the personnel came from the PLA Headquarters, Beijing Military Command, Beijing Garrison and the Chemical Defence Regiment of the Beijing Military Command.[58]

---

7 January 2008, available at <http://www.mindef.gov.sg/imindef/press_room/official_releases/nr/2008/jan/07jan08_nr/07jan08_fs.html> (accessed 9 March 2014).

[56] "Permanent Secretary (Defence) Signs Agreement on Defence Exchanges and Security Cooperation with China at Inaugural Defence Policy Dialogue", Singapore's Ministry of Defence website, 7 January 2008, available at <http://www.mindef.gov.sg/imindef/press_room/official_releases/nr/2008/jan/ 07jan08_nr.html> (accessed 9 March 2014).

[57] The participating troops from SAF were from the 2nd People's Defence Force and the SAF Chemical, Biological, Radiological and Explosives Defence Group. On China's side, the personnel came from the PLA Emergency Response Office and Guangzhou Military Region. "SAF and PLA to Conduct Joint Counter-Terrorism Training Exercise", Singapore's Ministry of Defence website, 18 January 2009, available at <http://www.mindef.gov.sg/imindef/press_room/official_releases/nr/2009/ jun/18jun09_nr.html> (accessed 9 March 2015).

[58] "SAF and PLA in Joint Counter-Terrorism Training", *Pioneer*, 19 November 2010, available at <http://www.mindef.gov.sg/imindef/resourcelibrary/cyberpioneer/topics/articles/news/2010/november/19nov10_news.html> (accessed 9 March 2015).

Moving beyond counter-terrorism, and in an indication of their desire to step up the level of cooperation, the two countries have embarked on conventional training in their third bilateral training exercise. In November 2014, the SAF and PLA took part in a company-level infantry exercise that featured a live firing demonstration in Nanjing, China. The number of personnel that participated from each side also increased from the previous two counter-terrorism exercises of 60 to around 70.[59] Defence Minister Ng Eng Hen witnessed the live firing exercise as part of his official visit to China in the same month of November.

In addition to practical areas of cooperation, the two sides hold regular high-level meetings and strategic consultations. Foremost among them is the Defence Policy Dialogue (DPD) inaugurated in 2008 that is led by the permanent secretary for defence on the Singapore side and the deputy chief of general staff of the PLA on the Chinese side. The DPD provides a regular platform for both countries to discuss issues of mutual interests such as the regional security situation as well as bilateral defence exchanges. So far, five such DPDs had been held.[60]

Apart from bilateral cooperative platforms, Singapore and China have also collaborated at various multilateral fora. For instance, when Singapore took over command of the Combined Task Force 151 to fight piracy off the Gulf of Aden in 2011 (sanctioned by the United Nations),[61] the officers of the Republic of Singapore Navy and the PLA Navy Task Force CTF 526 had the opportunity to interact and share their operational experiences.[62]

---

[59] The SAF was represented by personnel from the 5th Battalion, Singapore Infantry Regiment and 3rd Singapore Division. Their Chinese counterparts were from the PLA 179th Brigade and Nanjing Military Region. See "SAF and PLA Conduct Bilateral Training Exercise", Singapore's Ministry of Defence website, 2 November 2014, available at <http://www.mindef.gov.sg/imindef/press_room/ official_releases/nr/2014/nov/02nov14_nr.html> (accessed 9 March 2015).

[60] The five meetings were held in 2008 (in Beijing), 2009 (in Singapore), 2010 (in Beijing), 2012 (in Singapore) and 2014 (in Beijing).

[61] The Combined Task Force (CTF) 151 is a multi-national task force established by the Combined Maritime Forces in January 2009 to conduct counter-piracy operations in the Gulf of Aden, Somali Basin and Arabian Sea. Singapore took over command of CTF 151 in March 2011.

[62] "Commander CTF 151 Visits Chinese Independent Warship", Combined Maritime Forces website, 15 May 2011, available at <http://combinedmaritimeforces.com/2011/05/15/commander-ctf-151-visits-chinese-independent-warship/> (accessed 9 March 2015).

Singapore and China further participated in the first ever combined 18-nation ASEAN Defence Ministers Meeting Plus (or ADMM-Plus) Humanitarian Assistance and Disaster Relief (HADR) and Military Medicine Exercise — both table top and full troop — in Brunei in 2013.[63] This exercise saw the deployment of approximately 3,200 personnel, seven ships, 15 helicopters as well as military medical, engineering and search and rescue teams, and assets from the 18 nations in scenarios relating to collapsed buildings, landslides and flash floods. The multi-national forces exercised the evacuation of casualties and displaced personnel, as well as the delivery of aid to affected communities.[64]

In addition, China has been a regular participant at the annual Shangri-La Dialogue (or SLD which is organised by the London-based International Institute for Strategic Studies in Singapore) that provides an informal platform for key players to exchange views and explore ways to enhance regional security. At SLD 2015, the Chinese delegation was led by Admiral Sun Jianguo (deputy chief, General Staff Department, PLA) who is ranked higher than China's head of delegation at the 2014 dialogue.[65] This shows that China regards the SLD as a viable platform to exchange views with other countries. Likewise, Singapore has accorded importance to similar platforms for regional defence engagement led by China. Defence Minister Ng Eng Hen attended the Fifth Xiangshan Forum in Beijing in November 2014, the first time this forum was upgraded from Track Two to a Track 1.5 forum.[66]

Singapore's increasing defence ties with China is consistent with its overall relationship with China, which has been growing. It defence relationship with China is also not mutually exclusive, i.e. its closer defence ties with China does

---

[63] The 18 nations included the 10 countries of ASEAN plus China, Japan, South Korea, Australia, New Zealand, India, Russia and the United States.

[64] "SAF and Other Militaries Conclude the ADMM-Plus HADR/MM Exercise", Singapore's Ministry of Defence website, 20 June 2013, available at <http://www.mindef.gov.sg/imindef/press_room/official_releases/nr/2013/jun/20jun13_nr.html> (accessed 9 March 2015).

[65] At SLD 2014, the Chinese delegation was led by Lieutenant-General Wang Guanzhong and deputy chief, General Staff Department, PLA. Although Lieutenant-General Wang shares the same designation as Admiral Sun Jianguo who are both deputy chief of the General Staff Department, rank-wise he is lower than Admiral Sun.

[66] At previous forums, invitations were extended only to foreign scholars. For the Fifth Xiangshan Forum, China extended invitations to senior official representatives from several countries. The same forum also decided to increase the frequency of the forum to an annual affair, up from biennially.

not preclude Singapore from developing its defence ties with other countries. Other countries, on their part, are also seeking closer ties with China.

From personal interaction to institutional framework

At the political level, there have been frequent exchanges of visits by the leaders, ministers and officials of Singapore and China. Such exchanges are very important to building personal relationships, promoting better understanding and ties between the two countries. In the earlier years, there were strong personalities on both sides such as Deng Xiaoping and Lee Kuan Yew that were instrumental in moving the relationship forward. For instance, Deng Xiaoping had visited Singapore in November 1978 when he saw first-hand how far Singapore had progressed since independence in 1965. Then Prime Minister Lee Kuan Yew believed that what Deng saw and experienced in Singapore at that time had left an indelible impression on him. Lee observed that after Deng returned to China, the *People's Daily* (China's party newspaper) changed its attitude towards Singapore. Singapore was no longer excoriated as 'running dogs of the American imperialists'. Instead Singapore was described as a garden city and a model for developing good housing for the people and for tourism. Lee regarded Deng as the 'most impressive leader' he had met.[67]

Furthermore, Deng's mention of Singapore as a reference for China in his Southern Tour speech in early 1992 led to more than 400 Chinese delegations visiting Singapore in that year to study various aspects of Singapore's development experience.[68] His remarks further provided a political window of opportunity for Singapore to explore deeper collaboration with China. This led to Singapore's embarking on its first government-to-government project with China in the form of the SIP in 1994.

Today, the context and dynamics of the relationship has changed as there are no strong or charismatic personalities on both sides to drive the relationship. Furthermore, China is no longer as dependent on Singapore as it was in the past when it was much less integrated with the world economy. In this context, the role of institutional mechanisms in providing the momentum for bilateral cooperation has become more important for augmenting the personal ties and rapport between the leaders, ministers and officials on both sides.

---

[67] Lee Kuan Yew, *From Third World to First: The Singapore Story,* pp. 601–602.
[68] Speech by Senior Minister Lee Kuan Yew at the International Conference on National Boundaries and Cultural Configurations for the 10th Anniversary Celebration of the Centre for Chinese Language and Culture, Nanyang Technological University, 23 June 2004.

The institutional framework for bilateral cooperation was gradually built up over the years. Beginning from the SIP project, an institutional platform for both sides to engage each other on the project was agreed upon in 1994.[69] It has three levels. At the top is the Joint Ministerial Council (JMC), jointly headed by then Deputy Prime Minister Lee Hsien Loong and Vice Premier Li Lanqing. The JMC sets the overall direction and scope of the project, and approve necessary resources and review progress periodically. It provides coordination at the highest level by bringing together various ministries and agencies from both sides to facilitate the development of the SIP.[70] On the Chinese side, officials from the Jiangsu government and Suzhou municipal government are involved in driving this project as well.

Below the JMC is the Joint Working Committee (JWC) that translates the overall direction and scope of the SIP project as decided by the JMC into specific plans and oversees the implementation of these plans. The JWC was then jointly headed by a senior representative from the Jurong Town Corporation and a senior official from the Suzhou municipal government. The JWC reports to the JMC. At the third level, there was a project office on each side that was responsible for jointly identifying areas for software transfer (relating to Singapore's public administration and economic management).

The JMC, now known as the Joint Steering Council or JSC, had continued to meet regularly over the years. It held its 16th meeting in Suzhou in October 2014 co-chaired by Singapore's Deputy Prime Minister, Coordinating Minister for National Security and Minister for Home Affairs Teo Chee Hean and China's Vice Premier Zhang Gaoli. The meeting coincided with the 20th anniversary of the SIP.

---

[69] This framework was formalised in an agreement signed by both the Chinese and Singapore sides in February 1994.

[70] Today, the ministries and agencies on the Chinese side include the Ministry of Commerce, Ministry of Foreign Affairs, National Development and Reform Commission, Ministry of Science and Technology, Ministry of Finance, Ministry of Land and Resources, Ministry of Housing and Urban-Rural Development, General Administration of Customs, and General Administration of Quality Supervision, Inspection and Quarantine. The Singapore side includes the Ministry of Trade and Industry, Ministry of Home Affairs, Prime Minister's Office, Ministry of Education, Ministry of National Development, Ministry of Finance, Ministry of Transport, Ministry of Foreign Affairs, Ministry of Culture, Community and Youth, Ministry of Environment and Water Resources. See Suzhou Industrial Park Administrative Committee website, available at <http://www.sipac.gov.cn/english/InvestmentGuide/SinoSingapore Cooperation/201107/t20110704_102985.htm> (accessed 11 March 2015).

The institutional framework that started with the SIP has since been upgraded. In November 2003, Prime Minister Goh Chok Tong and Premier Wen Jiabao launched the Joint Council for Bilateral Cooperation (JCBC), the highest level governmental body between the two countries to promote and facilitate bilateral cooperation. The JCBC was then co-chaired by Deputy Prime Minister Lee Hsien Loong and Vice Premier Wu Yi.[71] A total of 11 JCBC meetings have since been held to discuss areas of cooperation and explore new ones.[72] Some of the key areas discussed and agreements reached included an update of the double taxation agreement between the two countries, banking supervisory cooperation that covers crisis management, bilateral FTA, technical assistance to third countries, cooperation to develop China's western and northeast regions, deepening software collaboration, enhancement of banking service cooperation, promotion of the internationalisation of the Chinese currency, RMB, for trade and investment (including direct currency trading between the Chinese Yuan and Singapore Dollar), and discussion of a third government-to-government project between Singapore and China.

Under JCBC's purview is the JSC and other bilateral cooperation bodies (see diagram). At present, there are two JSCs: one is the JSC that oversees the SIP (mentioned earlier) while the other is the JSC that overlooks the development of the Sino-Singapore Tianjin Eco-city, the second flagship project between the two countries, mooted in April 2007. The JSC for the Eco-city was formalised in a framework agreement signed in November 2007. The designated co-chairs of this JSC were Deputy Prime Minister Wong Kan Seng and Vice Premier Wu Yi. Similar to the JSC for the SIP, the JSC for the Eco-city brings together relevant government ministries and agencies from both countries that are needed for the comprehensive development of this project.[73] Under the JSC is a JWC that is co-chaired by Singapore's Minister for National Development and China's Minister of Housing and Urban-Rural Development. The JWC is responsible for the implementation of the project and the achievement of its key milestones.

---

[71] The Singapore co-chairs of the JCBC were Deputy Prime Minister (DPM) Lee Hsien Loong, DPM Wong Kan Seng and DPM Teo Chee Hean (current). The China co-chairs were Vice Premiers Wu Yi, Vice Premier Wang Qishan and Vice Premier Zhang Gaoli.

[72] The 11th JCBC was held in Suzhou in October 2014 to coincide with the 20th anniversary of the establishment of the SIP.

[73] On the Singapore side, the Ministry of National Development is the lead agency for the project while the lead agency on China's side is the Ministry of Housing and Urban-Rural Development.

```
┌─────────────────────────────────────────────────┐
│   Joint Council for Bilateral Cooperation (JCBC)  │
│        11th meeting in Suzhou (Oct '14)           │
└─────────────────────────────────────────────────┘
```

Joint Steering Council (JSC) on Suzhou Industrial Park 16th meeting in Suzhou (Oct'14)	Joint Steering Council (JSC) on Sino-Singapore Tianjin Eco-city 7th meeting in Suzhou (Oct'14)	Other bodies

Other bodies:

Singapore-Shandong Business Council (1993)

Singapore-Sichuan Trade and Investment Committee (1996)

Singapore-Liaoning Economic and Trade Council (2003)

Singapore-Zhejiang Economic and Trade Council (2003)

Singapore-Tianjin Economic and Trade Council (2007)

Singapore-Jiangsu Cooperation Council (2007)

Singapore-Guangdong Collaboration Council (2009)

Singapore-China Investment Promotion Committee (2007)

Joint Working Committee

Joint Working Committee

Software Project Office

JV Company

JV Company

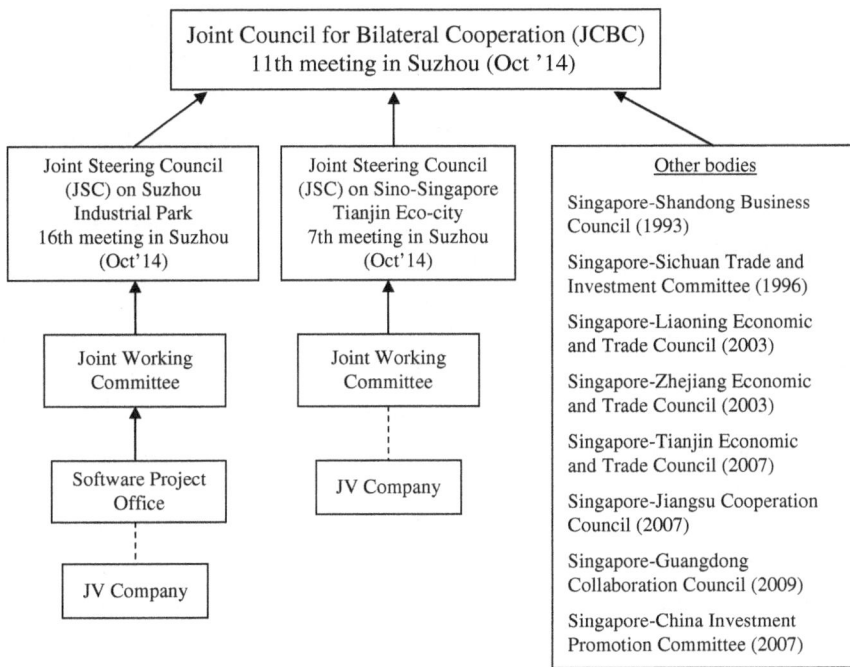

Diagram: Overview of Bilateral Cooperation Mechanism

Source: Authors' own.

There is also a Joint Venture (JV) company involved in the development of the SIP and the Sino-Singapore Tianjin Eco-city. The participation of the private sector underscores the importance of ensuring that these two projects are commercially viable even though they are government-to-government projects. Strictly speaking, the JV companies are not part of the official bilateral cooperation mechanism. They do not need to report to the JWC or to the JSC though there would be informal channels of communication between the company representatives on the one hand and government leaders and officials on the other hand. Hence, this relationship is represented by a dotted line.

In addition to the national level framework, Singapore has established bilateral cooperation mechanisms with seven other provinces in China. The provinces are Shandong (1993), Sichuan (1996), Liaoning (2003), Zhejiang (2003), Tianjin (2007), Jiangsu (2007) and Guangdong (2009). They are respectively co-chaired by Minister of State (MOS) for Trade and Industry Teo Ser Luck and Shandong Vice Governor Xia Geng; Minister for Culture, Community and Youth, and Second Minister for Communications and

Information Lawrence Wong and Sichuan Vice Governor Gan Lin;[74] Minister for Manpower Tan Chuan-Jin and Liaoning Governor Li Xi; Minister, Prime Minister's Office, Second Minister for the Environment and Water Resources, and Foreign Affairs Grace Fu and Zhejiang Vice Governor Liang Liming; Minister for National Development Khaw Boon Wan and Tianjin Mayor Huang Xingguo;[75] Minister for Education Heng Swee Keat and Jiangsu Governor Li Xueyong;[76] and Minister of Transport Lui Tuck Yew and Guangdong Vice Governor Zhao Yufang.

Each of the seven bilateral cooperation mechanisms is co-chaired by officials at either the ministerial or vice-ministerial level, thus affording Singapore additional avenues to get to know and collaborate with Chinese leaders at the sub-national levels. While most of these cooperation mechanisms have a pre-dominant focus on pursuing economic, business and trade-related cooperation, the Singapore-Jiangsu Cooperation Council and Singapore-Guangdong Collaboration Council, which were formed in the later years, have a focus extending beyond economics to include training, tourism and education exchanges.

Furthermore, the bilateral cooperation that is pursued at these platforms does not only benefit government linked corporations and big businesses. There is also a conscious effort to build and strengthen linkages between the small and medium-sized enterprises (SMEs) on both sides. For instance, Minister Tan Chuan-Jin remarked in his facebook post on 28 August 2013 (immediately after the conclusion of the Seventh Singapore-Liaoning Economic and Trade Council meeting) that the council and other provincial level coopera-tion mechanisms were 'useful platforms' for Singapore to work with China on projects of mutual benefit. He said that they have enabled Singapore companies 'of all sizes including SMEs, to expand and make forays into China' and in the process create 'good jobs for Singaporeans'. He singled out the example of a consortium of eight Singapore childhood education and enrichment SMEs that had set up a JV with a Chinese counterpart in Shenyang, the capital city of Liaoning.[77]

---

[74] The co-advisers to the Singapore-Sichuan Trade and Investment Committee are Minister in the Prime Minister's Office Lim Swee Say and Sichuan Governor Wei Hong.

[75] The vice chairmen of the Singapore-Tianjin Economic and Trade Council are Senior Minister of State for National Development and Trade and Industry Lee Yi Shyan, Tianjin Vice Mayor Ren Xuefang and Tianjin Binhai New Area Party Secretary Yuan Tongli.

[76] The vice co-chairmen of the Singapore-Jiangsu Cooperation Council are Minister of State for Trade and Industry Teo Ser Luck and Jiangsu Vice Governor Fu Ziying.

[77] "Some Thoughts from Liaoning…", Minister Tan Chuan-Jin's Facebook Post, 28 August 2013, available at <https://www.facebook.com/TanChuanJin1/posts/590331744342938>

Apart from Singapore's cooperation with China's seven provinces, there are other bilateral cooperation platforms. One of them is the Singapore–China Investment Promotion Committee (IPC) established in 2007. The committee, co-chaired by Minister for Trade and Industry Lim Hng Kiang and China's Minister of Commerce Gao Hucheng, offers a platform for Singapore and China to promote greater investment flows between the two countries by collaborating in promising sectors. The committee meets once every two years.[78]

Additional bilateral platforms have been created over the years to address new and common development challenges faced by Singapore and China. In 2009, the two countries held an inaugural Singapore–China Forum on Leadership co-chaired by Deputy Prime Minister Teo Chee Hean and Head of China's Central Organisation Department Li Yuanchao.[79] The purpose of the forum is to share experiences on leadership planning and development issues.[80] Apart from ministers, the forum is attended by senior civil servants from both sides. So far, five such forums had been held on themes like leadership selection and development (in 2009), harmonious society and the development of leadership (in 2010), leadership development in the age of new media (in 2012), fostering integrity in government (in 2013), and forging consensus with the people and building national unity (2015).

In 2012, Singapore and China established the Singapore–China Social Management Forum which is also pegged at the deputy prime minister level.[81] The forum seeks to share experiences on pertinent social issues brought about by challenges such as rising social expectations, increasing migrant flows, impact of globalisation and widespread use of information technology. Two such forums had been held in 2012 and 2014 on topics such as inclusive

---

(accessed 12 March 2015). The eight Singapore SMEs are Climb Asia, Cristofori Music, Dancepointe, Genius R Us, Gowfe Pro Academy, Kidz Education City, LEAP SchoolHouse Pte Ltd and WOW! Learning Centre Pte Ltd. They signed an agreement with Shenyang Duo Duo Kids World Business Management Company Ltd to set up an enrichment cluster in Shenyang's Star Mall on 28 August 2013.

[78] The IPC met four times in January 2007 (Beijing), April 2010 (Beijing), May 2012 (Beijing) and June 2014 (Singapore).

[79] In 2012, when Li Yuanchao was elevated to the post of vice president, Zhao Leji took over as head of China's Central Organisation Department.

[80] The forum was first proposed by Senior Minister Goh Chok Tong in September 2008 when he met Political Bureau Member and Head of China's Central Organisation Department Li Yuanchao in Beijing.

[81] The Singapore side is led by Deputy Prime Minister Teo Chee Hean while the Chinese side is led by Political Bureau Member and Secretary of the Political and Legal Affairs Committee of the Central Committee of the Chinese Communist Party Meng Jianzhu.

growth and income gap, innovation in social management and building a harmonious society, social governance and the rule of law.[82]

Conclusion

Singapore's relations with China have become much more broad-based and deeper over the years. This is a remarkable and even commendable achievement when not too long ago such as in the 1950s, 1960s and even 1970s, the two countries were at opposing ends of the political and ideological spectrum.

Without overlapping with the contribution of other authors in this book, this chapter has highlighted the areas where the relationship has extended into such as cultural exchange (including the setting up of a China Cultural Centre), panda diplomacy and military cooperation. It has also provided an overview of the bilateral cooperation mechanisms that have been built up over the years. Several of these mechanisms are led at the deputy prime minister level such as the JCBC, the JSC on the SIP and the JSC on the Sino-Singapore Tianjin Eco-city, and the separate forums on leadership and social management. It is extremely unique for a small country like Singapore to have that many high-level platforms with a big country like China. They speak volumes of Singapore's relevance to China and the constant effort to make this possible.

At the strategic and political level, these bilateral platforms are invaluable to enabling Singapore's leaders, ministers and officials various avenues to interact and build ties with their Chinese counterparts. They also provide a convenient platform for both sides to meet regularly to review existing areas of cooperation and explore new areas of collaboration. They are likely to become more important in augmenting the personal ties and rapport of the leaders and policy-makers on both sides.

---

[82] "Speech by Mr Chan Chun Seng, Acting Minister for Community Development, Youth and Sports & Senior Minister of State, Ministry of Defence, at the Singapore–China Social Management Forum, 22 September 2012 at the St Regis Hotel, Singapore", available at <http://app.msf.gov.sg/Press-Room-Archives/Singapore-China-Social-Management-Forum> (accessed 12 March 2015). See also "The Opening Ceremony of the Singapore–China Social Governance Forum on 'Social Governance and the Rule of Law' — Opening Speech by Deputy Prime Minister, Coordinating Minister for National Security and Minister for Home Affairs, Mr Teo Chee Hean", Singapore's Ministry of Home Affaris website, 28 July 2014, available at <http://www.mha.gov.sg/news_details.aspx?nid=MzIxNQ%3D%3D-RNh0YuIb C6Y%3D> (accessed 12 March 2015).

Bilateral ties have indeed come a long way. There remains much potential for both countries to work together for mutual benefit. For Singapore, it is in its long-term interest to constantly stay relevant to China's growth. As for China, a giant in many ways, the building of a strong and comprehensive relationship with Singapore on the basis of mutual respect and mutual benefit will help to underscore China's pledge to peaceful development and to treat other countries, however small, on an equal basis.

Chapter 2

Lee Kuan Yew: The Special Relationship with China

ZHENG Yongnian and LIM Wen Xin

Singapore's first Prime Minister Lee Kuan Yew met five generations of Chinese leaders including Mao Zedong, Deng Xiaoping, Jiang Zemin, Hu Jintao and Xi Jinping. Xi said Lee was an old friend of the Chinese people and the founder and mover of China–Singapore relationship. Indeed, Lee had laid the foundation for strong bilateral ties. Chinese leaders are always keen to learn from the Singapore model, especially Lee's brand of 'soft authoritarianism'. Lee's unique background as a Cambridge-educated Chinese and his farsightedness made him an impressive interlocutor to foreign leaders. Despite the passing away of Lee, Singapore is likely to continue to be an active actor in China's 'going global' initiatives.

A Special Relationship

'No foreign country other than Britain has had a greater influence on Singapore's political development than China, the ancestral homeland of three-quarters of our people', the late Singapore's former Senior Minister Mentor Lee Kuan Yew mentioned in his memoir[1] when he recounted bilateral relations between China and Singapore. The deep, instrumental and intricate relationship between China, one of the largest countries in the world, and Singapore, a red dot in Southeast Asia, has been widely regarded as a special one. Certainly, Lee Kuan Yew was the veteran architect and engineer who built and moulded such a relationship.

In the past few decades, China has successfully engaged in two simultaneous transformations. Internally, it has lifted itself from one of the poorest economies

---

[1] Lee Kuan Yew, *From Third World to First, The Singapore Story: 1965–2000*, Singapore, Singapore Press Holdings Limited, 2000, p. 635.

to the number two in the world. Externally, it has escaped isolation and become a part of the international system; it now plays an increasingly important role in the world. Why had Singapore under Lee succeeded in building a special relationship with China? The answer is simple: Lee (and Singapore) as a strategic visionary and symbolic figure had been an integral part of China's dual transformations.

Lee once said to Tom Plate:

> The Chinese know I have helped them in the past. The ideas that Deng Xiaoping formed, if he had not come here (in the 1970s) and seen the Western multinationals in Singapore producing wealth for us, training our people so as a result we were able to build a prosperous society, then he might never have opened up…opening up the coastal SEZs (Special Economic Zones) that eventually led to the whole of China opening up by joining the World Trade Organisation… The relationship with me goes back a long way, opening windows for them.[2]

The deep-rooted friendship was forged during Lee's first visit to China in 1976. It then spanned over three decades where he made more than 30 visits to China, meeting the five generations of Chinese leaders including Mao Zedong, Deng Xiaoping, Jiang Zemin, Hu Jintao as well as the current President Xi Jinping.[3] Undeniably, Lee's incessant efforts and contributions in constructing a special relationship with China is the cornerstone of strong China–Singapore ties today. He was one of the first to raise the seminal view and recognise China's potential as a nascent economic power. Reciprocally, despite the absence of formal diplomatic relations before 1990, Deng Xiaoping regarded Lee as his unofficial mentor, seeking Lee's unvarnished opinions on China's mammoth economic reform plans.[4] In fact, Lee was one of the few foreign leaders he consulted and both came to share a special bond.

In this chapter, through examining the various aspects of Singapore's founding father — Lee Kuan Yew — we aim to buttress and underscore the vital role of Lee in shaping a special relationship between the two nations despite the significant disparity in size. More specifically, we aim to discuss how Lee's

---

[2] Tom Plate, *Giants of Asia: Conversation with Lee Kuan Yew: Citizen Singapore: How to Build a Nation*, Singapore, Marshall Cavendish, 2010, pp. 61–62.

[3] Jeremy Koh, "Lee Kuan Yew 'Laid Foundation for Strong Singapore–China Ties'", *Channel News Asia*, 25 March 2015.

[4] Graham Allison and Robert D Blackwill, "Lee Kuan Yew, Grand Master of Asia", *The National Interest*, 1 March 2013.

personality, the principles that he firmly upheld, his positive contributions under different periods of the Chinese leadership and the successful Singapore model under his governance had successfully engaged one of the most powerful countries in the world, China, in a special relationship.

The pre-Deng era

Chinese official media China Central Television (CCTV) ran tributes repeatedly on 23 March 2015, the day Lee passed away, lionising the late leader by quoting President Xi Jinping's reference to Lee as an 'old friend of the Chinese people' in his condolence message to President Tony Tan of Singapore.[5]

Chinese leaders since the late Deng have shown their appreciation of Lee's contribution to China's modernisation[6] and viewed Lee as a close friend of their country. While such a close relationship began with Deng, the first contact between China and Singapore was through the 'ping-pong diplomacy' in 1971 when Singapore's ping-pong team accepted an invitation to play at the Afro-Asia Table Tennis Friendship Games in Beijing.[7] In the following year, a few months after President Nixon went to China, Singapore also accepted a Chinese offer to send its ping-pong team for a friendly visit to Singapore.[8]

Lee's sentiments towards China were underpinned by a complex set of calculations. He was not into communism and had to wrestle the control of Singapore from communist insurgents in the early days. During the entire Cold War period, Southeast Asia (SEA) remained extremely wary of China simply because Mao wanted to promote a Communist movement which threatened the survival of newly formed governments in the region. Up to 1970, China did not recognise the existence of Singapore as an independent country and Lee was often derided as a 'running dog of US and British imperialism'[9] by those who held a vitriol stance. Singapore, according to Lee in his memoir, also decided strategically to be the last ASEAN country to exchange diplomatic representations with China. 'We would establish diplomatic relations

---

[5] "Mr Lee Kuan Yew Was an 'Old Friend' to China: President Xi", *Channel News Asia*, 23 March 2015.
[6] Graham Allison, "The Sayings of Lee Kuan Yew, the Sage of Singapore", *Los Angeles Times*, 24 March 2015.
[7] Lee Kuan Yew, *From Third World to First, The Singapore Story: 1965–2000*, p. 638.
[8] Lee Kuan Yew, *From Third World to First, The Singapore Story: 1965–2000*, p. 638.
[9] Ian Storey, *ASEAN and the Rising China*, New York: Routledge, 2013, p. 232.

with China only after Indonesia had done so. We had to avoid any suspicion that Singapore was influenced by kinship ties with China'.[10]

When the United States began to normalise its ties with China under President Nixon, Lee saw an opportunity to improve Singapore's relations with China. Lee's China policy was based on his strong sense of Singapore's long term national interest, his clear big-picture vision and his extraordinary strategic leadership. While President Nixon wanted to ally with China against the then other super power, the Soviet Union, Lee prognosticated the inevitable rise of China and foresaw that China would eventually adopt an open-door policy to reconnect itself with the world. He believed that Singapore as a peripheral city-state had to establish good relations with a China that would eventually become strong in the future.

Lee's influence in China could be traced four decades back during his path-breaking visit and meetings with an ailing Mao Zedong and his successor, Hua Guofeng in 1976.[11] He made a speech at the Great Hall of the People on 11 May 1976 to assure the Chinese that Singapore did not view a strong China with suspicion:

> Singapore would not be anti-China. The stronger China became, the better and more equal the balance between the United States, the Soviet Union and China. This would be safer for the world and for Singapore. If China concluded that an independent Singapore was not against China's interest, then many of the differences between our two countries would diminish. On the other hand, if it believed that an independent Singapore was against its interest or if China therefore wanted to help install a communist government, then disagreements were bound to increase.[12]

Lee was among the few international leaders to engage with China's leaders. Since Lee's visit to China in 1976, he had made it a point to visit the country regularly — once a year if possible.[13] Upon his return from his first visit to

---

[10] Lee Kuan Yew, *From Third World to First, The Singapore Story: 1965–2000*, p. 640.

[11] Before Lee Kuan Yew's first visit to China, Zhou Enlai had sent him a few invitations to Beijing after meeting with S Rajaratnam. S Rajaratnam repeated Singapore's position to Zhou: that Singapore would establish diplomatic relations with China only after Indonesia had done so. Premier Zhou said China respected Singapore as an independent state. However, before Zhou and Lee could settle a date to meet in Beijing, Zhou passed away: see Lee Kuan Yew, *From Third World to First, The Singapore Story: 1965–2000*, p. 640.

[12] Lee Kuan Yew, *From Third World to First, The Singapore Story: 1965–2000*, p. 643.

[13] Lee Kuan Yew, *One Man's View of the World*, Singapore, Straits Times Press, 2013, p. 29.

China, Lee called for a review of and eventually removed the restriction which deterred Singaporeans under the age of 30 from visiting China so as to promote a more realistic understanding of Chinese society.[14] Although the discussions that Lee had with Mao and Hua did not amount to anything substantial, ties between the two countries gradually improved. As the Prime Minister of Singapore at that time, Lee had sown the seeds for good relations between the two countries today. Lee's visit to Beijing was a political breakthrough as it was the first visit made by a Singapore prime minister to China. The visit also paved the way for Singapore to establish stronger commercial and economic ties with China.[15]

Needless to say, the change in the Singapore–China relationship took place only after Deng Xiaoping returned to power in the late 1970s.

Deng and Lee Kuan Yew

The story of good relations between the two great leaders, Deng and Lee, is well-known. Deng was the Chinese leader whom Lee most respected. Although Deng did not make any published comment on Lee, he spoke about Singapore during his landmark Southern Tour to Chinese cities in 1992: 'There is good social order in Singapore. They govern the place with discipline. We should draw from their experience, and do even better than them'.[16] Lee's Singapore must have left an indelible mark in Deng's memory during his visit to the island in 1978. The year of 1992 was a critical point in China's post-Mao transformation. The crackdown on the pro-democracy movement in 1989 led to the West-led international sanctions on China and to the rise of a conservative leadership. In order to initiate a new wave of reform and open-door policy, Deng went to China's southern coastal cities to tap local dynamics. For Deng, economic development and social order must be achieved at the same time. While calling for radical economic reform, Deng believed that good governance was also desirable. In this context, he referred to Singapore.

---

[14] Lee Kuan Yew, *From Third World to First, The Singapore Story: 1965–2000*, p. 656.

[15] In December 1979, Singapore and China signed a trade agreement that provided a framework for increased trade and economic cooperation. This trade accord was signed by Singapore's Finance Minister Hon Sui Sen and Chinese Foreign Trade Minister Li Qiang in a ceremony attended by Vice-Premier Deng Xiaoping. In June 1980, the two countries signed a bilateral agreement to set up commercial representative offices in each other's country.

[16] Leong Wee Keat, "MM Lee: This Century's Most Important Relationship", *Singapura Kini*, 10 April 2009.

Deng's comment on Singapore soon unleashed a wave of Chinese learning from Singapore in the early 1990s. Yet, the Republic had influenced Deng's reform initiatives much earlier on in 1978 to allow foreign businesses to set up shop in China. Deng visited Singapore in November 1978 when the Chinese leadership held a working conference between 10 October and 15 December 1978. During his stay, Deng showed great interest in Singapore's social and economic development experience. In Singapore, Deng witnessed how a tiny island without sufficient natural resources was able to create a good life for its people by bringing in foreign investments, proper management and technical expertise.[17] Singapore's unique development trajectory and governance model of a prevailing single-party rule under the system of free economy in a Chinese-majority society greatly inspired and reaffirmed the late Chinese strongman's will to embrace market economy. A few weeks after Deng's visit to Singapore, the *People's Daily* changed its line when reporting on Singapore; it described Singapore as a 'garden city worth studying for its greening, public housing and tourism'.[18]

Indeed, Deng's public comment to emulate Singapore in 1992 was a reaffirmation of the favourable Singapore model he had witnessed in Singapore 14 years earlier. Deng's trust in Lee and his Singapore model could be seen in three dimensions. First, both leaders had a strong missionary zeal in building their respective nations. As Tom Plate commented after he interviewed Lee, the two leaders 'had in common extreme ambition, a determination not to let anything or anyone get in their way, and a shared sense of the Chinese people, everywhere, deserving a special place on the world stage'.[19] Deng called himself 'the son of the Chinese people', showing his determination to build a strong China:

> Deng deserves most of the credit for putting China on a different trajectory. When he wanted to open up, many Old Guard leaders were opposed to it. But he was a strong-willed character. He brushed them aside and went ahead and did it. Without him, the turnaround would not have happened so fast, because he was the only one with the Long March credentials to override the doubters. A physically small man, but a giant of a leader — Deng is undoubtedly the most impressive international leader I have ever met. [20]

---

[17] Lee Kuan Yew, *One Man's View of the World*, pp. 30–31.

[18] Lee Kuan Yew, *From Third World to First, The Singapore Story: 1965–2000*, p. 668.

[19] Tom Plate, *Giants of Asia: Conversation with Lee Kuan Yew: Citizen Singapore: How to Build a Nation*, p. 59.

[20] Lee Kuan Yew, *One Man's View of the World*, p. 31.

Second, both leaders considered their country's long term national interest as a priority. Lee's engagement with China during the Cold War was in line with Singapore's national interest and so was Deng's engagement with Lee. Deng listened to Lee as Lee's analysis of the world was in China's national interest. Similarly, to learn from Singapore was to serve the purpose of ensuring China's orderly development.

Third, the two great leaders shared a high level of mutual trust and mutual respect, partly due to their similar pursuit of national interest and shared pragmatism in seeking solutions for pertinent problems in their countries. In his memoirs, Lee recounted how Deng, a chain smoker who had a spittoon beside him wherever he went, refrained from lighting up or spitting in the presence of Lee when he visited Singapore in 1978.[21] In his meeting with Deng during the same visit, Lee told Deng that, 'China wanted SEA countries to stand by its side to isolate the "Russian bear", Singapore's neighbors wanted Singapore to unite and isolate the "Chinese dragon"'.[22] Lee said, 'Association of Southeast Asian Nations (ASEAN) governments regarded radio broadcasts from China appealing directly to their ethnic Chinese as dangerous subversion. Deng listened silently. He had never seen it in this light…He knew that I had spoken the truth. Abruptly, he asked: "What do you want me to do?" … I said, "Stop such radio broadcasts; stop such appeals. It will be better for the ethnic Chinese in ASEAN if China does not underline their kinship and call upon their ethnic empathy"'.[23] Not long after Deng's return to China, the broadcasting to SEA was ceased. Since then, the pragmatic Lee had developed a rapport with the equally pragmatic Deng.[24] Despite coming from very different perspectives and background — one as the descendant of a Hakka trading family, and the other as a Chinese revolutionist — the two leaders shared a pragmatic streak and got along well with each other.

Lee held Deng in high regard as he described Deng as a five-footer, but a giant among men in his memoir:

> I do not know how Chinese historians will evaluate his role. I consider Deng a great leader who changed the destiny of China and of the world… Deng was

---

[21] Lee Kuan Yew, *From Third World to First, The Singapore Story: 1965–2000*, p. 660.

[22] Lee Kuan Yew, *From Third World to First, The Singapore Story: 1965–2000*, pp. 663–664.

[23] Lee Kuan Yew, *From Third World to First, The Singapore Story: 1965–2000*, p. 665.

[24] Rachel Lu, "Was Lee Kuan Yew an Inspiration or a Race Traitor? Chinese Can't Agree", *Foreign Policy*, 23 March 2015, available at <http://foreignpolicy.com/ 2015/03/23/ was-lee-kuan-yew-an-inspiration-or-a-race-traitor-chinese-cant-agree/> (accessed 10 April 2015).

the only leader in China with the political standing and strength to reverse Mao's policies. Like Mao, Deng fought to destroy the old China. But he did what Mao did not do. He built the new China, using free enterprise and the free market "with Chinese characteristics"… Twenty years after Deng's open-door policy, China shows every promise of becoming Asia's largest and most dynamic economy… When he died, Deng left the Chinese people a huge and promising legacy.[25]

Lee and Deng's mutual respect and strong rapport paved the way for better bilateral and economic ties between Singapore and China. As a result, Lee captured the opportunity and ride on the bandwagon of China's reform and opening up policy to advance China–Singapore partnership and collaboration. During Deng's rule, Singapore became a major investor in China, building infrastructure, shopping malls, office towers and airline projects in mainland China.[26]

Post-Deng

On 11 August 1990, Premier Li Peng visited Singapore and invited Lee to visit China in mid-October.[27] Lee paid his last visit to Beijing as prime minister to formalise and establish diplomatic relations on 3 October 1990.[28] This move came shortly after Indonesia resumed formal relations with China in the same year.

In 1992, before Deng Xiaoping's retirement from his formal power positions in the Central Advisory Committee and the Central Military Commission, the Chinese Communist Party (CCP) held its 14th National Congress and formally incorporated Deng's theory of a socialist market economy into the party's charter. Deng fully retired from politics and rarely appeared in public scene thereafter. Nevertheless, the solid foundation laid by Deng and Lee continued to drive bilateral relations. As China continued its steady rise as a nascent superpower, economic and business ties between the two countries have been deepened.

The main reason is that ever since the 1976 Lee-Deng meeting, Singapore has constantly made itself relevant to China's development, demonstrating

---

[25] Lee Kuan Yew, *From Third World to First, The Singapore Story: 1965–2000*, pp. 694–695.

[26] Christopher Bodeen, "Singapore's Lee Seen as an Inspiration for Modern China", *Yahoo News*, 23 March 2015.

[27] Lee Kuan Yew, *From Third World to First, The Singapore Story: 1965–2000*, p. 701.

[28] Lee Kuan Yew, *From Third World to First, The Singapore Story: 1965–2000*, p. 702.

flexibility and resilience by sharing valuable experiences and best practices. In his numerous visits to China, Lee had told Chinese leaders: 'Singapore is willing to tap into the full potential of economic cooperation, adding that it will focus on sustainable development and economic transformation'.[29] Indeed, Singapore has a strong presence in China. In 1994, when China initiated a new wave of industrialisation, the Singapore-Suzhou Industrial Park (SIP) was established. Backed by Lee and Deng, this industrial park aimed to replicate Singapore's DNA and tapped on Singapore's successful experience in industrialisation.

Nevertheless, the relationship between Singapore and China was not without hurdles. The SIP took off with great enthusiasm on both sides but soon ran into difficulties. It is recorded in Lee's memoir that:

> Chinese local officials used their association with Singapore to promote their own industrial estate, Suzhou New District (SND), undercutting SIP in land and infrastructure costs, which they controlled. This made the SIP less attractive than SND… The five years in Suzhou educated us on the intricacies of their multi-layered administration and flexible business culture. [30]

Lee's wisdom and farsightedness allowed Singapore to resolve this unpleasant experience between the two countries. According to Education Minister Heng Swee Keat, 'Instead of hoping that time would resolve this, Mr Lee raised issues at the highest levels, and made the disagreements public. Mr Lee was unfazed that going public could diminish his personal standing. Mr Lee proposed to the Chinese, among others, two radical changes: To swap the shareholding structure so that the Chinese had majority control, and to appoint the CEO of the rival park to head the Suzhou Industrial Park … the changes created the necessary realignment and put the project back on track'.[31] Lee himself also mentioned the SIP project in an interview with Tom Plate:

> When my own officers ask me, why do we teach them and then they will outdo us and then we are in trouble? I told them, this is a chance for us to get a foot

---

[29] Zhang Yunbi and Wu Jiao, "Beijing Seeks to Cement Relations with Singapore," *China Daily*, 27 August 2013.

[30] Lee Kuan Yew, *From Third World to First, The Singapore Story: 1965-2000*, pp. 722–724.

[31] Ministry of Education Singapore, "Speech by Heng Swee Keat: An Unwavering Dedication to Singapore", 16 September 2013, available at <http://www.moe.gov.sg/media/speeches/2013/09/16/speech-by-mr-heng-swee-keat-at-the-big-ideas-of-mr-lee-kuan-yew-conference.php> (accessed 29 April 2015).

in China at a time when they don't know how to do it. But they've got so many bright fellows and they are going to go all around the world, and you can't prevent them from coming to Singapore with a camcorder and taking pictures and studying us. So, we might as well do this for them; make a great impact on them and the leadership.[32]

As such, Singapore engages China at various levels. Apart from sharing its industrialisation experience through the SIP, Singapore has helped to develop other projects to share various aspects of Singapore's experiences. In 2007, when China's environmental problem became a hot issue before the 2008 Olympics, the idea to jointly build an eco-city to tackle the environmental problem was broached and later developed into the Singapore-Tianjin Eco-city. Besides these two hallmark government-to-government projects, Singapore has embarked on various key projects in China in accordance to the mutual needs of both countries, such as the Sino-Singapore-Guangzhou Knowledge City, Singapore-Chengdu High-Tech Park and the Sino-Singapore Jilin Food Zone. These iconic projects are not only perceived as tangible achievement of modernisation for China, but more importantly, an extant testimony to the veritable cooperation between China and Singapore. Such a partnership also provides avenues for existing and aspiring leaders at different levels from both sides to strengthen personal ties and foster deeper relationship.

Emeritus Senior Minister Goh Chok Tong highly appraised Lee's contribution to Singapore–China relations when he said: 'Mr Lee's good relations with China's leaders enabled Singapore and the leaders who came after Mr Lee to ride on those good relationships'.[33]

The successful Singapore model

Singapore's per capita gross domestic product today is one of the world's highest. It is not only an international port, but also the third-largest oil refiner in the world. Moreover, it is renowned as a financial hub with an excellent workforce and education system. To a great degree, Singapore's success is a

---

[32] Tom Plate, *Giants of Asia: Conversation with Lee Kuan Yew: Citizen Singapore: How to Build a Nation*, p. 66.

[33] Teo Xuan Wei, "All I Can Say Is, I Did My Best", News Clip, 29 March 2015, available at <http://heresthenews.blogspot.sg/2015/03/all-i-can-say-is-i-did-my-best.html>.(accessed 10 April 2015).

good mix of Western practice with Asian values, crafted under Lee's governing philosophy. Despite receiving his education in Cambridge, with a demeanour of a British aristocrat, Lee remained very Chinese in many ways.[34] Lee propounded the Confucian culture (also known as the Asian values) as he believed that there can be an alternative to Western-style liberal democracy and that the Western model is not the only feasible way to development and prosperity. He held the belief that 'Asian countries did not need to completely follow Western values, and felt that Western democracy could not be forced on Asian people'.[35] Lee successfully married Asian virtues including filial piety, diligence, collectivism and family culture with Western concepts such as the rule of law, transparency, productivity and effectiveness. His legacy, the Singapore model, gives Chinese leaders reasons to carve out its own development path.

Despite being small in geographical size, Singapore's success in economic development, state-led marketisation and clean governance under a one-party dominant ruling system are of China's interest. Singapore's experience, especially Lee's peculiar brand of 'soft authoritarianism' and paternalistic approach, which extols one-party rule and an uncompromising line on dissent without succumbing to rampant corruption, resonates well in China.[36] Being a practitioner, Lee's adamant and unyielding effort in realising the material well-being of Singapore keeps the economy going. The system undeniably appeals to the Chinese leaders who are eager to expand the economic base but abhor electoral democracy and party competition.

In order to emulate the successful Singapore model, China seeks Singapore's assistance in administrative management expertise and civil servant training. The first of these classes began in the 1980s after Lee's visit to Beijing in September 1985 when he suggested to Zhao Ziyang that they might like to send some of their public sector managers to Singapore.[37] Since then, waves of Chinese officials including top brass from the provincial and regional government

---

[34] Joel Kotkin, "Singapore after Lee Kuan Yew: Future Is Uncertain for the Utilitarian Paradise He Created", *Forbes*, 23 March 2015.

[35] Duncan Hewitt, "Lee Kuan Yew's Death: China's Leaders, Media Avoid Sensitive Topics in Mourning Singapore Leader", *International Business Times*, 23 March 2015.

[36] Carlton Tan, "Lee Kuan Yew Leaves a Legacy of Authoritarian Pragmatism", *The Guardian*, 23 March 2015.

[37] Lee Kuan Yew, *My Lifelong Challenge: Singapore's Bilingual Journey*, Singapore: The Straits Times Press, 2011, p. 206.

organs have visited Singapore to learn from Singapore's experiences. Singapore President Tony Tan mentioned at Nankai University on 1 July 2015:

> Human resource development is a key pillar of China–Singapore bilateral cooperation. Since the mid-1990s, close to 50,000 Chinese officials and cadres have visited Singapore for study trips and courses in areas such as urban and city planning, social governance, and public administration.[38]

Singapore's institutions such as the Lee Kuan Yew School of Public Policy in the National University of Singapore, Nanyang Technological University and the Civil Service College offer public administration programmes and courses specially tailored to the needs of Chinese officials. Such intensive training programmes cover multi-layered and wide-ranging subjects ranging from economic policy, capacity building, urban planning, project management and anti-corruption to community management.[39] As such, there is an institutionalised and systematic transfer of ideational expertise and technical knowledge from Singapore to China.[40]

In commemorating Lee's passing on 23 March 2015, *People's Daily* highlighted his four major legacies that can be observed in China today:

> China's ruling Communist Party has implied it will follow and emulate some of Lee Kuan Yew's political legacies, saying the late Singaporean leader's governing theory inspires and offers much to today's China. The four legacies include maintaining social stability, achieving a smooth and orderly transition of political power, building a clean and uncorrupted government, and introducing the rule of law.[41]

The CCP which has been selective in reading Lee's legacy sees Singapore as a mirror of its future: the perpetuation of its authoritarian rule in a prosperous market-driven society. Chinese President Xi Jinping is seeking a transformative

---

[38] Speech by President Tony Tan Keng Yam at the Honorary Doctorate Conferment Ceremony by Nankai University on 1 July 2015, The Istana, available at <http://www.istana.gov.sg/news/speeches/2015/speech-president-tony-tan-honorary-doctorate-conferment-ceremony-nankai> (accessed 8 July 2015).

[39] Zha Daojiong, "Lee Kuan Yew: A Towering Inspiration for China", China US Focus, 31 March 2015, available at <http://www.chinausfocus.com/culture-history/lee-kuan-yew-a-towering-inspiration-for-china/> (accessed 10 April 2015).

[40] Zha Daojiong, "Lee Kuan Yew: A Towering Inspiration for China".

[41] Cary Huang, "How Lee Kuan Yew's Political Legacies Have Rubbed Off on China", *South China Morning Post*, 25 March 2015.

agenda heavily influenced by the Singapore model — a relentless anti-corruption drive, a broad suppression of dissent and a comprehensive deepening of pro-market economic reforms.[42] China's recent efforts in fighting graft among senior officials show no signs of abating. The nationwide campaign to aggressively crack down both 'tigers' and 'flies' is equivalent to Lee's 'netting big fish'.[43] Moreover, Lee's legacy of the rule of law also inspired China to improve its judicial system. The CCP recently trumpets a new agenda, making a renewed call for the rule of law reform during the fourth plenum of the Communist Party's Central Committee held in October 2014. Overall, it is said that both countries observed the same rules which suit their long-term national interest and meet their needs of the times.

Bridging the gap between China and Taiwan

While China always regards the Taiwan issue as its internal affairs, Lee actually played an important role in re-connecting mainland China with Taiwan. Lee, with his charismatic personality, had helped to thaw the formerly icy cross-strait ties by facilitating the ground-breaking Wang-Koo Summit (*wangguhuitan*) in Singapore in 1993, a historical and peaceful dialogue to develop and promote cross-strait relations. With this move, the statesman was said to have unveiled a new epoch in cross-strait relations by supporting and creating a mutually beneficial communication platform for China and Taiwan to vigorously seek cooperative measures and peaceful conversations. In a press release by the Executive Yuan, Premier Mao Chi-kuo said:

> The death of Mr Lee has cost international society the loss of a wise man and the loss of a close friend of the Republic of China. The ROC government and its people will always remember Lee Kuan Yew's contributions to the promotion of Taiwan-Singapore relations and the peace between the two sides of the Taiwan Strait. [44]

Being a consummate politician, Lee is able to manoeuvre and strike a good balance between China and Taiwan. This is due to his pragmatic and

---

[42] Pei Minxin, "The Real Singapore Model", *The Straits Times*, 31 March 2015.

[43] Cary Huang, "How Lee Kuan Yew's Political Legacies Have Rubbed Off on China", *South China Morning Post*, 25 March 2015.

[44] "Lee Kuan Yew's Passing Mourned in Taiwan", *Want China Times*, 23 March 2015, available at <http://www.wantchinatimes.com/news-subclasscnt.aspx?id=20150323000150 &cid= 1101> (accessed 11 April 2015).

non-ideological approach to foreign policy. While Singapore adheres to the 'One-China' policy, it has maintained friendly and long-term relations with Taiwan in the military[45] and economic spheres.[46]

His contribution to making the first high-level dialogue possible deserved enormous credit as it had a remarkable impact on the region as well as cross-strait developments. The first cross-strait talks took place in Singapore in April 1993 between the two respective heads of quasi-official organisations: Straits Exchange Foundation Chairman Koo Chen-fu and Chairman of China's Association for Relations across the Taiwan Straits Wang Daohan.[47] Four agreements were signed at the first meeting to promote economic ties, trade and people-to-people exchanges.[48]

Lee had this to say on cross-strait relations: 'China does not need to use force to achieve unification; gradual economic integration would bring the two sides closer'.[49] Indeed, since Taiwan President Ma Ying-jeou took office in 2008, cross-strait economic links have improved significantly. Under the Kuomintang administration, the Wang-Koo Summit had resumed to boost trade and investment, and resultant economic and social integration on both sides of the strait.

Lee Kuan Yew as China's interlocutor to the world

Lee had often been regarded as an 'influential world class statesman and strategist'[50] whose foreign policy for Singapore reflected his 'broad global perspective and also a positive strategic mindset'.[51] Singapore's relationship with China is special because Lee (and Singapore) have not only contributed to China's

---

[45] For nearly 30 years, due to the lack of space for large-scale military manoeuvres, Singapore has trained its troops in Taiwan under the code name Operation Starlight; see Fayen Wong, "Singapore Military Juggles Ties with Taiwan and China", *Reuters*, 27 August 2006.

[46] Fayen Wong, "Singapore Military Juggles Ties with Taiwan and China".

[47] Shih Hsiu-chuan and Loa Lok-sin, "Government, Politicians Mourn Death of Lee Kuan Yew", *Taipei Times*, 24 March 2015.

[48] "First Straits Talks in 9 Years Open", *Xinhua News Agency*, 12 June 2008.

[49] "Integrated Economy will Unite China and Taiwan: Lee Kuan Yew", *Want China Times*, 9 August 2013, available at <http://www.wantchinatimes.com/news-subclass-cnt.aspx?id=20130809000075&cid=1101> (accessed 11 April 2015).

[50] Kor Kian Beng and Esther Teo, "China Officials Pay Tribute to 'World Class Strategist' Lee Kuan Yew", *The Straits Times*, 24 March 2015.

[51] Kor Kian Beng and Esther Teo, "China Officials Pay Tribute to 'World Class Strategist' Lee Kuan Yew".

modernisation, but also helped the world, particularly the West and China, to understand each other.

Externally, Singapore strives to maintain productive and fruitful relationships with major powers to maximise its national interests and avoid risks. Singapore's foreign policy towards the West and the East abides by a few fundamental principles. It stresses on maintaining a balance of power and a pragmatic non-alignment approach to ensuring its autonomy, security, economic sustainability and liberalism.[52] The pragmatic and realistic approaches to not becoming a de facto vassal of any dominant power have allowed Singapore to navigate smoothly between the United States and China.

Singapore has foreseen the rise of China as a driver for regional economic development and its large market as an opportunity for mutual cooperation and gains. There is a fundamental conviction that China shares the political stability and economic growth imperatives of regional countries. As a result, whilst Singapore-US relationship is long established across the military, security, economic and diplomatic spheres, Singapore has unhesitatingly engaged in a deep relationship with China through bilateral trade, investments, cultural exchanges, economic collaboration and multilateral regional institutions. In the Working Paper series of the Institute of Defence and Strategic Studies of Singapore, Evelyn Goh commented in her paper, *Singapore's Reaction to Rising China*:

> Singapore places great importance on China becoming a second benign great power in the region, balanced tacitly by, and enjoying a modus vivendi with, the benign superpower. China apparently recognises that Singapore — while possessing close military ties with the US — is a fairly 'independent', 'objective' voice in international relations. Thus, it provides a useful bridge between the 'Asian way' and the 'western style' of diplomacy and politics, and acts as an 'honest broker' and even 'interpreter' for the two sides.[53]

No leader appears to be as candid as Lee when it comes to China's external affairs; he provided his insights and reminded China of how to integrate itself into the world. For instance, during Deng's visit to Singapore in 1978, Lee convinced Deng of the need for China to stop its communist propaganda in

---

[52] Robyn Klingler-Vidra, "The Pragmatic 'Little Red Dot': Singapore's US Hedge against China" in *IDEAS reports — Special Reports SR015*, Nicholas Kitchen (ed.) LSE IDEAS, London School of Economics and Political Science, London, the United Kingdom, 2012.

[53] Evelyn Goh, "Singapore's Reaction to Rising China: Deep Engagement and Strategic Adjustment, Working Paper of Institute of Defence and Strategic Studies Singapore 67, May 2004, p. 9.

SEA if it wanted to improve ties with the region. During Jiang Zemin's leadership, Jiang often sought Lee's views on America and the West over dinner as China did not understand the West adequately at the time. Lee recalled in his book: 'Once, Jiang held my hand and asked me, "Tell me, what does the West really think of us?" I said to him, "Really, they're fearful of you once you get your act going"'.[54] For its own national interest, Singapore very much wanted China to play a constructive role in the region. At times, Lee's blunt comments ruffled feathers, particularly among the younger generation of Chinese. Nevertheless, China's leaders understood that Lee's comments were made in Singapore's interest.

In the same way, Lee has helped the West understand China by threading the policy needle between the United States and China. Since Deng's open-door policy, the West has frequently dismissed China's growth and its sustainability, with some even arguing that the country faced fragmentation. Lee would tell the Americans and Europeans that China's growth was indeed real and it would be the biggest thing that had ever happened in recent history. He also cautioned the United States against underestimating China and its attempt to contain this rising power.

Due to his innate understanding of China, Lee's views were sought and closely listened to by other world leaders. Former German Chancellor Helmut Schmidt first met and became friend with Lee when the latter was in his late 70s. Schmidt said, 'It was under the influence of Lee Kuan Yew that I visited China a dozen or 15 times or so in the last 30 years … I met Deng Xiaoping and I was greatly impressed … I think that the modern development of China is due to the genius of Deng Xiaoping. And Harry Lee was one of those who rather early understood the enormous importance of Deng Xiaoping'.[55] Graham Allison of Harvard University also wrote that, '[n]o one outside the United States has had a greater influence on American policy towards a rising China than Mr Lee'.[56]

Singapore's language planning and policy adopted by Lee, which aims to facilitate effective communication by emphasising bilingual education, has provided a competitive edge for Singapore to serve as a bridge between the United States and China. Today, even though China's leaders no longer need

---

[54] Lee, *My Lifelong Challenge: Singapore's Bilingual Journey*, p. 211.

[55] "Four Friends — Helmut Schmidt, Lee Kuan Yew, Henry Kissinger and George Shultz", SG Hard Truth, available at <http://www.sghardtruth.com/2012/08/13/four-friends-helmut-schmidt-lee-kuan-yew-henry-kissinger-and-george-shultz/> (accessed 15 April 2015).

[56] Han Fook Kwang, "What's Next for Singapore after Lee Kuan Yew", *The Straits Times*, 4 April 2015.

Singapore as much to help them understand America, the ability to converse in Mandarin is still helpful. 'When President Hu Jintao was in Singapore in 2009 for the APEC Summit, he sat next to Prime Minister Lee Hsien Loong at a dinner. Their speaking in Mandarin to each other created a different relationship. If we spoke no Mandarin at all, the relationship would be more formal and distant',[57] Lee vividly recalled.

While English, the international lingua franca is heavily emphasised in Singapore, the government encourages the teaching of mother tongue languages, especially the mastery of Mandarin, as Chinese constitutes the largest percentage of Singapore's total population. Robyn Klingler Vidra wrote in his paper, 'Singapore's language selection is telling of its pragmatism and balancing of Chinese and English markets with economic relevance'.[58] A point made by Robyn Klingler Vidra in her publication with the London School of Economics and Political Science, *The New Geopolitics of South-east Asia*, depicts how Singapore's language selection and cultural background have been effective in managing its international relations with other countries including China and the United States:

> Singapore hedges its cultural, spatial and economic proximity to China with robust diplomatic, military and economic relations with the US and through regional participation in ASEAN and international organisations.[59]

By strengthening its bicultural and bilingual capabilities, Lee and his political peers thus guarantee Singapore's economic and cultural relevance to the East and the West, enabling the tiny island to establish an economic and cultural bridge between China and the world.

Conclusion

After more than three decades of opening up, China has now become an important player on the world stage and its leaders can directly talk or negotiate with world leaders everywhere. However, Chinese leaders continue to appreciate Singapore's view of the world. Lee said in his book *My Lifelong Challenge: Singapore's Bilingual Journey*: 'Then Vice President Xi Jinping told me in 2008: "We will need you for a long time. I have been to Singapore, I know

---

[57] Lee, *My Lifelong Challenge: Singapore's Bilingual Journey*, pp. 211–215.

[58] Robyn Klingler-Vidra, "The Pragmatic 'Little Red Dot': Singapore's US Hedge against China".

[59] Robyn Klingler-Vidra, "The Pragmatic 'Little Red Dot': Singapore's US Hedge against China".

what you have and our people want to learn. We get more from you than from America"'. [60] Indeed, Lee as Singapore's founding father and guiding light had exerted an influence disproportionate to the size of his small city state. His dedication and contribution to shaping a constructive China–Singapore relationship are admirable.

In a book published in 2013, *Lee Kuan Yew: The Grand Master's Insights on China, the United States, and the World*, Lee held heady hopes for Xi: 'He has iron in his soul. I would put him in Nelson Mandela's class of persons. He is a person with enormous emotional stability who does not allow his personal misfortunes or sufferings to affect his judgment. In other words, he is impressive'.[61] Lee, who had witnessed the glory of five generations of Chinese leadership had developed a good understanding of China's system and always manage to stay onside with both Beijing and Washington. Chinese leaders have seen how Singapore has assimilated Western ways and adapted them in an Asian context.

With the passing of Lee, China–Singapore relationship will enter a new stage. As China's political and economic influence continues to grow. It is a fast learner who has learned a great deal from the world. With time, in some areas, China has begun to offer its own experiences to the outside world. Will such developments make Singapore's experiences less relevant to China? Or, will China become less interested in Singapore's experiences?

Certainly, it is a great challenge for Singapore to retain its relevance to China, not only in economic terms, but also in political and strategic terms. Nevertheless, the prospects of China–Singapore relations are positive. Internally, what China called the Singapore model of governance has been evolving. As long as Singapore is capable of integrating 'best practices' from the West and Asian values, as Lee did in the past decades, China will retain its interest in the Singapore model. As Chinese society becomes more complicated, there is a need to learn from the world on governance. Externally, Singapore will remain as one of the main gates to the international community, particularly Southeast Asia. This is especially true when China is 'going global', as its latest initiative of 'One Belt, One Road' showed. Singapore has been an active actor in China's domestic modernisation. It will certainly be an active actor in facilitating China's 'going global' initiatives.

---

[60] Lee, *My Lifelong Challenge: Singapore's Bilingual Journey*, p. 209.
[61] Lee Kuan Yew, *Lee Kuan Yew: The Grand Master's Insights on China, the United States, and the World*, Belfer Centre Studies in International Security, p. 17.

Chapter 3

Resilient and Enduring Singapore–China Bilateral Economic Relations

Sarah Y TONG

Bilateral economic ties between China and Singapore predate the establishment of bilateral diplomatic relations in 1990. Since the late 1970s, bilateral economic exchange had advanced and cooperation expanded at both the government and business levels. Bilateral economic relations have further deepened since Singapore and China formally set up diplomatic ties in 1990. Bilateral trade has grown in volume and scope. Capital flows between the two countries, in the forms of direct investment and equity investment, have also surged. Both sides have enhanced their financial cooperation in recent years. The future witnesses great potential in further strengthening of their economic ties, although challenges exist.

Economic pragmatism triumphs over political differences

While diplomatic relations between Singapore and China started only in 1990, high-level bilateral contacts had already taken place before both sides' official recognition of each other. The first state delegation led by the then Singapore Minister for Foreign Affairs S Rajaratnam to China in 1975, the then Prime Minister Lee Kuan Yew's first visit in 1976, and the visit to Singapore by China's then Senior Vice Premier Deng Xiaoping in 1978, Prime Minister Lee Kuan Yew's second visit in 1980, and Premier Zhao Ziyang's visit in 1981 are a testament to close contacts established before relations were formalised.

More significantly, bilateral economic relations have proven to be even more enduring. Indeed, before Southeast Asian countries began to normalise their political relations with China in the 1970s, "the Sino-Pan-Malayan (Malaysia and Singapore) trade has been the most durable in the sense that it has survived the most stormy period of the late 1950s…Indeed, Malaysia and Singapore are rare examples of countries, including the socialist states, which have success-fully maintained continuous trade relations with China without having suc-cumbed to the interferences of the Cold War…".[1] Between 1950 and 1966, Singapore's imports from China grew at an average annual rate of over 8% a year in nominal terms.[2]

Since Singapore's separation from Malaysia on 9 August 1965, economic ties between Singapore and China continued to grow and have advanced considerably. Not only trade in commodities rapidly expanded, trade in ser-vices as well as in cross-border equity investment and direct investment also developed significantly. Moreover, closer bilateral economic relations have contributed to the promotion of the Sino-ASEAN (Association of Southeast Asian Nations) economic cooperation and regional economic integration in East and Southeast Asia.

It is therefore justified to claim that bilateral economic relations over the past five decades are overall stable and have been enhanced considerably in the last 25 years since 1990. As Singapore and China enter the next quarter century of their diplomatic relations, it is in their respective interests to reinforce bilat-eral ties. From China's perspective, maintaining robust bilateral economic relations is essential for the country's further development and modernisation. It is, first of all, consistent with China's domestic development agenda. China envisages the positive aspects of maintaining closer economic relations with Singapore, such as a more balanced trade, increased trade in services and grow-ing bilateral investment, particularly from China to Singapore. These are the structural changes that China attempts to promote in further opening up its economy.

Second, China's close economic relations with Singapore has also significantly facilitated its efforts in advancing economic ties with its Asian neighbours in general and with ASEAN in particular. Singapore, a long-term advocate of economic integration in Asia, is one of the most open and most developed

---

[1] John Wong, *The Political Economy of China's Changing Relations with Southeast Asia*, London, MacMillan Press, 1984, p. 67.
[2] As calculated by the author using data from Table 3.1 in John Wong's book; see John Wong, *The Political Economy of China's Changing Relations with Southeast Asia*, p. 202. Exports fluctuated much more and grew on average by 1.6% per year.

countries in Asia. Together with China, Singapore can provide strong backing to help bridge closer economic cooperation between China and Southeast Asia.

Furthermore, building strong bilateral ties is also instrumental to facilitating regional economic integration in East and Southeast Asia. There are at present numerous initiatives that involve countries in the region, including the Trans-Pacific Partnership (TPP), the Regional Comprehensive Economic Partnership (RCEP) and the Free Trade Area of the Asia-Pacific (FTAAP).[3] Singapore is involved in all of the initiatives, of which it is also a key party.

Similarly, maintaining stronger economic ties with China has provided Singapore impetuses to sustain its growth and development. As China's economy becomes not only larger but also increasingly open and consumption-oriented, it begins to serve as an important market for Singapore's goods and services as well as a destination for Singapore investment. Second, closer Sino-Singapore bilateral economic relations could help promote closer ties between ASEAN and China in the development of regional production networks. This could also facilitate intra-regional economic integration within ASEAN and enhance the region's competitiveness. Third, closer economic cooperation between China and ASEAN is pivotal to the promotion of economic integration in greater Asia as well as between Asia and the rest of the world.

Persistent economic relations during the pre-1990 years

The People's Republic of China was established in 1949 and Singapore separated from Malaysia in 1965. Although ties were only formally established in 1990, economic exchanges between China and Singapore had already developed substantially due largely to the economic pragmatism exercised by both governments. As such, bilateral economic relations have enjoyed five decades of development, although with ups and downs.

---

[3] The four original signatory countries of the TPP are Brunei, Chile, New Zealand and Singapore; the other eight countries under negotiation are the United States, Australia, Peru, Vietnam, Malaysia, Mexico, Canada and Japan. In 2013, South Korea and Taiwan also announced their interests in joining. In the case of RCEP, 16 countries are involved — the 10 ASEAN member states, three countries in East Asia (China, Japan and South Korea), India, Australia and New Zealand. FTAAP, on the other hand, aims to form free trade areas among member economies of the Asia-Pacific Economic Cooperation (APEC), including Australia, Brunei, Canada, Indonesia, Japan, South Korea, Malaysia, New Zealand, the Philippines, Singapore, Thailand, the United States, Taiwan, Hong Kong, the People's Republic of China, Mexico, Papua New Guinea, Chile, Russia and Vietnam.

Between 1965 and the late 1970s, when ideological differences and Cold War hostility dominated political relations between China and Singapore, two-way trading activities in fact took place, albeit at a low level. There are several contributing factors. From Singapore's perspective, its separation from Malaysia had actually given it a free rein to trade with China and to deal independently with any related issues without being hamstrung by pressure from Kuala Lumpur. Furthermore, as a city-state with no natural resources, Singapore has to retain its open economy and free enterprise system.[4]

While China's economy at the time remained largely inward-oriented, it nonetheless had demand for trade. Essentially, it needed to import certain raw materials and capital goods to sustain its industrialisation. As the country's political relations with the former Soviet Union deteriorated since the late 1950s, it had to export food products and light manufactured goods to earn the hard currency for its imports. Overall, Southeast Asia was important in China's trade, as a market for China's manufactured goods and source of imports for raw materials such as rubber.

Singapore was particularly significant to China economically. Singapore, being more developed and the region's most important entrepôt, is not only an important market for Chinese products, but also serves as the gateway for China's trade with the rest of Southeast Asia.[5] In 1970, Singapore's imports from China mainly consisted of food (21.5%), light manufactured products (paper and textile, 25.6%) and miscellaneous manufactures (including clothing, 12.4%).[6] Trade between the two countries expanded steadily throughout the 1970s, at an average annual rate of over 20%.

Nonetheless, before the late 1970s, economic exchange between China and Singapore remained relatively small in size and complementary in nature. First, China adopted Soviet-style economic system, characterised by central planning domestically and autarky, or self-reliance, externally. Second, as China conducted trading in order to achieve its industrial policies objectives, it preferred to trade with the communist bloc. Therefore, economic exchange with non-communist countries was mostly at a supplemental and secondary level, at least

[4] John Wong, *The Political Economy of China's Changing Relations with Southeast Asia*, p. 92.
[5] In 1975, for example, Singapore's exports to China amounted to S$98.5 million, of which around 30% were domestic export and 70% were re-exports of products imported from other countries. As calculated by the author using data from Table 4.9 in John Wong, *The Political Economy of China's Changing Relations with Southeast Asia*, p. 213.
[6] See Table 4.4 in John Wong, *The Political Economy of China's Changing Relations with Southeast Asia*, p. 207.

until the 1960s when Sino-Soviet relations soured. Since the early 1970s, China had become more receptive towards trade, which was essential for China in order to fulfil its ambition to modernise its economy. This also coincided with China's warming relations with the United States, following Nixon's visit to Beijing in 1972. China's exports to Southeast Asia, including Singapore, began to increase so that the country could earn the foreign currency needed to import capital goods from advanced economies such as Japan.

Before 1978, despite a lack of official exchange between the Chinese and Singapore governments which viewed each other with much animosity, trading activities grew considerably. Between 1966 and 1978, total bilateral trade and Singapore's imports from China rose by about 7% and 9%, respectively, annually on average in nominal terms. However, it is noteworthy that trade volumes experienced drastic fluctuations during this period, especially with respect to Singapore's exports to China.[7] Overall, Singapore imported far more from China than it exported to China and bilateral trade deficit amounted to around two-thirds of total trade (Table 1). This is, in part, due to Singapore's role as an entrepôt, where a portion of imports from China were re-exported to other parts of Southeast Asia.

Since the late 1970s, Sino-Singapore bilateral economic relations were enhanced. First, Southeast Asian countries including Singapore began to improve their political ties with China. Second, China launched its "reform and opening-up" in 1978, adopting a more open and outward-looking economic strategy. Indeed, Sino-Singapore economic relations entered a new phase in late 1979, when a bilateral trade agreement was signed. The trade pact provided a legal basis for the expansion of mutual economic cooperation

Table 1 Singapore's Trade with China, 1965–2014: Annual Growth and Net-to-Total Ratio (%)

Year	Total Trade	Imports	Exports	Balance/Total
1966–1978	6.9	9.1	−0.4	−65.9
1978–1990	15.7	14.1	22.2	−43.5
1990–2001	14.2	11.8	18.7	−12.7
2001–2007	26.4	24.5	28.8	−3.7
2007–2014	4.1	2.3	5.9	3.8

Source: Author's calculation using data in Table 11 in the Appendix.

---

[7] See Table 11 in Appendix for further details.

in the absence of a formal diplomatic framework. Moreover, under the pact, both countries were committed to extend the "most-favoured nation" (MFN) treatment to each other.[8] The two sides established their Commercial Representatives' Office in each other's country in 1981 and started their air service in 1985. Also in 1985, Singapore's former Deputy Prime Minister and Finance Minister Dr Goh Keng Swee was asked to serve as economic adviser on the development of China's coastal provinces and economic zones.[9]

Although China and Singapore did not normalise diplomatic relations until 1990, bilateral trade had accelerated. Between 1978 and 1990, total trade expanded by 15% annually on average, more than double that of the 1966–1978 period. More significantly, Singapore's exports to China expanded much faster than its imports from China, at 22% and 14% per year on average, respectively. During the 1978–1990 period, Singapore continued to incur trade deficit with China in absolute terms, at around S$1.5 billion per year on average, though the net-to-total trade ratio declined considerably to about 44% of total trade on average during the period.

Robust trade relations since 1990

China and Singapore have enjoyed enduring trade relations for the past five decades even during times of hostile political climate. During the first 25 years (from 1965), bilateral trade fluctuated and grew gradually in the first decade but picked up speed since the late 1970s. In 1990, the two countries established diplomatic ties, providing a strong and new momentum for bilateral economic relations. Trade between Singapore and China has since developed significantly in volume and in scope.

Between 1990 and 2001, total bilateral trade volume grew by 14% annually on average, from S$5 billion to S$20 billion. However, growth during the 1990–2001 period, in comparison to the 1978–1990 period, was slightly slower due partly to the Asian financial crises in 1997 and 1998. Meanwhile, Singapore's imports from and exports to China grew annually at 12% and 19%, respectively. As a result, Singapore's trade deficit with China continued to shrink in relative terms, equivalent to 13% of total trade volume on average for the 1990–2001 period (Table 1).

---

[8] John Wong, *The Political Economy of China's Changing Relations with Southeast Asia*, p. 100.
[9] Saw Swee-Hock and John Wong, eds., *Advancing Singapore–China Economic Relations*, Singapore, East Asian Institute and Institute of Southeast Asian Studies, 2014, p. 35.

China's accession to the World Trade Organization (WTO) in late 2001 marked its entry into a new era of economic opening and integration with the world economy. In 2003, China signed a free trade agreement with ASEAN, which took effect in July 2005. As China's trade growth accelerated, bilateral trade with Singapore also gathered pace. Between 2001 and 2007, total bilateral trade grew by 26% annually, reaching over S$90 billion. Singapore's exports to China, at an annual growth rate of 29%, continued to outpace its imports from China, which grew 25% annually. As a result, bilateral trade had largely achieved a balance, with the ratio of trade deficit to total trade reduced to less than 4%.

Growth in bilateral trade slowed down sharply since 2008, when the world economy was severely affected by the global financial and economic crisis. Total bilateral trade rose by 4% annually between 2007 and 2014, while Singapore's imports from and exports to China rose by 2.3% and 5.9%, respectively. Since 2009, Singapore has recorded growing trade surplus with China, amounting to S$65 billion in 2014. During the 2007–2014 period, the ratio of surplus to total trade was around 3.8%.

Overall, bilateral economic relations between China and Singapore have survived and thrived over the years, having overcome both bitter political tensions and severe external shocks. Based on trade data reported by Singapore government, trade expanded by 16% per year on average for the period between 1966 and 2014. Singapore's exports to China grew faster than its imports from China at 18% and 15% annually, respectively. In addition, bilateral trade has become increasingly balanced — in the earlier years, China exported to Singapore more than it imported from Singapore but the recent years witnessed a reverse in the trend whereby Singapore exports to China slightly more than it imports from China, with Singapore recording a small surplus.

Table 2 China's Trade with Singapore, 1993–2014: Annual Growth and Net-to-Total Ratio (%)

Year	Total Trade	Imports	Exports	Balance/Total
1993–2001	5.9	4.1	7.6	1.9
2001–2007	27.6	22.7	31.3	8.2
2007–2014	7.8	8.4	7.4	19.4

Source: Author's calculation using data in Table 12 in the Appendix.

Although trade data from China are only available since 1993, calculations had demonstrated relatively similar trends of growth. First, total trade growth was the fastest from 2001 to 2007 at 27% annually on average (Table 2), comparably close to that recorded by Singapore government. Second, trade growth decelerated sharply since 2007 to less than 8%. This is consistent with that reported by Singapore, although the values are different. Third, between 2007 and 2014, China's imports from Singapore grew faster than its exports to Singapore. The figures are once again comparable to those reported by Singapore.

There are however discrepancies between the two sets of values. For example, from 1990 to 2014, Singapore data have shown that the country's exports growth outperformed its imports growth from China. Data from China, on the other hand, have shown that its imports from Singapore slightly outpaced its exports to Singapore only for the 2007–2014 period. As a result, data on trade balance from the two sides differed greatly. Singapore reported a decline in the deficit-to-total trade ratio over the decades and a mild surplus in recent years. Data from China showed that its trade surplus with Singapore continues to increase in both absolute volume and in relation to total trade. To a large extent, the data disparity could be attributed to the middleman role that Singapore played in China's trade with Southeast Asia. In fact, this mirrored the case of mainland China's trade with Hong Kong, where a considerable volume of shipment to Hong Kong for re-export to a third market is recorded as exports to Hong Kong.

In sum, bilateral trade relations between Singapore and China has been resilient for the past five decades and grown even stronger since the normalisation of diplomatic relations. Economic pragmatism of the two governments, geographical proximity and shared historical and cultural ties of the peoples have largely contributed to strong bilateral trade ties. China's economic reform and opening-up in the late 1970s and its entry to WTO membership in 2001 were also important driving forces behind the strengthened bilateral trade ties.

Economic significance of bilateral trade to both countries

After decades of development, trade between China and Singapore have become increasingly important to both sides. Between 1999 and 2014, China's share in Singapore's total exports rose from 3.4% to 12.6%, while the share in Singapore's exports to Asian countries increased from less than 6% to 17%

Table 3 Percentage Share of Trade with Mainland China and Hong Kong in Singapore's Total Trade, 1999–2014

	Percentage Share in Singapore's Exports to			
	Asia		World	
	Exports to Mainland China	Exports to Mainland China and Hong Kong	Exports to Mainland China	Exports to Mainland China and Hong Kong
1999	5.9%	19.2%	3.4%	11.1%
2002	8.6%	23.0%	5.5%	14.6%
2005	12.6%	26.3%	8.6%	18.0%
2008	13.1%	27.9%	9.2%	19.6%
2011	14.6%	30.1%	10.4%	21.5%
2014	17.1%	32.0%	12.6%	23.6%

	Percentage Share in Singapore's Imports from			
	Asia		World	
	Imports from Mainland China	Imports from Mainland China and Hong Kong	Imports from Mainland China	Imports from Mainland China and Hong Kong
1999	8.0%	12.5%	5.4%	8.4%
2002	11.4%	15.0%	7.9%	10.4%
2005	14.4%	17.4%	10.4%	12.5%
2008	15.3%	16.8%	10.7%	11.9%
2011	15.0%	16.3%	10.5%	11.4%
2014	17.8%	19.1%	12.4%	13.3%

Note: Trade data before 2003 does not include Singapore's trade with Indonesia.
Source: Singapore Department of Statistics, SingStat Table Builder.

(Table 3). Singapore's imports from China are also equally important. China's share in Singapore's imports from Asia rose from 8% in 1999 to 18% in 2014, and the share in Singapore's total imports increased from 5% to 12%. The mainland China and Hong Kong's combined share of trade with Singapore is also reportedly higher, accounting for one-third of Singapore's exports to Asia and one-fifth of Singapore's imports from Asia.

In terms of non-oil domestic exports, China is seen to be even more important to Singapore as a market. Between 1988 and 1997, Singapore's

Table 4 Percentage Share of Selected Economies in Singapore's Non-oil Domestic Exports, 1988–2014

	United States	European Union	Mainland China and Hong Kong		
			Mainland	Hong Kong	Total
1988	39.8%		2.4%	4.7%	7.0%
1993	31.1%	18.7% (1995)	1.4%	6.8%	8.2%
1998	29.7%	21.6%	3.3%	5.8%	9.2%
2003	17.3%	17.8%	6.8%	7.3%	14.1%
2008	12.8%	15.4%	10.0%	7.3%	17.4%
2013	9.3%	11.5%	14.0%	9.2%	23.3%
2014	9.5%	11.1%	15.3%	7.3%	22.7%

Note: Trade data before 2003 does not include Singapore's trade with Indonesia.
Source: Singapore Department of Statistics, SingStat Table Builder.

non-oil domestic exports to China was between 1% and 3% of its total, in contrast to its exports to the United States at between 30% and 40% and to the European Union (EU) at nearly 20%. However, China's share in Singapore's non-oil domestic exports has since risen steadily, reaching 15% in 2014. Indeed, since 2009, mainland China and Hong Kong together accounted for around one-fifth of Singapore's total non-oil domestic exports — slightly lower than that of the United States and EU combined (Table 4).[10] It is also higher than that of Indonesia, Malaysia and Thailand combined.

From China's perspective, the trend however appeared to be slightly different. As China expands its trade relations with the rest of the world, its share of trade with many Asian countries out of its total trade has declined to some extent, although trade volume has increased significantly. From 1993 to 2014, Asia's share in China's total exports and imports dropped by around five percentage points, from 57% to 51% and from 60% to 55%, respectively (Table 5). China's trade with Japan in proportion to its total trade experienced the sharpest decline over the same period, from 17% to 6% for exports and from 22%

---

[10] China's share in Singapore's domestic exports also increased significantly, accounting for 18% of Singapore's exports to Asia and 12% of Singapore's total exports to the world. In terms of mainland China and Hong Kong combined trade, the share would be 29% and 19% of Singapore's exports to Asia and to the world in 2014, respectively. See Table 12 in Appendix for further details.

Table 5 Asia's Trade Share in China's Trade, 1993–2014

| | Total | | Japan | | Korea | | ASEAN | | | |
| | | | | | | | Total | | Singapore | |
	Exports	Imports	Exports	Imports	Exports	Imports	Exports	Imports	Exports	Imports
1993	57.4%	60.4%	17.2%	22.4%	3.1%	5.2%			2.4%	2.5%
1994	60.7%	59.5%	17.8%	22.8%	3.6%	6.3%			2.1%	2.1%
1995	61.8%	59.1%	19.1%	22.0%	4.5%	7.8%			2.4%	2.6%
1996	60.4%	60.1%	20.4%	21.0%	5.0%	9.0%			2.5%	2.6%
1997	59.6%	62.1%	17.4%	20.4%	5.0%	10.5%	6.6%	8.6%	2.4%	3.1%
1998	53.5%	62.1%	16.2%	20.2%	3.4%	10.7%	5.9%	9.0%	2.1%	3.0%
1999	52.6%	61.6%	16.6%	20.3%	4.0%	10.3%	6.2%	8.9%	2.3%	2.4%
2000	53.1%	62.8%	16.7%	18.4%	4.5%	10.3%	6.9%	9.8%	2.3%	2.2%
2001	53.0%	60.4%	16.9%	17.6%	4.7%	9.6%	7.0%	9.5%	2.2%	2.1%
2002	52.3%	64.5%	14.9%	18.1%	4.8%	9.7%	7.2%	10.6%	2.1%	2.4%
2003	50.8%	66.1%	13.6%	18.0%	4.6%	10.4%	7.1%	11.5%	2.0%	2.5%
2004	49.8%	65.9%	12.4%	16.8%	4.7%	11.1%	7.2%	11.2%	2.1%	2.5%
2005	48.1%	66.9%	11.0%	15.2%	4.6%	11.6%	7.3%	11.4%	2.2%	2.5%
2006	47.1%	66.4%	9.5%	14.6%	4.6%	11.3%	7.4%	11.3%	2.4%	2.2%
2007	46.6%	64.8%	8.4%	14.0%	4.6%	10.9%	7.7%	11.3%	2.4%	1.8%
2008	46.4%	62.1%	8.1%	13.3%	5.2%	9.9%	8.0%	10.3%	2.3%	1.8%
2009	47.3%	60.0%	8.2%	13.0%	4.5%	10.2%	8.9%	10.6%	2.5%	1.8%
2010	46.4%	59.9%	7.7%	12.7%	4.4%	9.9%	8.8%	11.1%	2.1%	1.8%
2011	47.4%	57.8%	7.8%	11.2%	4.4%	9.4%	9.0%	11.1%	1.9%	1.6%
2012	49.1%	57.3%	7.4%	9.8%	4.3%	9.3%	10.0%	10.8%	2.0%	1.6%
2013	51.4%	56.0%	6.8%	8.4%	4.1%	9.4%	11.0%	10.3%	2.1%	1.5%
2014	50.7%	55.4%	6.4%	8.3%	4.3%	9.7%	11.6%	10.6%	2.1%	1.6%

Source: Author's calculation using data from CEIC Data Manager.

to 8% for imports. In contrast, China's trade with Korea in proportion to its total trade had risen considerably till the mid-2000s but that also began to fall.

ASEAN as a whole has become an increasingly important trading partner to China, especially as a market for China's exports. Between 1997 and 2014, the share of China's exports to ASEAN in the country's total rose from 6.6% to 11.6%, while that of China's imports from ASEAN climbed from 8.6% to 10.6% (Table 5). Within ASEAN, Singapore's share of trade in China's overall trade has declined slightly but remained substantial. In 2014, China's trade with Singapore accounted for about 2% of China's overall trade, down from around 2.5% in 1993. In 1997, China's exports to and imports from Singapore both accounted for over one-third of China's trade with ASEAN, but in 2014, the corresponding proportions were 18% and 15%. It should however be noted that trade volume between China and Singapore has been growing over the years despite the declining growth rate (Table 1 and Table 2), suggesting that China's trade relations with ASEAN's less developed members have grown even stronger.

Considerable structural changes in bilateral trade

As bilateral trade between China and Singapore expanded since the early 2000s, the composition of product types in China's exports to and imports from Singapore has changed markedly.

In 1993, China's top four export products to Singapore were "mineral products" (13.2%), "textile and textile article" (11.9%), "machinery and electrical equipment" (10%) and "base metal and article" (8.3%) (Table 6). These four categories remained as key export items in 2005 but their percentage share has changed greatly — i.e. "machinery and electrical equipment" accounted for one-third of its total exports to Singapore, followed by "textile and textile article" (5.3%), "mineral product" (4.4%) and "base metal and article" (3.8%).

China's exports to Singapore continued to undergo structural changes due to the changing domestic economic dynamics and the world economy. "Machinery and electrical equipment" continue to be China's leading exports to Singapore, accounting for more than one-quarter of its total exports to Singapore in 2014. "Vehicle, aircraft, vessel and transport equipment", constituting 6.9% of China's export to Singapore in the same year, are China's second-largest export item, followed by "base metal and article" (6%), "mineral product" (5.3%) and miscellaneous manufacturing article (5.3%) and "textile and textile article" (2.9%).

Table 6 Singapore's Trade Share in China's Trade, by Main Harmonised System (HS) Section and Division, 1993–2014

	Exports to Singapore						Imports from Singapore					
	1993	1995	2000	2005	2010	2014	1993	1995	2000	2005	2010	2014
Live Animal, Animal Product	0.7%	0.5%	0.4%	0.2%	0.1%	0.3%	0.2%	0.1%	0.1%	0.0%	0.0%	0.0%
Vegetable Product	5.0%	3.9%	0.8%	0.3%	0.4%	0.4%	0.0%	0.1%	0.1%	0.0%	0.0%	0.0%
Animal or Vegetable Fat and Oil	0.1%	0.0%	0.0%	0.0%	0.0%	0.0%	1.0%	1.0%	0.1%	0.0%	0.0%	0.0%
Prepared Foodstuff, Beverage and Tobacco	6.7%	5.3%	0.9%	0.5%	0.4%	0.6%	0.3%	0.1%	0.2%	0.3%	1.1%	0.8%
Mineral Product	13.2%	5.5%	6.1%	4.4%	6.0%	5.3%	36.2%	21.8%	9.7%	7.6%	10.8%	9.5%
Product of Chemical or Allied Industry	3.5%	2.9%	2.1%	1.6%	1.9%	2.4%	1.9%	3.9%	4.4%	5.0%	6.4%	8.9%
Plastic, Rubber and Article Thereof	1.4%	1.6%	1.3%	0.8%	1.0%	1.7%	2.8%	3.2%	6.0%	6.2%	6.4%	8.9%
Raw Hide and Skin, Leather	0.6%	0.5%	0.4%	0.3%	0.4%	0.8%	0.0%	0.1%	0.2%	0.2%	0.0%	0.0%
Wood and Article, Charcoal	0.3%	0.3%	0.3%	0.2%	0.2%	0.3%	0.3%	0.3%	0.1%	0.0%	0.0%	0.0%
Pulp of Wood, Paper and Paperboard	1.1%	1.2%	0.3%	0.2%	0.3%	0.7%	0.3%	0.3%	0.4%	0.1%	0.2%	1.0%
Textile and Textile Article	11.9%	9.8%	6.1%	5.3%	2.0%	2.9%	0.3%	0.4%	0.5%	0.2%	0.1%	0.1%
Footwear, Headgear, Umbrella	1.0%	0.7%	0.5%	0.2%	0.6%	1.1%	0.0%	0.0%	0.0%	0.0%	0.0%	0.0%
Article of Stone, Cement, Glass	1.0%	1.0%	0.6%	1.0%	0.8%	1.9%	0.1%	0.2%	0.2%	0.1%	0.1%	0.1%
Pearl, Precious Stone and Metal	2.7%	2.4%	0.3%	0.1%	0.1%	0.2%	1.5%	0.9%	0.9%	0.1%	0.1%	0.1%
Base Metal and Article	8.3%	7.0%	4.1%	3.8%	3.9%	6.0%	1.5%	2.3%	1.3%	1.2%	0.9%	1.5%
Machinery, Electrical Equipment	10.0%	21.5%	29.5%	33.1%	29.9%	26.6%	7.2%	17.3%	31.2%	34.0%	30.0%	26.3%
— Nuclear Reactor, Machinery	4.0%	10.5%	11.6%	10.3%	13.2%	11.3%	3.6%	8.4%	14.6%	12.0%	9.7%	8.3%
— Electrical Machinery and Equipment	6.0%	10.9%	17.9%	22.7%	16.7%	15.3%	3.6%	8.8%	16.6%	21.9%	20.3%	17.9%
Vehicle, Aircraft, Vessel and Transport Equipment	2.4%	2.7%	2.3%	2.9%	10.3%	6.9%	1.6%	7.4%	0.3%	0.1%	0.2%	0.7%
Optical, Photographic, Musical Instrument	1.1%	1.2%	1.8%	1.5%	1.1%	1.4%	0.4%	0.8%	1.9%	1.7%	1.4%	3.1%
Miscellaneous Manufacturing Article	1.9%	1.5%	1.1%	0.6%	2.2%	5.3%	0.1%	0.2%	0.1%	0.0%	0.0%	0.0%

Source: Author's calculation using data from CEIC Data Manager.

China has clearly made remarkable achievement in upgrading its industries and exports in the past two decades as evident in the decline in relative importance of its export of resource materials and products of low technology intensity and the corresponding increase in manufactured goods of medium to high technology intensity.

The composition of China's imports from Singapore also reflected interesting changes during the past two decades. In 1993, China's imports from Singapore was largely "mineral products", about one-third of total imports from Singapore, followed by "machinery and electrical equipment" (7.2%) and "plastic, rubber and article thereof" (2.8%).

In the decade since 1993, "mineral products" no longer constituted China's dominant imports from Singapore as its percentage share in China's imports dipped to roughly 10% in 2000 and has since remained at that level. China's leading imports from Singapore were "machinery and electrical equipment", making up to over 30% of the total between the late 1990s and 2007 but that have since declined slightly to between 26% and 30% in recent years. Instead, China has significantly increased its imports of "product of chemical or allied industry", "plastic, rubber and article thereof" and "optical, photographic, musical instrument" from Singapore.

Overall, two-way trade in "machinery and electrical equipment" is one of the most important constituents in Sino-Singapore bilateral trade relations. As a large portion of the trade in this sector involves exchanges of parts and components, its dominance in bilateral trade suggests not only the strong interdependence between the two countries but also their integration into the regional production network. In addition, bilateral trade has become broader based, beyond resource-based products or low-skilled manufacturing.

Accelerated growth in trade in services

As bilateral trade witnessed an expansion and diversification of product types, services trade has become increasingly important for both countries. Between 2000 and 2013, Singapore's service exports grew faster than its imports, at an annual rate of 12.6% and 11.6%, respectively. By contrast, China's service imports outpaced its exports, at an annual growth rate of 18.4% and 14%, respectively.

More significantly, Singapore and China have substantially enhanced their bilateral trade in services. Indeed, Singapore's service trade with China had increased more rapidly than that with the rest of the world. As a result, China's share as a proportion to Singapore's services trade with Asia rose considerably

Table 7 Percentage Share of Selected Regions and Countries in Singapore's Service Trade, 2000–2013

	Africa	Europe	North America	Oceania	South and Central America and the Caribbean	Asia Total	China	Japan	ASEAN
							Percentage share of		
Import of services									
2000	0.5%	19.1%	45.6%	2.7%	1.3%	30.8%	2.3%	7.4%	9.3%
2001	0.5%	20.3%	40.3%	3.4%	3.5%	32.0%	2.4%	6.0%	10.0%
2002	0.5%	21.3%	38.0%	3.7%	4.0%	32.6%	2.5%	6.5%	9.9%
2003	0.5%	26.7%	34.6%	3.7%	4.2%	30.3%	3.3%	6.7%	8.3%
2004	0.7%	25.1%	31.1%	3.6%	4.7%	34.9%	4.2%	9.6%	8.8%
2005	0.9%	27.7%	29.6%	3.4%	4.9%	33.6%	4.0%	8.2%	8.5%
2006	1.3%	29.5%	26.9%	3.5%	5.0%	33.9%	3.8%	9.7%	7.6%
2007	1.0%	27.6%	28.1%	3.9%	5.6%	33.8%	4.6%	7.7%	7.8%
2008	1.1%	30.0%	25.3%	3.7%	6.5%	33.5%	4.8%	6.9%	8.0%
2009	1.2%	27.0%	27.7%	4.0%	7.6%	32.5%	5.3%	6.0%	7.4%
2010	1.2%	27.9%	26.0%	3.9%	8.3%	32.8%	5.4%	5.8%	7.2%
2011	1.4%	29.0%	19.8%	5.3%	11.0%	33.6%	6.2%	6.7%	7.1%
2012	1.4%	28.2%	23.8%	5.4%	10.4%	30.7%	6.0%	5.3%	6.7%
2013	1.4%	30.7%	21.8%	5.4%	10.4%	30.2%	6.1%	4.8%	6.7%
Export of services									
2000	0.9%	20.3%	22.1%	5.1%	2.7%	49.0%	6.6%	20.5%	31.3%
2001	0.8%	20.8%	20.8%	5.4%	2.9%	49.3%	7.6%	18.8%	32.8%
2002	1.1%	21.7%	19.8%	6.1%	3.0%	48.2%	7.2%	18.0%	33.0%
2003	1.1%	23.2%	18.8%	6.7%	3.5%	46.6%	9.8%	18.3%	30.6%
2004	1.2%	22.6%	17.5%	6.7%	3.6%	48.4%	10.4%	21.5%	29.2%
2005	1.3%	21.9%	18.1%	7.2%	3.8%	47.7%	10.4%	20.5%	28.7%
2006	1.8%	22.3%	19.6%	6.7%	4.0%	45.6%	10.2%	20.7%	28.4%
2007	1.5%	24.4%	17.1%	6.5%	4.4%	46.2%	12.6%	18.9%	26.8%
2008	2.3%	26.3%	16.0%	7.4%	3.9%	44.1%	13.5%	16.4%	27.7%
2009	2.2%	26.0%	15.1%	9.4%	3.5%	43.8%	13.6%	13.4%	30.0%
2010	1.9%	24.5%	15.8%	9.7%	3.8%	44.3%	16.3%	14.3%	26.6%
2011	2.2%	24.8%	15.3%	10.9%	4.4%	42.4%	14.4%	15.5%	28.2%
2012	2.3%	23.6%	16.4%	11.5%	4.6%	41.5%	14.8%	15.1%	30.8%
2013	3.5%	23.1%	16.0%	10.9%	5.2%	41.4%	15.9%	15.3%	30.9%

Source: Singapore Department of Statistics, SingStat Table Builder.

(Table 7). Between 2000 and 2013, China's share in Singapore's total imports of services rose from 2.3% to 6.1%. Incidentally, during the same period, the percentage share of Singapore's services imports from Japan dropped from 7.4% to 4.8%, and the percentage share of Singapore's services imports from ASEAN also decreased, from 9.3% to 6.7%. However, the share of Asia as a whole remained largely stable. Beyond Asia, Europe's share had risen considerably, whereas North America's share had dipped significantly.

A similar trend is observed for Singapore's exports of services over the same period. China's share in Singapore's service exports had more than doubled, from 3.2% in 2000 to 6.6% in 2013, while the share of Asia as a whole in Singapore's service exports declined from 49% to 41.4%. The share of Japan and ASEAN in Singapore's service exports also slumped by three to four percentage points. The share of North America in Singapore's service exports declined and that of Europe rose. It is worth noting that countries in Oceania accounted for over 10% of Singapore's service exports in 2013, doubling that in 2000.

Surging capital flows

Apart from bilateral trade, capital flows like equity investment and foreign direct investment (FDI) between Singapore and China have also expanded rapidly in recent years, particularly those from Singapore to China. For example, between 1994 and 2013, Singapore's outward equity investment as a share in China's total more than quadrupled, from around 5% to over 20%. In 2013, China accounted for more 37% of Singapore's total outward equity investment to Asia, while ASEAN accounted for 35% (Table 8).

Singapore channelled an overwhelming proportion, about 90%, of its total outward FDI to Asia, and China has become an increasingly important destination. In fact, since the mid-1990s, China has overtaken ASEAN to be the most important destination for Singapore's outward FDI, accounting for over two-fifths of Singapore's total FDI outflow and nearly half of that to Asia (Table 9).

China has also accelerated its efforts to promote its outward FDI (OFDI), particularly those by the country's large state-owned enterprises, since the early 2000s. A large majority of China's OFDI were channelled to Asia. The percentage share of Singapore in China's OFDI remains small, but the total in absolute amount has risen significantly. Between 2003 and 2013, Asia's share in China's total OFDI declined, from four-fifths to about three-fourths. Meanwhile, China's investment to Singapore rose from US$165 million to US$15 billion, while its percentage share rose from less than 1% to over 3%. Singapore's share

Table 8 Percentage Share of Singapore's Direct Equity Investment Abroad, 1994–2013

	As a Percentage of Singapore's Total Outward Equity Investment			As a Percentage of Singapore's Outward Equity Investment to Asia	
		Percentage Share			
	Asia	China	ASEAN	China	ASEAN
1994	59.5%	5.3%	33.6%	8.9%	56.4%
1995	60.6%	8.1%	34.0%	13.3%	56.2%
1996	59.6%	12.7%	31.1%	21.3%	52.1%
1997	56.7%	14.7%	25.8%	25.9%	45.5%
1998	62.4%	18.4%	25.0%	29.5%	40.0%
1999	64.1%	17.7%	24.9%	27.6%	38.8%
2000	60.9%	17.5%	23.9%	28.8%	39.3%
2001	48.5%	12.0%	18.9%	24.7%	39.0%
2002	48.5%	12.8%	20.3%	26.5%	41.9%
2003	50.5%	13.7%	21.7%	27.1%	42.9%
2004	49.8%	13.1%	22.0%	26.3%	44.1%
2005	53.2%	14.4%	23.1%	27.0%	43.4%
2006	50.8%	15.0%	22.1%	29.6%	43.6%
2007	48.9%	13.9%	21.5%	28.5%	44.0%
2008	59.3%	19.6%	23.7%	33.1%	40.0%
2009	57.8%	19.1%	23.3%	33.0%	40.2%
2010	55.4%	19.1%	21.8%	34.5%	39.4%
2011	59.6%	20.8%	22.0%	34.9%	36.9%
2012	58.5%	20.8%	21.9%	35.5%	37.5%
2013	57.9%	21.2%	20.4%	36.7%	35.2%

Source: Singapore Department of Statistics, SingStat Table Builder.

in China's OFDI to Asia was computed to be 8% if China's direct investment to Hong Kong was included, but the value would be over 20% if China's direct investment to Hong Kong was excluded. Indeed, Singapore ranked second in Asia since 2007 as the most important investment destination for China's OFDI.

Table 9 Singapore's Direct Investment Abroad, 1994–2013

| | As a Percentage of total OFDI | | | As a Percentage of OFDI to Asia | |
| | | Percentage Share of | | | |
	Asia	China	ASEAN	China	ASEAN
1994	92.3%	11.1%	70.0%	12.0%	75.8%
1995	93.7%	14.9%	68.1%	15.9%	72.7%
1996	90.2%	32.0%	47.2%	35.4%	52.3%
1997	92.5%	42.7%	35.9%	46.1%	38.8%
1998	90.9%	40.9%	34.8%	45.0%	38.3%
1999	92.1%	39.7%	34.0%	43.1%	37.0%
2000	92.0%	40.1%	32.9%	43.5%	35.8%
2001	90.5%	35.1%	35.8%	38.8%	39.6%
2002	88.8%	36.2%	37.8%	40.8%	42.5%
2003	90.7%	38.8%	37.6%	42.8%	41.4%
2004	89.6%	36.8%	36.6%	41.1%	40.8%
2005	89.2%	37.5%	35.8%	42.1%	40.1%
2006	89.4%	39.6%	34.3%	44.3%	38.3%
2007	83.2%	35.3%	33.9%	42.4%	40.7%
2008	94.2%	44.6%	35.2%	47.4%	37.4%
2009	92.1%	44.0%	35.0%	47.8%	38.0%
2010	88.5%	42.9%	32.9%	48.4%	37.2%
2011	96.4%	49.1%	34.8%	51.0%	36.1%
2012	91.5%	45.5%	33.0%	49.6%	36.1%
2013	87.2%	44.0%	30.6%	50.4%	35.1%

Source: Singapore Department of Statistics, SingStat Table Builder.

From Singapore's perspective, China's importance as a source of FDI inflow has been enhanced in recent years but remains relatively low. Between 1998 and 2012, Asia's share of Singapore's total FDI inflow declined from 30% to 24%, while China's FDI into Singapore rose from 0.5% to about 2% (Table 10). China's share of Singapore's total FDI inflow in 2012 (2%) was much smaller than those of ASEAN (4.7%) and Japan (7.9%). Hence, compared to ASEAN and Japan, China remains a minor player in investing in Singapore. However, it is noteworthy that the percentage share of Japan's FDI to Singapore between 1998 and 2012 had dropped markedly from 18% to 8%. The percentage share

Table 10 Percentage Share of Selected Regions and Countries' FDI to Singapore, 1998–2012

	Africa	Europe	North America	Oceania	South and Central America and the Caribbean	Total	Asia Percentage share of China	ASEAN	Japan
1998		34.4%			13.6%	30.3%	0.5%	6.2%	18.1%
1999	0.8%	36.7%			15.5%	28.0%	0.6%	5.4%	16.8%
2000	1.2%	37.2%			15.9%	25.8%	0.5%	4.6%	15.2%
2001	1.3%	39.0%			16.0%	23.6%	0.4%	4.2%	13.8%
2002	1.5%	40.2%			16.9%	23.8%	0.4%	3.8%	14.4%
2003	1.6%	42.2%	16.1%	1.1%	15.5%	23.5%	0.3%	3.2%	13.8%
2004	1.9%	43.5%	15.8%	1.2%	15.1%	22.5%	0.1%	3.0%	13.5%
2005	2.3%	43.2%	13.3%	1.5%	15.5%	24.2%	0.3%	3.5%	13.8%
2006	1.6%	47.0%	11.1%	1.5%	16.4%	22.3%	0.5%	3.3%	12.1%
2007	1.9%	42.5%	11.7%	1.6%	19.5%	22.6%	0.5%	3.5%	10.2%
2008	2.4%	39.9%	10.9%	1.6%	21.4%	23.5%	0.9%	3.7%	9.9%
2009	2.2%	38.6%	10.8%	1.7%	21.2%	25.4%	1.7%	4.1%	8.8%
2010	2.5%	36.9%	11.3%	2.0%	23.1%	24.4%	2.2%	3.7%	8.6%
2011	2.1%	38.0%	11.7%	2.0%	22.1%	24.1%	2.0%	4.0%	7.9%
2012	2.1%	35.0%	14.9%	2.1%	21.3%	24.4%	1.9%	4.7%	7.9%

Source: Singapore Department of Statistics, SingStat Table Builder.

of ASEAN's FDI to Singapore also declined, although not as sharply. As such, China has made important gains in its direct investment in Singapore relative to other Asian countries.

Growing financial cooperation

The Chinese and Singapore governments have in recent years worked together to promote financial cooperation besides expanding bilateral capital flows. Financial cooperation has so far encompassed increasing the amount of bilateral currency swap, expanding transactions in renminbi, promoting international use of renminbi through Qualified Foreign Institutional Investor scheme, and experimenting cross-border renminbi transactions in Suzhou Industrial Park and Sino-Singapore Tianjin Eco-city.

On 23 July 2010, at the Seventh Joint Council for Bilateral Cooperation (JCBC) Meeting between China and Singapore, the People's Bank of China

(PBoC) and the Monetary Authority of Singapore (MAS) announced the establishment of a bilateral currency swap arrangement to promote bilateral trade direct investment between the two countries. The bilateral currency swap arrangement would provide renminbi liquidity of up to RMB150 billion and Singapore dollar liquidity of up to S$30 billion. In March 2013, the arrangement was expanded, doubling to RMB300 billion and S$60 billion.

In October 2012, Bank of China (BOC) and the Industrial and Commercial Bank of China (ICBC) were granted full banking license in Singapore. On 2 April 2013, the MAS and PBoC signed a memorandum of understanding (MOU) on RMB Business Cooperation. Under the MOU, MAS and PBoC will cooperate closely in reviewing the conduct of renminbi businesses and clearing arrangements in Singapore. PBoC also signed a renminbi clearing agreement with ICBC Singapore branch which was appointed as the renminbi clearing bank in Singapore on 8 February 2013.[11] In April 2014, Singapore reportedly overtook London to rank second globally as a clearing centre for renminbi, according to SWIFT, a global transaction services organisation.[12]

On 22 October 2013, at the Tenth JCBC, Singapore and China agreed on new initiatives to strengthen cooperation on financial sector development and regulation. One initiative aimed to promote the international use of the renminbi through Singapore. China will extend its RMB Qualified Foreign Institutional Investor (RQFII) programme to Singapore, with an aggregate quota of RMB50 billion. This allows qualified Singapore-based institutional investors to channel offshore renminbi from Singapore into China's securities markets and help diversify the base of investors in China's capital markets.[13]

In addition, it is reported that China has allowed cross-border renminbi transactions for clients in Suzhou Industrial Park and Sino-Singapore Tianjin

---

[11] Monetary Authority of Singapore, "Monetary Authority of Singapore and the People's Bank of China Sign an MOU on Renminbi Business Cooperation, 2 April 2013, at <http://www.mas.gov.sg/news-and-publications/media-releases/2013/mas-and-the-people-bank-of-china-sign-an-mou-on-renminbi-business-cooperation.aspx> (accessed 10 May 2015).

[12] "Singapore Pips London as Yuan Clearing Center Helped by ICBC", *Reuters*, 28 April 2014, at <http://www.reuters.com/article/2014/04/28/markets-offshore-yuan-idUSL3N0NK0X C20140428> (accessed 10 May 2015).

[13] Monetary Authority of Singapore, "New Initiatives to Strengthen China–Singapore Financial Cooperation", 22 October 2013, at <http://www.mas.gov.sg/news-and-publications/media-releases/2013/new-initiatives-to-strengthen-china-singapore-financial-cooperation.aspx> (accessed 10 May 2015).

Eco-city.[14] As of October 2014, about 30 companies from the Suzhou Industrial Park and Tianjin Eco-city have borrowed nearly RMB2 billion from banks in Singapore through the cross-border renminbi lending initiative. Indeed, according to Ms Jacqueline Loh of MAS, "financial cooperation has become a pillar for Sino-Singapore bilateral relations. As China proceeds with its structural transformation and financial reform, financial cooperation between the two countries will grow in importance and mutual benefit".[15]

Great potential to enhance bilateral economic relations

Both China and Singapore regard their bilateral economic relations as among the strongest with other countries. The resilience in their economic exchange in times of hostile political climate is a testament to their pragmatic and strong relations. More importantly, both countries have strengthened their status as key trading partners and important investors with increased bilateral trade and investment in recent years.

China and Singapore's strong and comprehensive economic ties can be attributed to several factors. First of all, the shared historical and cultural ties as well as common language of the peoples have provided a strong foundation for bilateral relations to deepen. Second, the two countries are at different stages of economic development and thus there is a high complementarity in their industrial structures that enables mutually beneficial economic relations to thrive. Third, both governments share the same belief in economic pragmatism and have placed economic development at the top of their agenda.

Looking ahead, there is much potential to further enhance Sino-Singapore economic relations. First, Asia has become an integrated part of the world economy, thus providing strong foundation for intra-regional economic co-operation. Indeed, over the past decades, the world's economic centre of the gravity has shifted significantly eastward, and Asia has obviously become the most prosperous and dynamic region. Second, China is now the world's second-

---

[14] "China's Tianjin Eco-City Gets Go-ahead for Yuan Deals with Singapore", *Reuters*, 8 July 2014, at <http://www.reuters.com/article/2014/07/08/china-yuan-singapore-idUSL4N0PJ1K 620140708> (accessed 10 May 2015).

[15] Monetary Authority of Singapore, "Singapore and China Further Strengthen Financial Cooperation through New Initiatives", 27 October 2014, at <http://www.mas.gov.sg/news-and-publications/media-releases/2014/singapore-and-china-further-strengthen-financial-cooperation-through-new-initiatives.aspx> (accessed 10 May 2015).

largest economy after more than three decades of rapid economic development. As a regional economic power and a global heavyweight, China has the capability and political will to play a pivotal role in promoting regional economic cooperation and integration. Third, Singapore, as a key member of ASEAN and the most developed country in Southeast Asia, can play an instrumental role to help reinforce China's economic relations with Southeast Asia. Fourth, Singapore, as a highly developed and open economy, has much to offer to China in its aspiration to become an affluent society.

Despite the potentials, there are challenges to further strengthening of bilateral relations. First, China's growing economy has resulted in narrowing the development gap and increasing the competition with its neighbours in Asia, Singapore included. Second, Asia as a whole has yet to develop a strong consumer demand and the region continues to depend on advanced countries in Europe and North America for its huge and competitive production. As such, China's bilateral economic relations with its Southeast Asian neighbours are constrained by economic circumstances outside the region to a certain extent. Third, for both countries, economic calculations may not be in line with strategic considerations, thus requiring careful adjustment and delicate balancing. For China, its challenge entails taking into consideration the concerns of its smaller neighbours. For Singapore, as well as other countries in Southeast Asia, they probably have to make adjustments to accommodate China's rising economic power and influence.

The difficulties in reaching an agreement in and the heated debates surrounding the Trans-Pacific Partnership (TPP) partly reflect the mounting challenges, as it is sometimes seen as a US effort to retain its influence in the region by excluding China. Conversely, China's "One Belt, One Road" initiative and the establishment of the Asian Infrastructure Investment Bank have raised concerns from the United States whether the two strategic initiatives represent China's intention to flex its economic muscle to project its strategic influence.

Appendix

Table 11 Singapore's Trade with China, 1965–2014 (S$ million)

Year	Total Volume	Imports	Exports	Balance
1965	246.9	224.5	22.6	−201.9
1966	408.9	271.7	137.2	−134.5
1967	481.6	385.8	95.8	−290
1968	541.2	460.0	81.2	−378.8
1969	593.3	418.5	174.8	−243.7
1970	454.9	385.5	69.4	−316.1
1971	453.3	406.7	46.6	−360.1
1972	456.5	399.1	57.4	−341.7
1973	701.6	573.2	128.4	−444.8
1974	769.7	643.9	125.8	−518.1
1975	780.5	682.0	98.5	−583.5
1976	754.4	659.0	95.4	−563.6
1977	815.1	670.4	144.7	−525.7
1978	906.2	775.5	130.7	−644.8
1979	1,263.7	894.1	369.6	−524.5
1980	1,990.0	1,332.1	657.9	−674.2
1981	2,007.1	1,629.8	377.3	−1,252.5
1982	2,397.0	1,881.0	516.7	−1,364.3
1983	2,197.0	1,747.2	449.8	−1,297.4
1984	3,400.4	2,881.1	519.3	−2,361.8
1985	5,701.8	4,971.7	730.2	−4,241.5
1986	4,353.4	3,109.6	1,243.8	−1,865.8
1987	4,522.6	2,975.8	1,546.8	−1,429.0
1988	5,754.2	3,385.6	2,368.6	−1,017.0
1989	5,645.3	3,310.8	2,334.5	−976.3
1990	5,216.8	3,773.4	1,443.4	−2,330.0
1991	5,323.5	3,838.8	1,484.7	−2,354.1
1992	5,479.0	2,976.0	1,811.0	−1,165.0
1993	6,945.0	3,668.0	3,068.0	−600.0
1994	7,619.0	3,877.0	3,207.0	−670.0

(Continued)

Table 11   (*Continued*)

Year	Total Volume	Imports	Exports	Balance
1995	9,640.0	4,412.0	3,911.0	−501.0
1996	11,043.0	5,730.0	4,784.0	−946.0
1997	14,484.0	6,259.0	6,038.0	−221.0
1998	14,196.9	8,122.6	6,794.3	−1,328.3
1999	16,291.6	9,648.9	6,642.7	−3,006.2
2000	21,563.7	12,278.7	9,285.0	−2,993.7
2001	22,445.3	12,900.3	9,545.0	−3,355.3
2002	28,121.5	15,853.4	12,268.1	−3,585.3
2003	36,914.6	19,276.3	17,638.2	−1,638.1
2004	53,328.8	27,356.7	25,972.1	−1,384.6
2005	67,079.1	34,169.8	32,909.3	−1,260.5
2006	85,255.3	43,194.3	42,061.0	−1,133.3
2007	91,562.9	48,013.4	43,549.5	−4,463.9
2008	91,412.5	47,594.6	43,817.9	−3,776.7
2009	75,710.5	37,585.3	38,125.1	539.8
2010	95,312.2	45,844.3	49,467.9	3,623.6
2011	101,398.5	47,747.7	53,650.7	5,903.0
2012	103,822.8	48,950.2	54,872.7	5,922.5
2013	115,199.7	54,669.1	60,530.6	5,861.5
2014P	121,467.7	56,247.7	65,220.0	8,972.3

Note: P denotes projected.

Source: Data for 1965–2001 are extracted from Table 1 in Shee Poon Kim, "Singapore–China Special Economic Relations: In Search of Business Opportunities", *Ritsumeikan International Affairs*, vol. 3, 2005, p. 176. Data for 2002–2014 are extracted from Economic Survey of Singapore 2005, 2008, 2011, 2014, at <http://www.mti.gov.sg> (accessed 20 April 2015). See <http://www.tablebuilder.singstat.gov.sg/publicfacing/mainMenu.action> (accessed 20 April 2015).

Table 12 China's Share in Singapore's Domestic Exports, 1980–2014

	As a Percentage of Singapore's Domestic Exports to Asia		As a Percentage of Singapore's Domestic Exports to the World	
	Mainland China	Mainland China and Hong Kong	Mainland China	Mainland China and Hong Kong
1980	1.7%	21.2%	0.9%	11.2%
1981	0.7%	20.4%	0.4%	11.4%
1982	0.7%	17.1%	0.4%	9.8%
1983	0.7%	15.0%	0.4%	8.1%
1984	1.2%	15.0%	0.6%	7.6%
1985	2.5%	15.1%	1.2%	7.5%
1986	5.7%	19.7%	2.7%	9.3%
1987	6.0%	20.3%	2.7%	9.2%
1988	6.2%	20.9%	2.7%	9.2%
1989	6.2%	21.4%	2.8%	9.7%
1990	3.0%	17.6%	1.4%	8.2%
1991	2.8%	17.8%	1.3%	8.6%
1992	3.4%	20.4%	1.5%	9.4%
1993	6.0%	24.4%	2.9%	11.8%
1994	4.6%	21.9%	2.4%	11.2%
1995	4.6%	21.1%	2.4%	10.9%
1996	5.3%	23.0%	2.7%	12.0%
1997	6.5%	25.7%	3.3%	13.1%
1998	7.7%	25.0%	3.6%	11.9%
1999	6.9%	22.4%	3.4%	11.0%
2000	7.2%	21.5%	3.9%	11.6%
2001	8.0%	23.6%	4.5%	13.2%
2002	10.6%	26.3%	5.9%	14.8%
2003	11.2%	26.6%	6.7%	15.8%
2004	13.2%	28.2%	7.9%	16.8%
2005	13.8%	29.1%	8.5%	17.9%
2006	14.3%	29.9%	8.7%	18.1%
2007	14.1%	29.3%	8.5%	17.6%
2008	13.4%	29.6%	8.1%	17.9%
2009	14.7%	31.6%	9.0%	19.4%
2010	15.5%	32.1%	9.7%	20.0%
2011	16.3%	31.4%	10.1%	19.5%
2012	16.3%	31.2%	10.3%	19.6%
2013	17.1%	31.5%	11.1%	20.6%
2014	17.9%	29.0%	11.9%	19.2%

Source: Singapore Department of Statistics, SingStat Table Builder.

Chapter 4

Tourism Exchange between Singapore and China: Smooth Expansion and Bright Prospects

CHIANG Min-Hua

China–Singapore tourism exchange formally began when the two countries established diplomatic relations in 1990. Since 2003, China has become Singapore's second-largest tourism source market, behind Indonesia. Singapore, despite its tiny population, accounted for an important share in China's inbound tourism compared to other Southeast Asian countries. In addition to the growing inbound tourists from mainland China that would sustain the development of Singapore's tourism industry, China's inbound and domestic tourism also offers opportunities for Singapore companies to invest in China's tourism industry. Both countries will continue to benefit from mutual cooperation in terms of China's enormous market and Singapore's more mature management skills and marketing strategies in tourism promotion.

Introduction

Tourism has become one of the most important economic connections between China and Singapore since the establishment of diplomatic ties in 1990. The tourism industry has played an essential role in supporting Singapore's economic development over the past few decades. In recent years, as a result of rising income, relaxation of travel restrictions and more holidays, China has become one of Singapore's largest inbound tourism source markets. According to China Outbound Tourism Research Institute, 98 million Chinese travelled abroad in 2013.[1] China, registering

---

[1] China Outbound Tourism Research Institute, Information Services, at <http://www.china-outbound.com/informationservices.html?&L=1%20onfocus%3DblurLink%28this%29%3B%2F> (accessed 1 February 2015).

US$128.6 billion in tourism expenditure in 2013, is the largest outbound tourism market in the world. While outbound tourism expenditure in other countries have grown slowly, China's quick continuous expansion has widened the gap in tourism expenditure. In 2013, the expenditure gap between China and the second-largest tourist spender (i.e. the United States) increased to over US$42 billion, from US$18.9 billion in 2012.[2] As one of the most important tourism hubs in the world, Singapore will continue to benefit from this rising tide of Chinese tourists. In addition, the rise of China's tourism industry in recent years also provides Singapore further tourism business development opportunities in China. China's population of over 1.3 billion is an incompa-rably large domestic tourism market. China's enormous market, coupled with Singapore's more mature management skills and marketing strategies in tour-ism, will enable both countries to benefit from this booming industry via mutual cooperation.

This chapter discusses the tourism exchange between China and Singapore over the past few decades, including the tourist flow and achievements both countries have made thus far, that has laid the foundation for further bilateral tourism development. The first section outlines the economic contribution of Chinese tourists to Singapore's tourism industry; the second discusses some specific features of Chinese tourists in Singapore; and the third examines the profile of Singaporean tourists in China. The fourth section studies Singapore's investment in China's tourism industry and some tourism-related investment promotion between both countries. The final section provides some future perspectives based on recent development and policy orientation.

The rising importance of Chinese tourists to Singapore

Singapore's promotion of inbound tourism started as early as in the 1960s. Due to diverse global and regional changes, the then Singapore Tourism Promotion Board (STPB and now the Singapore Tourism Board or STB) had sought to adapt to the transforming external environment by implementing different tourism policies. Tourism in Singapore initially acted as a means to create employment, develop its economy and reconfigure its urban and industrial infrastructure. The slowdown in manufacturing production and decreasing competitiveness in labour-intensive sectors later highlighted the importance of developing its service industry, including tourism. The city-state has made

---

[2] United Nations World Tourism Organization, *UNWTO Tourism Highlights 2014*, 2014, p. 13.

much efforts in the last few decades to enhance and diversify its attractiveness by increasing tourist facilities, strengthening infrastructure and launching various marketing strategies. Singapore has changed its tourism marketing strategies several times — from "Instant Asia" in the 1970s, "Shopping Paradise" in the 1980s, "Gastronomic Fantasy Land" in the 1990s, "Arts City" in 2000, to the recent "Uniquely Singapore" and "Your Singapore" — in order to adapt to different environments. In addition to changing marketing slogans, tourism-related facilities have also undergone constant innovation in order to keep Singapore's tourism sector "fresh" for visitors. As a result, visitor arrivals and tourism receipts have increased progressively. According to the World Tourism Organization (WTO), Singapore had the third-highest international tourist arrivals and tourism receipts in Southeast Asia in 2012, behind Malaysia and Thailand.[3] The rapid growth of Chinese visitors had contributed most to Singapore tourism industry's development in recent years.

In 1990, Singapore was added to China's list for outbound travel. Tourists from mainland China to Singapore have since increased progressively. (Singapore, though not very rich in terms of tourist resources, is an important transit point in Asia.) In less than two decades, Chinese visitor arrivals to Singapore grew more than 10 times, from 202,000 in 1995 to over 2 million in 2013. Over the same period, the share of Chinese visitors in total visitor arrivals in Singapore also increased from a mere 3% to 15% (Figure 1). The rise in Chinese tourists to Singapore was particularly obvious after the 2000s. Since 2003, China has surpassed Malaysia as Singapore's second-largest tourism source market, behind Indonesia. Many Indonesians came to Singapore, because of its proximity to Indonesia and other factors such as to visit relatives or friends and shop for branded goods apart from sightseeing. The uptrend in mainland Chinese tourist arrivals in the past 15 years was temporarily dampened by the Severe Acute Respiratory Syndrome (SARS) outbreak in 2003 and the 2008–2009 global financial crisis, leading to a decline in the number of Chinese visitors to Singapore by 15% in 2003 and 13% in 2009.

From China's perspective, Singapore is a favourite foreign destination not only because of the proximity but also its modernity and diverse tourism offerings. When Resorts World Sentosa and Marina Bay Sands were opened in 2010, there was visible growth in visitors from China, at an annual growth rate of 25% in 2010, 34% in 2011 and 29% in 2012. In comparison, the annual growth rates of visitors from Indonesia increased to 32% in 2010 but slowed

---

[3] UN World Tourism Organization, *UNWTO Tourism Highlights 2014*, p. 9.

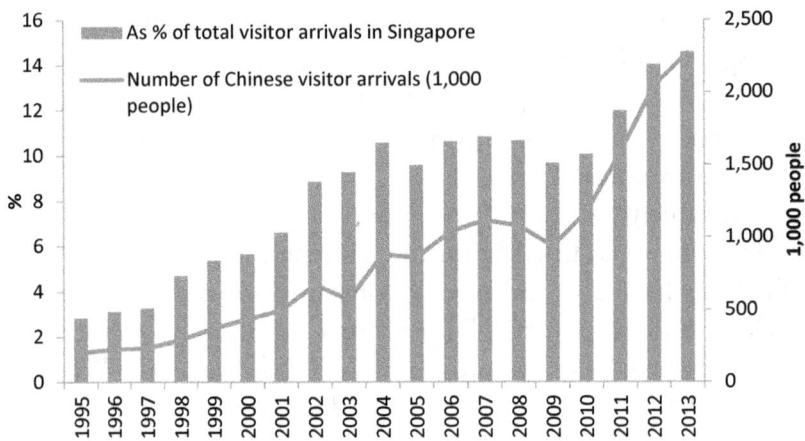

Figure 1 Chinese Visitor Arrivals in Singapore, 1995–2013

Source: Macroeconomic Database for Emerging and Developed Markets, CEIC Data, 2014, at <http://www.ceicdata.com/> (accessed 2 February 2015).

down to 12% in 2011 and 9% in 2012.[4] However, at an annual growth rate of 11% in 2013, the number of Chinese visitors to Singapore has apparently decelerated. In the first half of 2014, Chinese tourists to Singapore dropped by 30%. The disappearance of flight MH370 from Kuala Lumpur, the abduction of Chinese visitors in Sabah and the political unrest in Thailand in 2014 had a dampening effect on Chinese travel to the region.[5] Since most Chinese tourists visit Singapore, Malaysia and Thailand on package tours, the multiple incidents and events in Malaysia and Thailand have also affected Chinese tourists' interest to visit Singapore as a result.

The growing number of Chinese tourists was accompanied by rising tourism receipts. Between 1995 and 2003, there was no clear growth in Chinese tourist expenditure (Figure 2). Following a sharp increase to S$574 million in 2004 from S$270 million in 2003, Chinese tourist expenditure in Singapore has been on the ascent since 2004, hitting S$2,516 million in 2012. In 2013, China, whose tourist expenditure in Singapore was S$2,981 million, outpaced Indonesia (S$2,978 million) to become Singapore's largest tourism receipt

---

[4] Macroeconomic Database for Emerging and Developed Markets, CEIC Data, 2014, at <http://www.ceicdata.com/> (accessed 2 February 2015).

[5] "Decline in Chinese Tourists Hits Singapore Visitor Arrivals", *The Strait Times*, 15 October 2014, at <http://news.asiaone.com/news/travel/decline-chinese-tourists-hits-singapore-visitor-arrivals> (accessed 2 February 2015).

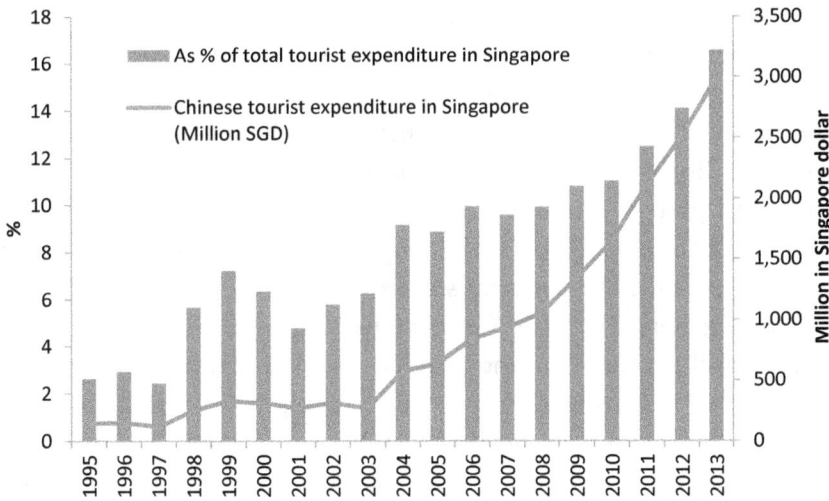

Figure 2 Chinese Tourist Expenditure in Singapore, 1995–2013

Source: Macroeconomic Database for Emerging and Developed Markets, CEIC Data, 2014, at <http://www.ceicdata.com/> (accessed 2 February 2015).

market. The share of Chinese tourist expenditure in total tourist expenditure in Singapore also grew from 3% in 1995 to 17% in 2013. The per capita tourist expenditure of Chinese visitors in Singapore tripled from S$467 in 2002 to S$1,313 in 2013. This has placed China the second-highest in 2013 in terms of per capita tourist expenditure, behind Vietnam (S$1,618).[6]

The Chinese government's successive deregulation for outbound travel has boosted the number of Chinese visitors going abroad. The implementation of several favourable measures for Chinese visitors has further contributed to a surge in Chinese tourists to Singapore. Since 2003, the visa application procedures for Chinese travellers in Beijing, Shanghai and Guangzhou to Singapore have been simplified. In 2010, both countries signed the "China–Singapore Visa Exemption Agreement" that allows Chinese and Singaporean diplomats and government officials enjoy visa waivers for a maximum of 30 days from 2011. In addition, the STB signed several memoranda of understanding (MOUs) with various cities in China. The most recent is an MOU between Singapore and Shandong province in April 2011 that commits both sides to

---

[6] Singapore Tourism Board, *Annual Report on Tourism Statistics 2013*, 2014, p. 9, at <https://www.stb.gov.sg/statistics-and-market-insights/marketstatistics/annual%20report_2013_f_revised.pdf> (accessed 11 May 2015).

invest in tourism promotion and strengthen knowledge of the travel trade and media. In order to provide better services for Chinese travellers in Singapore, the STB signed an MOU with China UnionPay Co Ltd (CUP) in 2011, a Chinese bankcard services provider, to further facilitate CUP bankcard services in Singapore. Both parties jointly promote the use of CUP bankcards in Singapore and plan to expand cooperation to other countries and regions. China UnionPay also issue new CUP-Singapore Tourism bankcards to provide a better and more efficient payment services to Chinese CUP bankcard holders travelling to Singapore. The STB's Greater China offices also work with Ctrip.com, the largest travel products online purchasing platform in China, to provide Chinese travellers a convenient way to purchase flight ticket and hotel packages in Singapore. Following the decline in Chinese tourists to Singapore since 2014, Changi Airport has decided to partner with STB to launch a new travel campaign with a total investment of S$1 million.[7]

Profile of Chinese tourists in Singapore

Unlike most other foreign travellers to Singapore, Chinese visitors spent more on shopping. In 2013, Chinese visitors spent S$1,399 million on shopping, more than double their expenditure on accommodation (Table 1). Chinese visitors spent 47% of their expenditure on shopping, 22% on accommodation, 9% on food and beverages, 3% on local transport and 1% on medical treatment. Chinese tourists are also the largest spenders in local shops. According to STB, in 2013, shopping spending from Chinese tourists accounted for 31% of Singapore's shopping receipts. Their favourite shopping items included fashion and accessories (35%), watches and clocks (32%) and cosmetic-related products (10%), accounting for about 77% of total shopping expenditure of Chinese tourists in Singapore in 2013. Chinese tourists' list of favourite shopping items in 2002 was, however, vastly different, which included consumer electronics products, apparels and genuine jewellery, accounting for 62% of total shopping expenditure (Table 2). Chinese visitors' expenditure on consumer electronics products as a percentage of their total shopping expenditure declined significantly from 29% in 2002 to 3% in 2013. Their expenditure on genuine jewellery had obviously dropped too, from 17% in 2002 to 8% in

---

[7] "$1-million Drive to Woo Chinese Tourists Back to Singapore", *The Sunday Times*, 24 June 2014, at <http://www.straitstimes.com/news/singapore/more-singapore-stories/story/1-million-drive-woo-chinese-tourists-back-singapore-2014> (accessed 2 February 2015).

Table 1   Chinese Tourist Expenditure by Items in Singapore, 2013

Items	Amount (S$ million)	Share of total amount (%)
Shopping	**1,399**	**47**
Accommodation	654	22
Food and Beverage	265	9
Local Transport	90	3
Medical	28	1
Others	545	18
Total	2,981	100

Note: "Others" include expenditure on airfares, port taxes, business, education and transit visitors.
Source: Singapore Tourism Board, *Annual Report on Tourism Statistics 2013*, 2014, p. 51.

Table 2   Comparison of Chinese Tourists' Profile in Singapore in 2002 and 2013

(unit: %)

	2002	2013		2002	2013
Mode of Arrival	**100**	**100**	**Shopping items**	**100**	**100**
Air	73	72	Fashion and accessories	n/a	35
Land	25	25	Watches and clocks	11	32
Sea	2	3	Cosmetics, perfumes toiletries/ health-care and wellness products	8	10
Age group	**100**	**100**	Genuine jewellery	17	8
24 and below	12	16	Consumer electronics products	29	3
25–44	51	43	Confectionary and food items	7	4
45–64	32	33	Souvenir and gifts	7	3
>65 or not stated	5	8	Handbag, wallet and other leather goods	2	n/a
Main purpose of visit	**100**	**100**	Apparel	16	n/a
Holiday	61	40	Others	2	5
Business and MICE	8	25			
Visit friends/relatives	4	15	**Length of stay**	**100**	**100**
Education	2	3	1 day and less	77	66
Others or not stated	13	17	2 to 4 days	10	21
In transit	12	n/a	5 days and more	13	13

Sources: Singapore Tourism Board, *Annual Report on Tourism Statistics 2002*, pp. 18, 34; and Singapore Tourism Board, *Annual Report on Tourism Statistics 2013*, 2014, pp. 27, 36 and 44.

2013. On the contrary, they had shown strong inclination to spend on watches and clocks, which registered an increase in expenditure from 11% in 2002 to 32% in 2013.

That Chinese tourists spend disproportionately more on shopping is not unique in Singapore. Chinese tourists have been a key source of revenue for retailers across the globe thanks largely to their fondness for buying luxury goods abroad. According to Hurun report, Chinese shoppers were ranked world's No. 1 in 2013 in terms of spending in tax-free shops, accounting for 27% of all tax-free shopping purchases, followed by Russian (17%) and Indonesian shoppers (4%). Singapore was ranked Chinese millionaires and billionaires' third-most favoured destination in 2013, behind France and the United States, to shop for luxury items.[8] Chinese tourists' penchant for shopping could be attributed to several factors. First is China's gift-giving culture. The Chinese are fond of buying "local brands", such as Burberry, Clarks shoes and Scotch whisky, as gifts for their relatives back home. Second is China's high tax on luxury goods. For example, luxury goods in China cost 45%, 51% and 72% higher than those in Hong Kong, the United States and France, respectively.[9] Third is the Chinese unique consumption behaviour. As outbound travel is still considered a privilege enjoyed largely by the middle to upper classes in China, purchases made abroad are perceived as a symbol of class and status.[10] Fourth is the inclusion of shopping in travel itineraries, thereby stimulating Chinese tourists' shopping expenditure. In most "zero-dollar tours", travel agents make their profits by diverting Chinese travel groups to shops that give them a commission on sales.[11] Fifth is the distrust of Chinese-made products,

[8] "2014 The Chinese Luxury Traveler", *Hurun Report*, at <http://up.hurun.net/Humaz/201406/20140603152517230.pdf> (accessed 2 February 2014).
[9] The Chinese government had recently decided to cut luxury goods tax to encourage Chinese people to purchase luxury items at home. See "China to Cut Tax on Luxury Items", *China Daily*, 20 June 2011, at <http://www.chinadaily.com.cn/china/2011-06/20/content_12735947.htm> (accessed 27 June 2011).
[10] Alice Ekman, "The Distinctive Features of China's Middle Classes", *Asie Vision*, vol. 69, IFRI Centre for Asian Studies, June 2014, p. 18, at < https://www.ifri.org/sites/default/files/atoms/files/ifri_av69_thedistinctivefeaturesofchinasmiddleclasses_ekman.pdf> (accessed 11 May 2015).
[11] "Chinese Tourists Getting a Bad Image", *The New York Times*, at <http://www.nytimes.com/2005/10/21/business/worldbusiness/21iht-tourists.html?_r=0> (accessed 7 June 2011). Interview with Mr Robert Khoo, chief executive officer of the National Association of Travel Agents Singapore, on 25 April 2011.

leading many Chinese tourists to buy better-quality health products and other high-end products overseas.[12]

Although Chinese visitors' expenditures are generally quite substantial, most of them do not stay in Singapore for long period of time. In 2013, 66% of Chinese visitors stayed in Singapore for only a day or less. This could be explained by the fact that many Chinese visitors travel in package tours organised by travel agencies in China that, as a measure of cost reduction, arrange for tourists to make a brief stopover in Singapore but stay overnight in other Southeast Asian countries with lower accommodation costs, such as Thailand and Malaysia. Putting up in other less expensive Southeast Asian countries is a possible reason why Chinese visitors' expenditure on accommodation in Singapore accounts for a less important proportion of their total expenditure. In 2013, accommodation only accounted for 22% of total expenditure by Chinese visitors in Singapore, far less than that spent by visitors from Taiwan (41%), Hong Kong (40%), South Korea (37%) and Japan (36%).[13] In terms of length of stay, while 77% of Chinese visitors stayed in Singapore a day or less in 2002, that percentage had however dropped in 2013. There is in fact an increasing number of Chinese visitors staying more than two days in Singapore. In 2013, 21% of Chinese tourists chose to stay in Singapore between two and four days, compared to only 10% in 2002 (Table 2). Of noteworthy is the share of Chinese visitors on holiday in Singapore, which decreased from 61% in 2002 to 40% in 2013, whereas the share of Chinese visitors on business trips and meetings, incentives, conferences, and exhibitions (MICE) increased from 8% to 25%. The share of Chinese visitors who came to visit friends and relatives had also increased from 4% in 2002 to 15% in 2013 (Table 2).

Singaporean tourists in China

China's economic reform in 1978 was a turning point for its development of inbound tourism. With the opening up of China, international visitor arrivals have grown steadily. Chinese official statistics' record of Singaporean visitors to China appeared as early as in 1984. Within a decade, Singapore visitors grew from 37,400 in 1984 to 231,900 in 1994. Due to its tiny population, Singapore visitors constitute a very small percentage of total visitors to China. Nonetheless, compared to other Southeast Asian countries, Singapore accounted for an

---

[12] Lara Farrar, "On Tour in the US with China's New Rich", *Women's Wear Daily*, vol. 21, no. 74, 11 April 2011.

[13] Singapore Tourism Board, *Annual Report on Tourism Statistics 2013*, 2014, p. 51.

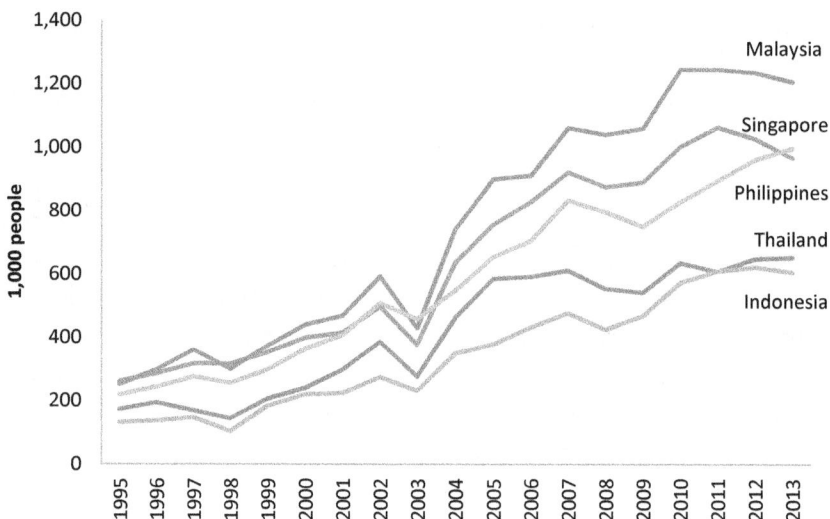

Figure 3 Number of Visitor Arrivals to China from Major Southeast Asian Countries

Source: Macroeconomic Database for Emerging and Developed Markets, CEIC Data, 2014, at <http://www.ceicdata.com> (accessed 2 February 2015).

important share. The number of Singaporean visitors to China increased sharply from 262,000 in 1995 to 1,063,000 in 2011 but slowed down to 967,000 in 2013. As shown in Figure 3, other Southeast Asian countries, such as Thailand, the Philippines and Indonesia have much larger population than Singapore but visitors from these countries to China are far fewer than that from Singapore. Malaysia's population is five times larger than Singapore's, but there were only 240,000 more Malaysian visitors to China than Singaporean visitors (Figure 3). Apart from leisure activities, close Sino-Singapore business relations could well explain the relatively high number of Singaporean visitors in China. According to China's official statistics, in 2012, 37% of Singaporeans visited China for sightseeing and leisure, 18% to attend meetings and business, 4% to visit relatives, 6% to work and 36% for other reasons. Singapore's percentage of visitors who attend meetings and business in China is especially high compared to visitors from Malaysia (10%), Thailand (6%), Indonesia (5%) and the Philippines (3%).[14]

China was the third-largest outbound travel destination for Singaporean travellers in 2013, after Malaysia and Indonesia. In terms of number of trips, 66% of Singapore outbound trips were made to Malaysia, 7% to Indonesia and

---

[14]National Tourism Administration of the People's Republic of China, *The Yearbook of China Tourism Statistics*, Beijing, China Travel and Tourism Press, 2012, pp. 38–39.

Table 3 Singapore's Outbound Tourism Destinations and Expenditures in 2013

	Departure by destinations (number of trips)	As % of total trips	Outgoing tourist expenditure by geography (S$ million)	As % of total outgoing tourist expenditure	Tourist expenditure per trip (S$ million)
Malaysia	12,885	66	11,844	59	0.9
Indonesia	1,450	7	528	3	0.4
China	904	5	943	5	1.0
Thailand	877	4	950	5	1.1
Australia	363	2	679	3	1.9
Others	3,029	16	5,230	26	1.7

Note: S$1 = US$0.75, Monetary Authority of Singapore, 8 May 2015.
Source: Euromonitor International, "Tourism Flows Outbound in Singapore", 20 August 2014.

5% to China (Table 3). Like Malaysia, China is also a budget travel destination, especially for the older generation of Singaporeans who retain strong cultural and kinship ties with China. Beijing and Shanghai received relatively more Singaporeans than other cities in China. Some coastal provinces, such as Jiangsu and Zhejiang, and popular touristy inland provinces, like Yunnan, also received many Singaporean visitors. Fujian is another popular destination, partly due to familial ties.[15] In terms of tourism expenditure, Singaporean visitors in China spent S$943 million (US$707.5 million) in total in 2013, accounting for about 5% of Singapore's total outbound tourism expenditure. Singaporeans' outbound tourism expenditure in Malaysia was the highest, about 59%, in 2013 because a sizeable number of Singaporeans travelled to Malaysia to play golf and shop. Despite the higher number of trips and enormous expenditure, the tourist expenditure per trip in Malaysia was S$0.9 million (US$0.68 million), less than that in China (S$1.0 million or US$0.75 million), Thailand (S$1.1 million or US$0.83 million) and Australia (S$1.9 million or US$1.43 million).

Singapore's investment in China's tourism industry

Conventional perspectives suggest that developing the tourism industry will generate hard currency, increase employment, boost government tax revenue and increase gross domestic product (GDP). The positive economic contributions

---

[15] Macroeconomic Database for Emerging and Developed Markets, CEIC Data, 2014, at <http://www.ceicdata.com/> (accessed 2 February 2015).

from tourism are particularly important to developing countries whose tourism resources are abundant. In the case of China, given its large and diverse economy, the tourism industry's direct contribution to China's overall economic development is quite limited. Nonetheless, for inland regions with insignificant manufacturing production, tourism can be a potential leading industry that induces the development of other related industries. That the inland regions are rich in natural and cultural attractions and have potential to absorb agricultural labour force has made tourism attractive for the development of local economies.[16]

The Chinese government regards the tourism industry as strategically important because it has low resource consumption, provides abundant job opportunities and promotes development of other industries. As early as in 1986, the tourism industry was incorporated into the national development plan, namely the National Tourism Plan 1986–2000, with the aim of making China an advanced tourist-receiving country by improving infrastructure, tourist services and quality.[7] In 2009, China's State Council unveiled plans, namely Opinions of the State Council on Accelerating the Development of Tourism Industry, to boost the tourism industry. Domestic tourism was the main focus, followed by inbound tourism and outbound tourism. Chinese Vice Premier Wang Qishan further highlighted in March 2011 that China would "strive to develop tourism into a strategic pillar industry of the nation's economy over the 12th Five-Year Plan period from 2011 until 2015".[17] China's promotion of tourism industry provides Singaporean entrepreneurs plenty of opportunities to invest in tourism-related sectors, such as hotels, restaurants, transportation, travel agencies and other leisure services.

Since China's economic opening-up in the late 1970s, Singapore has been one of China's most important foreign investors. In 2013, Singapore was China's second-largest investor after Hong Kong, accounting for 6% of total foreign direct investment (FDI).[18] Although Singapore's investment in China

---

[16] J Jackson, "Developing Regional Tourism in China: The Potential for Activating Business Clusters in a Socialist Market Economy", *Tourism Management*, vol. 27, no. 4, 2006, pp. 695–706; and Wen JJ and CA Tisdell, *Tourism and China's Development: Policies, Regional Economic Growth and Ecotourism*, Singapore, World Scientific Publishing, 2001.

[17] "China Vows to Nurture Tourism into Pillar Industry over Next 5 Years", *Xinhua News*, 11 April 2011, at <http://news.xinhuanet.com/english2010/china/2011-04/11/c_13823828.htm> (accessed 10 June 2011).

[18] "Statistics on FDI in China 2014", at <http://www.fdi.gov.cn/1800000121_33_4320_0_7.html?style=1800000121-33-10000318> (in Chinese, accessed 2 February 2015).

Table 4 Singapore's Investment in China by Selected Sectors in 2011

Major source of FDI	Wholesale and retail services		Rental and business services		Transport, storage and post services		Accommodation and restaurant	
	US$ billion	As % of total FDI	US$ billion	As % of total FDI	US$ billion	As % of total FDI	US$ billion	As % of total FDI
Hong Kong	3.3	50	3.8	54	1.5	69	0.6	64
Virgin Islands	0.8	11	0.5	7	0.1	6	0.1	9
Japan	0.4	6	0.5	8	0.08	4	0.03	3
Singapore	0.3	4	0.3	4	0.05	2	0.06	7
USA	0.2	3	0.4	6	0.03	1	0.04	4

Source: Ministry of Commerce, People's Republic of China, *Report on Foreign Investment in China*, Tianjin, Nankai University Publishing, 2013.

continued to grow, the main investment target has gradually shifted from manufacturing to tourism-related services. In 2012, manufacturing sectors only accounted for 38% of total Singapore's investment in China, whereas services made up to 60% and agriculture, at 2%. Real estate is the largest investment item in services, accounting for 33% of Singapore's total FDI in China, followed by transport, storage and post services (8%), wholesale and retail services (5%), rental and business services (4%), financial services (2%) and other services (8%).[19]

According to World Travel and Tourism Council's (WTTC) definition, the sectors that have direct links to tourism industry include accommodation, food and beverage services, retail trade, transportation, cultural, sports and recreational services. Domestic consumption of goods and services by sectors that deal directly with tourists could also contribute indirectly to the tourism industry such as cleaning services procured by hotels or IT services procured by travel agents. Singapore is one of China's key sources of FDI in tourism-related sectors (Table 4). In terms of investment amount, Singapore invested the most in wholesale and retail services, and rental and business services (including machinery rental services, travel agencies, advertising, market consultation, legal services, etc.) in 2011, each at US$0.3 billion. Compared to Japan and the United States, Singapore is an important investor in accommodation and

---

[19] Ministry of Commerce, People's Republic of China, *Report on Foreign Investment in China*, Tianjin, Nankai University Publishing, 2013, p. 46.

restaurants (US$0.06 billion), accounting for 7% of total FDI in the sector, behind Hong Kong at 64%.

The growth potential of China's tourism industry is one main motivation behind Singapore firms' investment interests. The continued growth in inbound tourism and domestic tourism is expected to further spur future development in China's tourism industry. Many Singapore companies have made inroads into the Chinese tourism market. As China's economy continues to expand westwards from the eastern coastal region, Singapore companies have also transferred their investments from coastal cities to western and central China regions in recent years.[20] China, with 5,000 years of history, is inherently rich in tourism resources. It is ranked the second in 2014 for the number of sites on the World Heritage List, with 47 sites — which include 33 cultural heritage sites, 10 natural heritage sites and four mixed sites.[21] Since 2002, China has risen from fifth to fourth place in the World Tourism Organization's ranking of top tourist destination, based on international tourist arrivals and tourism receipts. With 57.7 million international visitor arrivals in 2013, China was the third-most popular tourist destination in the world, behind the United States and France. In terms of tourism receipts, China ranks fourth, after the United States, France and Spain.[22] Compared to domestic tourism, China's inbound tourism and tourism receipts are not significant. According to China National Tourism Administration (CNTA), there were 3.3 billion trips by domestic travellers in 2013, generating a revenue of nearly RMB2.6 trillion (US$420 billion) for the industry. China's domestic tourism market is the largest in the world in terms of tourist number.[23]

Beyond the business consideration, several policy initiatives have helped to promote investment in tourism services between China and Singapore. Based on the ASEAN–China Free Trade Agreement (ACFTA) signed in 2007, Singapore opened up tourism and travel-related services, recreational, cultural and sporting services and transport services to China, and China also started to open up its road transport services to Singapore (Table 5). In 2008, the China–Singapore

---

[20] "Singapore, China Witness Strong Bilateral Trade Growth: Singapore Minister", *People's Daily Online*, 6 February 2011, at <http://english.peopledaily.com.cn/90001/90776/90883/7280387.html> (accessed 23 May 2011).

[21] World Heritage Centre, at <http://whc.unesco.org/en/statesparties/cn> (accessed 11 May 2015).

[22] World Tourism Organization, *UNWTO Tourism Highlight*, 2014, p. 6.

[23] China National Tourism Administration, "China Tourism Statistics", 24 September 2014, at <http://www.cnta.com/html/2014-9/2014-9-24-%7B@hur%7D-47-90095.html> (in Chinese, accessed 3 February 2015).

Table 5 ASEAN-China FTA Trade in Services in 2007

Sectors	Sub-Sectors	China opens to Singapore	Singapore opens to China
Tourism and Travel-related Services	Travel Agent and Tour Operators Services		√
	Tourist Guide Services		√
Recreational, Cultural and Sporting Services (other than Audiovisual Services)	Entertainment Services		√
	Archive Services		√[a]
	Parks		√[b]
	Sporting and other recreational services		√[c]
Transport Services	Maritime Transport Services (passengers)		√
	Road Transport Services (passengers)	√	
	Rental Services of cars/buses and coaches with operators		√

Notes: [a] except for services specified under the National Heritage Board Act;
  [b] except for national parks defined under the Park and Trees Act; and
  [c] except for gambling and betting services.
Source: China FTA Network, at <http://fta.mofcom.gov.cn/english/index.shtml> (accessed 10 May 2011).

Free Trade Agreement (CSFTA) committed China and Singapore to strengthen tourism cooperation. In addition to road transport services which were already opened, China further opened up hotel and restaurant operations, travel agent and tour operator services, sporting and other recreational services and maritime transport services to Singapore (Table 6). The CSFTA came into force on 1 January 2009 and is the first comprehensive bilateral FTA that China has signed with an Asian country. In addition to the facilitation of bilateral flow of goods and services, CSFTA provides an ideal platform to boost the flow of investment in the tourism industry between both sides. The trade concession in tourism-related sectors between China and Singapore is detailed in Appendices 1 and 2.

Tourism development in perspective: China versus Singapore

With economic growth and rising income, tourism in both China and Singapore is expected to grow in the next few years provided the world is not

Table 6   China–Singapore FTA Trade in Services in 2008

Sectors	Sub-Sectors	China opens to Singapore	Singapore opens to China
Tourism and Travel-related Services	Hotels and Restaurants	√	√
	Travel Agent and Tour Operators Services	√	√
Recreational, Cultural and Sporting Services (other than Audiovisual Services)	Tourist Guide Services		√
	Entertainment Services		√
	Archive Services		√[a]
	Parks		√[b]
	Sporting and other recreational services	√	√[c]
Transport Services	Maritime Transport Services (passengers)	√	√
	Road Transport Services (passengers)	√	

Notes: [a] except for services specified under the National Heritage Board Act;
[b] except for national parks defined under the Park and Trees Act; and
[c] except for gambling and betting services.
Source: China FTA Network, at <http://fta.mofcom.gov.cn/english/index.shtml> (accessed 10 May 2011).

hit by sudden economic recession or crisis. According to the WTTC estimates, the direct contribution of travel and tourism to China's and Singapore's GDP is 8.1% and 5.8% in 2014, respectively. Travel and tourism also supported 22,780,000 jobs and 147,000 jobs in China and Singapore, respectively, which are projected to reach 26,819,000 and 178,000 in 2024.[24] The recent push for tourism development by both governments will also lead to its further expansion. The STB estimated that the Marina Bay Sand and Resorts World Sentosa integrated resorts can contribute an additional S$2.7 billion (US$2 billion) to Singapore's GDP in 2015, roughly between 0.5% and 1% of the city-state's GDP.

Both the Chinese and Singapore governments recognise the strategic importance of the tourism industry to their economies, as reflected in China and Singapore's development plans for tourism in Table 7. Both countries set targets to be achieved by 2015, including the number of tourists, tourism receipts and

---

[24] World Travel & Tourism Council, "Travel & Tourism: Economic Impact 2014 China"; and World Travel & Tourism Council, "Travel & Tourism: Economic Impact 2014 Singapore".

Table 7 Tourism Development Plans of China and Singapore for 2015

China	Singapore
Vision for Tourism in 2015	
1. To focus on domestic tourism	1. To become the leading convention and exhibition city in Asia
2. To promote China to international visitors	2. To become the leading Asian leisure destination
3. To progressively open up outbound tourism	3. To become the services centre of Asia
4. To develop local tourism	
5. To promote environment protection and sustainability of tourism industry	
Target for Tourism in 2015	
Inbound overnight tourists: In 2010: 55.7 million Target for 2015: 66.3 million	Visitor arrivals: In 2010: 12 million Target for 2015: 17 million
Domestic tourists: In 2010: 2.1 billion Target for 2015: 3.3 billion	N/A
Tourism employment: In 2008: 2.8 million Target for 2015: 15.3 million	Tourism employment: In 2008: 99,800 Target for 2015: 250,000
Tourism receipts: In 2010: US$45.8 billion Target for 2015: Above 12% of annual growth rate	Tourism receipts: In 2010: S$18.8 billion (US$14.1 billion) Target for 2015: S$30 billion (US$22.5 billion)
Initiatives for Developing Tourism	
1. Improvement of public transport service	1. Infrastructure development
2. Diversification of tourist destination	2. Capability development
3. Encouragement of private business in tourism	3. Anchoring iconic/major events
4. International tourism branding	4. Product development
5. International exhibition/cultural activities/ international sport event	
6. Product development	
7. Promotion of Hong Kong and Macao as destination to Chinese tourists	
8. Strengthening cross-strait cooperation in tourism	

Sources: China National Tourism Administration; Singapore Tourism Board; World Travel & Tourism Council; Ministry of Trade and Industry, "The Contribution of Tourism to the Singapore Economy", *Economic Survey of Singapore 2010*, Singapore, p. 75; The Central People's Government of the PRC, "Opinions of the State Council on Accelerating the Development of Tourism Industry", at <http://www.gov.cn/zwgk/2009-12/03/content_1479523.htm> (accessed 19 May 2011).

employment in tourism. Several similar initiatives, including infrastructure development, capability development and product development, were already implemented to further strengthen the tourism industry's competitiveness. China's diverse approach in tourism promotion, which includes developing domestic tourism, inbound and outbound tourism, is different from that of Singapore. China incorporates the promotion of Chinese tourists to Hong Kong and Macao and building strong tourism cooperation with Taiwan in its tourism development plan. In comparison Singapore positions itself as a leading tourism destination in Asia.

The future prospects for the development of tourism industry in both China and Singapore will be bright but their development paths will be very different. As China's tourism industry is still in its infancy, opportunities abound for tourism-related businesses to develop, such as hotels, travel agencies, restaurants and so on. First, in terms of market segments, the middle class in smaller cities and young adults are two major consumer groups that deserve attention. The middle class in smaller cities has been neglected by tourism service providers. However, as China's economy continues to develop, the consumption power and willingness to travel of the middle class are expected to grow. Second, travel habits of Chinese tourists are transforming, from travelling in organised groups to travelling independently.[31] Independent travel, which is increasingly preferred, will promote tourism in personal services, such as online booking services, personal financial services and so on. In addition, tourism, due to its connection with other sectors, is likely to become one of the major industries that will drive China's further economic development, especially in the inland region, which is less economically developed but possesses richer tourism resources.

Singapore, on the other hand, enjoys the edge of a comprehensive transportation and communication infrastructure, political stability, safe environment, multiculturalism and strategic location in developing its tourism industry. That said, it faces severe competition from neighbouring countries such as Thailand and Malaysia as a gateway to Southeast Asia. At present, it also has to deal with the competition from Taiwan, Hong Kong, South Korea and Japan for high-quality tourism services. Because of limited land and resources, Singapore is seeking to pursue high value-added tourism instead of increasing visitor arrivals. In other words, achieving the target of tourism receipts is far more important than the number of visitors. Given the geographic proximity, safe environment and absence of political control on tourists that may otherwise be imposed in their country of origin, casino tourism will more likely attract Asian visitors to

Singapore. Chinese students are also drawn to Singapore's English-speaking environment and reputable education services, and this has helped boost its education tourism. Health-care tourism will also have profound positive impact on Singapore's tourism development. Singapore thus needs to invest more in the provision of highly professional medical services. Singapore therefore has to differentiate itself in order to better compete with other Asian economies in medical tourism in the long run — such as South Korea, renowned for its plastic surgery; Taiwan, well-known for its trustworthy record in all aspects of medical services; and Thailand, known for budget tourism in health care.

Appendix 1

ASEAN-China Agreement on Trade in Services
(Only Tourism-Related Sector are Listed)

Sector	Sub-Sector	Limitations on Market Access	Limitations on National Treatment	Additional Commitments
		China opens to Singapore		
Transport Services	Passenger Transportation	(1) Unbound (2) Unbound (3) Only in the form of joint ventures, with foreign investment not to exceed 49%. Economic needs tests are required. (4) Unbound except as indicated in horizontal commitments.	(1) Unbound (2) Unbound (3) None (4) Unbound except as indicated in horizontal commitments.	
		Singapore opens to China		
Tourism and Travel-related Services	Travel Agent and Tour Operators Services	(1) None (2) None (3) None (4) Unbound except as indicated in the horizontal section.	(1) None (2) None (3) None (4) Unbound	
	Tourist Guide Services	(1) None (2) None (3) None (4) Unbound except as indicated in the horizontal section.	(1) None (2) None (3) None (4) Unbound	

Recreational, Cultural and Sporting Services (other than Audiovisual Services)	Entertainment Services (including theatre, live bands and circus services)	(1) None (2) None (3) None (4) Unbound except as indicated in the horizontal section.	(1) None (2) None (3) None (4) Unbound
	Archive Services except for services specified under the National Heritage Board Act	(1) None (2) None (3) None (4) Unbound except as indicated in the horizontal section.	(1) None (2) None (3) None (4) Unbound
	Parks except for national parks, nature reserves and parklands as defined under the National Parks Acts	(1) None (2) None (3) None (4) Unbound except as indicated in the horizontal section.	(1) None (2) None (3) None (4) Unbound
	Sports and Recreational Services except gambling and betting services	(1) Unbound (2) None (3) None (4) Unbound except as indicated in the horizontal section.	(1) Unbound (2) None (3) None (4) Unbound

(Continued)

Appendix 1 (*Continued*)

Sector	Sub-Sector	Limitations on Market Access	Limitations on National Treatment	Additional Commitments
Transport Services	International Maritime Transport (freight and passengers) excluding cabotage transport	(1) None (2) None (3) None (4) Unbound except as indicated in the horizontal section; unbound for intra-corporate transfers of ships of ships crews.	(1) None (2) None (3) None (4) Unbound	When the following services are not otherwise covered by the obligation enshrined in Article XXVIII(c) (ii) of General Agreement on Trade in Services in Annex 1B to the WTO Agreement, they will be made available to international maritime transport suppliers on reasonable and non-discriminating terms and conditions: — pilotage; towing and tug assistance; provisioning fuelling and watering; garbage collecting and ballast; waste disposal; port captain's services; navigation aids emergency; repair facilities; anchorage; and other shore-based operational services essential to ship operations, including communications, water and electrical suppliers.
	Rental Services of buses and coaches with operators	(1) Unbound (2) None (3) None (4) Unbound except as indicated in the horizontal section.	(1) Unbound (2) None (3) None (4) Unbound	

Source: "ASEAN-China Agreement on Trade in Services", China FTA Network, Ministry of Commerce, People's Republic of China, at <http://fta.mofcom.gov.cn/topic/chinaasean.shtml> (accessed 11 May 2015).

Appendix 2

China–Singapore Agreement on Trade in Services (Only Tourism-Related Sector are Listed)

		China opens to Singapore		
Sector	Sub-Sector	Limitations on Market Access	Limitations on National Treatment	Additional Commitments
Tourism and Travel-related Services	Hotels (including apartment buildings) and Restaurants	(1) None (2) None (3) Foreign services suppliers may construct, renovate and operate hotel and restaurant establishments in China. Wholly foreign-owned subsidiaries will be permitted. (4) Unbound, except as indicated in horizontal commitments and as follows: — Foreign managers, specialists including chefs and senior executives who have signed contracts with joint venture hotels and restaurants in China shall be permitted to provide services in China.	(1) None (2) None (3) None (4) Unbound, except as indicated in horizontal commitments.	

(Continued)

Appendix 2 (*Continued*)

Sector	Sub-Sector	Limitations on Market Access	Limitations on National Treatment	Additional Commitments
	Travel Agency and Tour Operator	(1) None (2) None (3) Foreign services suppliers who meet the following conditions are permitted to provide services in the form of joint venture travel agencies and tour operators in the holiday resorts designated by the Chinese government and in the cities of Beijing, Shanghai, Guangzhou and Xi'an: (a) a travel agency and tour operator or mainly engaged in travel business; (b) annual worldwide turnover exceeds US$40 million. The registered capital of joint venture travel agency/tour operator shall be no less than RMB2.5 million. Foreign majority ownership will be permitted. Within six years after accession, wholly foreign-owned subsidiaries will be permitted and geographic restrictions will be removed. The business scope of the travel agency/tour operator is as follows: (a) travel and hotel accommodation services for foreign travellers which can be made directly with transportation and hotel operators	(1) None (2) None (3) None except that joint ventures or wholly owned travel agencies and tour operators are not permitted to engage in the activities of Chinese travelling abroad and to Hong Kong China, Macao China and Chinese Taipei. (4) Unbound, except as indicated in horizontal commitments.	

in China covering such operations; (b) travel services and hotel accommodation services for domestic travellers which can be made directly with transportation and hotel operators in China covering such operations; (c) conducting of tours within China for both domestic and foreign travellers; and (d) travellers check cashing services within China. None within six years after accession, there will be no restriction on the establishment of branches of the joint venture travel agency/tour operator and the requirement on registered capital of foreign-invested travel agency/tour operator will be the same as that of Chinese travel agency/tour operator.

(4) Unbound, except as indicated in horizontal commitments.

Recreational, Cultural and Sporting Services (other than audiovisual services)	Sporting and other Recreational Services	(1) Unbound (2) Unbound (3) Wholly foreign-owned enterprises will be allowed. Economic needs tests are required. (4) Unbound, except as indicated in horizontal commitments.	(1) Unbound (2) Unbound (3) Unbound (4) Unbound, except as indicated in horizontal commitments.

(Continued)

Appendix 2 (*Continued*)

Sector	Sub-Sector	Limitations on Market Access	Limitations on National Treatment	Additional Commitments
Transport Services	Maritime Transport Services — International Transport (freight and passengers)	(1) (a) Liner shipping (including passenger transportation): None (b) Bulk, tramp and other international shipping (including passenger transportation): None (2) None (3) (a) Establishment of registered companies for the purpose of operating a fleet under the national flag of the People's Republic of China: — Foreign service suppliers are permitted to establish joint venture shipping companies. — Foreign investment shall not exceed 49% of the total registered capital of the joint venture. — The chairman of board of directors and the general manager of the joint venture shall be appointed by the Chinese side. (b) Other forms of commercial presence for the supply of international maritime transport services: Unbound.	(1) (a) None (b) None (2) None (3) (a) None (b) Unbound (4) (a) Unbound except as indicated in horizontal commitments. (b) Unbound except as indicated in horizontal commitments.	The following services at the port are made available to international maritime transport suppliers on reasonable and non-discriminatory terms and conditions: 1. Pilotage 2. Towing and tug assistance 3. Provisioning, fuelling and watering 4. Garbage collecting and ballast waste disposal 5. Port Captain's services 6. Navigation aids 7. Shore-based operational services essential to ship operations, including communications, water and electrical supplies 8. Emergency repair facilities 9. Anchorage, berth and berthing services.

(4) (a) Ship's crew: Unbound except as indicated in horizontal commitments.

(b) Key personnel employed by Commercial Presence as defined under mode (3) (b) above: Unbound except as indicated in horizontal commitments.

Road Transport Services Passenger Transportation	(1) Unbound (2) Unbound (3) Only in the form of joint ventures, with foreign investment not to exceed 49%. Economic needs tests are required. (4) Unbound except as indicated in horizontal commitments.	(1) Unbound (2) Unbound (3) None (4) Unbound except as indicated in horizontal commitments.

Singapore opens to China

Tourism and Travel-related Services	Hotel and other Lodging Services	(1) None (2) None (3) None (4) Unbound except as indicated in the horizontal section.	(1) None (2) None (3) None (4) Unbound
	Restaurant and Catering Services	(1) None (2) None (3) None (4) Unbound except as indicated in the horizontal section.	1) None 2) None 3) None 4) Unbound

(Continued)

Appendix 2 *(Continued)*

Sector	Sub-Sector	Limitations on Market Access	Limitations on National Treatment	Additional Commitments
	Travel Agent and Tour Operators Services	(1) None (2) None (3) None (4) Unbound except as indicated in the horizontal section.	(1) None (2) None (3) Unbound (4) Unbound	
	Tourist Guide Services	(1) None (2) None (3) None (4) Unbound except as indicated in the horizontal section.	(1) None (2) None (3) None (4) Unbound	
Recreational, Cultural and Sporting Services (Other than Audiovisual Services)	Entertainment Services (including theatre, live bands & circus services)	(1) None (2) None (3) None (4) Unbound except as indicated in the horizontal section.	(1) None (2) None (3) None (4) Unbound	
	Archive Services except for services specified under the National Heritage Board Act	(1) None (2) None (3) None (4) Unbound except as indicated in the horizontal section.	(1) None (2) None (3) None (4) Unbound	

	Parks except for national parks, nature reserves and parklands as defined under the National Parks Acts	(1) None (2) None (3) None (4) Unbound except as indicated in the horizontal section.	
	Sports and Recreational Services except gambling and betting services	(1) Unbound (2) None (3) None (4) Unbound except as indicated in the horizontal section.	
Transport Services	International Maritime Transport (freight and passengers) excluding cabotage transport	(1) None (2) None (3) None (4) Unbound except as indicated in the horizontal section; unbound for intra-corporate transfers of ships crews.	When the following services are not otherwise covered by the obligation enshrined in Article XXVIII(c) (ii) of General Agreement on Trade in Services in Annex 1B to the WTO Agreement, they will be made available to international maritime transport suppliers on reasonable and non-discriminating terms and conditions: — pilotage; towing and tug assistance; provisioning fuelling and watering; garbage collecting and ballast; waste disposal; port captain's services; navigation aids emergency; repair facilities; anchorage; and other shore-based

(*Continued*)

Appendix 2 *(Continued)*

Sector	Sub-Sector	Limitations on Market Access	Limitations on National Treatment	Additional Commitments
	Road Transport Services	(1) Unbound (2) None (3) None (4) Unbound except as indicated in the horizontal section.	(1) Unbound (2) None (3) None (4) Unbound	operational services essential to ship operations, including communications, water and electrical suppliers.
	Rental Services of buses and coaches with operators			

Source: "The China–Singapore Free Trade Agreement", China FTA Network, Ministry of Commerce, People's Republic of China, at <http://fta.mofcom.gov.cn/topic/ensingapore.shtml> (accessed 11 May 2015).

Chapter 5

Suzhou Industrial Park: More than Just a Commercial Undertaking

LYE Liang Fook

The Suzhou Industrial Park (SIP) has laid a good foundation for Singapore to broaden and deepen its relations with China, including enabling government and business leaders, ministers and officials from both sides to establish stronger political and economic ties. A high-level bilateral cooperation framework was thus created and subsequently expanded to oversee cooperation between the two countries. Apart from its political significance, the SIP has reaffirmed the Singapore brand name in China. Building on the success of the SIP, both countries have embarked on the Sino-Singapore Tianjin Eco-city, the second flagship project, and a third flagship project is in the pipeline. With cooperation being pursued on several fronts including several private sector-led projects, it is important to ensure SIP's continued success so as to add substance to the bilateral relationship.

Introduction

Most industrial parks are run on a commercial basis, with minimal or no governmental intervention. If the government is involved, its role is usually to provide a conducive regulatory framework or the right incentives to give industrial parks a head start in attracting investors or to maintain the momentum of development. Going by the laissez-faire principle, the less involved the government, the better it is for any industrial park to reach its full market potential.

Even so, the Suzhou Industrial Park (SIP), which Singapore and China embarked on in 1994, was and still is no ordinary industrial park. Like other industrial parks, it has to be commercially viable in order to be sustainable.

At the outset, the Singapore side stated clearly that the development of the park should be based on market principles and that the government should not intervene to bail it out if it runs into financial difficulties. This operating principle has not made the SIP any different from other industrial parks.

Unlike other industrial parks, however, the SIP served a broader strategic and political function that is less known. More specifically, it provided a platform for government and business leaders, ministers and officials, especially the younger generation, from both sides to join efforts and work on a common project. By working on the details and sorting out issues related to the project, both sides would understand and get to know each other better. This would lay the foundation for a long-term and robust relationship. More significantly, as a result of the SIP, a high-level bilateral cooperation framework was developed and consequently upgraded to oversee all areas of bilateral cooperation. Also, the Singapore brand name that is often associated with the project has generated positive mileage for both sides. On these counts, the SIP has achieved and served its role beyond that of a purely commercially-run industrial park.

This chapter examines the SIP in a broader context of the Sino-Singapore relationship, centring on the argument that the project has laid a strong foundation for the development of bilateral ties despite its initial difficulties. The author has identified four key aspects of the SIP to corroborate this argument. The first aspect is the highly unusual origins of the SIP, in particular the unique political context in which the Singapore and Chinese governments became actively involved in conceiving the project.

Second, a defining feature of the SIP project is the transfer of Singapore's economic management and public administration software apart from its physical development. It will also highlight one difficult issue faced by both sides in the implementation of Singapore's software. On surface, this issue reveals the gap that existed between the two countries in terms of their mindset and way of doing things. At a deeper level, and on hindsight, this difference underscored the value of the software that Singapore was transferring to the Chinese side. This value became increasingly apparent as years went by. Today, the success or appeal of the SIP can be attributed to the foundation laid in the early years.

Third, the SIP has made key achievements in terms of economic performance and, more importantly, non-economic indicators such as environmental protection and creating a quality environment for residents to live, work and play. The SIP's commendable record in the non-economic areas has differentiated it from other industrial parks in China.

Fourth, the SIP has engendered a level of political significance whose impact is still at play. This is evident in the high-level institutional mechanism set up initially to drive the SIP but was later upgraded to oversee other areas of bilateral cooperation. In addition, the success of the SIP today has generated greater awareness of the Singapore brand name in China, notwithstanding the teething problems encountered in the initial years. It is therefore important to ensure the SIP's continued success as it has a direct bearing on the bilateral relationship. The four key aspects are discussed as follows in greater detail.

A highly unusual origin

The origins of the SIP project could be traced as far back as November 1978 when Chinese paramount leader Deng Xiaoping's visit to Singapore left an indelible impression on him. Deng was unexpectedly impressed, or in some accounts shocked, by Singapore's socio-economic progress within such a short period of time since its independence in 1965. Deeply impressed, Deng kept abreast of developments in Singapore thereafter[1] and even specifically mentioned Singapore in his *Nanxun* (Southern Tour) 14 years later in 1992.

To be sure, Deng had even visited Singapore much earlier in 1920 when he was on his way to Marseilles in France to work and study after the end of the First World War. At the time, Singapore was still a British colony. When Deng met Prime Minister Lee Kuan Yew in 1978, Deng apparently told Lee that he was "glad he had come and seen Singapore again after 58 years". He remarked that Singapore had undergone a "dramatic transformation" and congratulated Lee, who replied that "Singapore was a small country with two and a half million people". To this, Deng sighed and said "If I had only Shanghai, I too might be able to change Shanghai as quickly. But I have the whole of China!"[2]

At the end of his visit, after Deng had boarded the plane departing from Singapore, Lee said to his colleagues that Deng's staff were going to get a

---

[1] Then Singapore Prime Minister Lee Kuan Yew met Deng Xiaoping in Beijing on three subsequent occasions in the 1980s. According to Lee, Deng kept up his interest in Singapore's developments. See "Speech by Senior Minister Lee Kuan Yew at the International Conference on National Boundaries and Cultural Configurations", at the 10th Anniversary Celebration of the Centre for Chinese Language and Culture, Nanyang Technological University, 23 June 2004, at <http://www3.ntu.edu.sg/corpcomms2/releases/Speech%20by%20SM%20Lee%20Kuan%20Yew%20at%20CCLC%20Conference.pdf> (accessed 26 March 2015).
[2] Lee Kuan Yew, *From Third World to First: The Singapore Story, 1965-2000*, Singapore, Singapore Press Holdings, 2000, pp. 667–668.

"shellacking" as Deng had witnessed a Singapore that "his brief had not prepared him for". Sure enough, after Deng's visit, articles in the *People's Daily*, the main newspaper of the Communist Party of China (CPC), took a different line and portrayed Singapore in a positive light. No longer seen simply as "running dogs of the American imperialists", Singapore was described as a "garden city worth studying for its greening, public housing and tourism".[3] Another evidence of Deng's positive impression of Singapore was his speech in October 1979 when he mentioned how Singapore had utilised foreign capital to generate revenue for the state and income for the workers, and promoted the growth of the service sectors.[4] To Deng, Singapore was a vivid example of a country that had done well after independence. More importantly, Singapore's experience could provide a reference for China.

Before arriving in Singapore in November 1978, Deng had visited Thailand and Malaysia. His impression of Southeast Asia before the tour was that it was a backward region as in the mind of many Chinese leaders in those days. But among the three countries he visited, Singapore is said to have left the deepest impression on him.[5] What Deng saw in Singapore and his frank discussion with Lee had "in some way convinced Deng to open up China". Lee also told Deng that "if Singaporeans, who were descendants of illiterate, landless peasants who had to leave China, could do it, then China with its progeny of scholars, mandarins and literati who had stayed home could certainly do it".[6] In other words, Singapore had shown China that it was possible to have a high level of socio-economic development under a strong and capable leadership. More precisely, a market economy was compatible with a one-party dominant state.

Fourteen years later, in 1992, Singapore was again mentioned in Deng's *Nanxun* speech when he sought to break out of the constraints of political

---

[3] Lee Kuan Yew, *From Third World to First*, p. 668.

[4] Lee Kuan Yew, *From Third World to First*, pp. 668–669.

[5] This view was expressed by Lü Yuanli, director of Singapore Research Centre at Shenzhen University. See "Deng-Lee Meeting Depicted in China TV Serial", *The Straits Times*, 27 August 2014, at <http://www.straitstimes.com/news/asia/east-asia/story/deng-lee-meeting-depicted-china-tv-serial-20140827> (accessed 26 March 2015).

[6] Mr Goh Chok Tong, then Senior Minister of State for Finance, was present at the historic meeting between Lee Kuan Yew and Deng Xiaoping when the latter visited Singapore in 1978. See "Speech by Mr. Goh Chok Tong, Senior Minister, at the Singapore-Guangdong Development Forum" (in Guangzhou), Prime Minister's Office website, 24 March 2009, at <http://www.pmo.gov.sg/mediacentre/speech-mr-goh-chok-tong-senior-minister-singapore-guangdong-development-forum-24-march> (accessed 26 March 2015).

conservatism and economic reform inertia China had slipped into following the 1989 Tiananmen incident and the 1991 collapse of the Soviet Union. Deng's *Nanxun* not only set China firmly on the path of economic reforms but also provided the political opening for China and Singapore to explore and expand cooperation with each other.

In his *Nanxun* speech, Deng said that "Guangdong should catch up with Asia's four dragons (Hong Kong, Singapore, South Korea and Taiwan) in 20 years, not only in economics but also in social order and social climate. China should do better than these countries in these matters".[7] In particular, Deng mentioned that "Singapore enjoys good social order. They govern the place with discipline. We should tap their experience and learn how to manage better than them" (新加坡的社会秩序算是好的，他们管得严，我们应该借鉴他们的经验，而且比他们管得更好*Xinjiapo de shehui zhixu suan shi haode, tamen guandeyan, women yinggai jiejian tamen de jingyan, erqie bi tamen guande genghao*).[8] Deng's particular reference to Singapore opened the political window for Singapore and China to cooperate further. It sparked off "Singapore fever" in China and led to numerous visits by Chinese delegations to Singapore. In 1992 alone, more than 400 delegations from China came to Singapore. They wanted to better understand how Singapore had established good social order alongside rapid economic growth.[9]

In September 1992, Zhang Xinsheng, the mayor of Suzhou, broached the idea of Singapore investing a part of its reserves to help Suzhou industrialise when Senior Minister Lee Kuan Yew visited Suzhou.[10] Zhang was cognisant of the improved political climate in China for foreign investments following Deng Xiaoping's *Nanxun* speech and he saw an opportunity for Suzhou to work with Singapore. Singapore was not immediately seized with the idea of collaborating with Suzhou as it was unclear then how much support Suzhou could obtain from the central government.[11] It took further discussions and several meetings later before the idea of developing an industrial park there was conceived.

---

[7] Lee Kuan Yew, *From Third World to First*, p. 714.

[8] Shenzhen Propaganda Department, ed., *Deng Xiaoping yu Shenzhen: 1992 Chun* (*Deng Xiaoping and Shenzhen: Spring 1992*), Shenzhen, Haitian chubanshe, 1992, p. 9.

[9] John Wong, "China's Fascination with the Development of Singapore", *Asia-Pacific Review*, vol. 5, no. 3, Fall/Winter 1998, pp. 51–63.

[10] Lee Kuan Yew, *From Third World to First*, p. 719. Lee was prime minister of independent Singapore from August 1965 to November 1990. From November 1990 to August 2004, he was Senior Minister. From August 2004 to May 2011, he was Minister Mentor.

[11] Ibid, p. 719.

On its part, Singapore leaders had since the late 1980s and early 1990s began to emphasise the importance of regionalisation, i.e. exhorting its businesses to venture into regional markets to develop a second wing to augment Singapore's small domestic market.[12] In a speech to cadres of the ruling People's Action Party (the ruling party in Singapore) in 1992, Senior Minister Lee Kuan Yew cited the success of Taiwan, Hong Kong and South Korea in building economies outside their geographical boundaries. He noticed that these newly-industrialising economies had "two wings with which to take flight. With only one wing, Singapore will stay on the ground and not get airborne".[13]

Likewise, at a regionalisation forum organised by the government in May 1993, Prime Minister Goh Chok Tong reiterated that going regional was part of Singapore's "long-term strategy to stay ahead".[14] He outlined a three-pronged approach on how Singapore businesses can venture abroad: (i) Singapore businessmen could follow their own instincts and go where they think they had the best chance of succeeding. This was what Singapore's small and medium-sized enterprises (SMEs) were doing; (ii) the government or a Singapore consortium could identify a few major projects in selected cities in different regions or countries. These projects should have economic linkages and spin-offs to a wide range of Singapore business entities; and (iii) select a suitable province or state which has the potential to be a newly industrialised economy and whose leaders are keen to tap Singapore's experience. This approach would enable Singapore to build up a broad and deep relationship with provincial leaders, who in turn could help Singapore businessmen secure some of their development projects. Prime Minister Goh also stressed that such collaboration with the province or state must have the full support of the central government of the country concerned.[15]

---

[12] Tan Chwee Huat, *Venturing Overseas: Singapore's External Wing*, Singapore, McGraw-Hill, 1995; "Singapore's Second Wing Looks Set to Take Flight", *The Straits Times*, 17 April 1994; "Ventures Abroad: Panel of Advisers Named", *The Straits Times*, 31 January 1993; and "SM Lee: Singapore will Become Failed NIE if its People do not Venture Abroad", *The Straits Times*, 3 January 1993.

[13] "SM: Singaporeans Must Now Build Up External Economy", *The Straits Times*, 16 November 1992. See also remarks by then Deputy Prime Minister Lee Hsien Loong in "Walking with Two Legs", *The Straits Times*, 9 November 2008.

[14] "Keynote Address by Prime Minister Goh Chok Tong at the Regionalisation Forum", National Archives of Singapore, 21 May 1993, at <http://www.nas.gov.sg/archivesonline/data/pdfdoc/gct19930521.pdf> (accessed 31 March 2015).

[15] Ibid.

The first strategy outlined by Prime Minister Goh in 1993 referred to the usual way that businesses, especially SMEs, would on their own accord go about in search of the most viable returns. In such instances, the government either would not be involved or would be minimally involved by assisting or facilitating their efforts through its agencies such as the Economic Development Board or Trade Development Board (now known as International Enterprise Singapore). The second strategy involved some form of governmental role in pinpointing projects in certain locations that would generate economic spin-offs for Singapore. The Batam Industrial Park, the Bintan Industrial Estate and the Wuxi-Singapore Industrial Park which were spearheaded by a Singapore-led consortium fell under this strategy. Finally, the third strategy required the government to play a much more active role in working with the counterparts in another country not only to implement a project but also develop a "broad and deep relationship". Singapore has adopted this approach in developing economic ties with Johor, Malacca and the Riau province. Likewise, the SIP falls into this category.

The SIP was thus conceived due to a fortuitous confluence of political factors on the part of Singapore and China. From China's perspective, Singapore (a young nation under a strong leadership that was capable of capitalising on the opportunities afforded by the free market) provided a useful reference for its economic development. Singapore had struck a positive image in Deng Xiaoping's mind since 1978 and Deng further gave it a ringing endorsement in 1992. Furthermore, Singapore was politically more acceptable to China compared to Hong Kong (which was still under the British rule at the time), Taiwan (which was regarded as a province of China) and South Korea (which did not establish diplomatic relations with China until August 1992).

From Singapore's perspective, Deng Xiaoping's special mention of Singapore in his 1992 speech was unexpected. It opened up a political window of opportunity for the two countries to explore ways of working together even more closely. It led to the idea of developing the SIP whereby both countries could reap mutual benefits by working on a common project together.

Software transfer in the SIP

The SIP had industrial, commercial and residential components. Beginning in 1994, the goal was to develop a 70-square kilometre site east of the old city of Suzhou in the direction of Shanghai. It was estimated to take 10 to 15 years to complete and to attract a total investment of US$20 billion. When ready, the township would be able to support a population of 600,000 and provide employment for more than 300,000 workers. On the surface, the SIP was no different from other industrial parks.

To understand why the SIP is different, there is a need to draw a distinction between its hardware development and software transfer. The hardware development of SIP refers primarily to the physical development or tangibles of the industrial park that includes the construction of factories and other buildings, the laying of roads, and other public infrastructure and amenities. The software transfer largely refers to the intangibles such as having the right mindset, the right attitudes and even value systems of the leaders and officials in handling any issue or problem encountered in the process of developing the SIP. The software aspect, which is a defining feature of the SIP and differentiates it from most other industrial parks in China, will be the focus here.

In the 1990s, many Chinese delegations came to Singapore to better understand how Singapore worked especially after Deng's *Nanxun* speech. However, it was uncertain how much learning they could absorb and bring back for adaptation in China during their short study visits. Hence, the governments on both sides recognised the value of working hands-on on a project, namely the SIP, through which Singapore could better share its experience in economic management and public administration with China. The Singapore experience, also better known as Singapore's "software", essentially embodies its laws, rules, regulations, as well as its efficient work processes and systems, and most important of all, the values and problem-solving attitudes of its experienced officers. The Changi International Airport is emblematic of Singapore's software often cited by Singapore leaders. Changi's reputation as a world-class airport did not come from the physical manifestations of its terminal buildings, but in its excellent software in terms of management mindset, leadership and efficiency.[16]

Some of the key values, concepts and practices that Singapore shared, particularly through the collaboration in the SIP, with their Chinese counterparts included the importance of conducting long-term planning; the provision of one-stop service; responsiveness to investors' needs; commitment to transparency and accountability; inculcating a sense of community among residents; and promoting environmental awareness through, for instance, greening efforts and setting aside sufficient green spaces. These may be standard practice or principles widely adopted today, but they were less understood then or even envisaged as alien ideas when proposed in Suzhou in 1994. Hence, understandably, Singapore encountered difficulties in introducing and implementing these

---

[16] Lee Kuan Yew, *From Third World to First*, pp. 230–232.

ideas and principles to guide the physical development of the SIP. In theory, software transfer and hardware development may seem to be two separate and distinct entities. In practice, however, they are closely intertwined as the values, concepts and practices that Singapore attempted to impart are linked to the physical development of the SIP. There is a correlation between software transfer and hardware development in that the sooner the Chinese imbibe the values, concepts and practices that Singapore sought to share, the sooner would the SIP's physical development attain a level comparable to the Singapore experience. This linkage shows the difficulty in implementing Singapore's software in the initial years of SIP's development as will be explained below.

One software concept which took longer time to gain traction with the Chinese side was promoting awareness of the importance of a master plan. At the time, "rolling development" (滚动式发展 *gundongshi fazhan*) was the common practice adopted in China's development zones. The approach, whereby land would be arbitrarily developed if there was a need or demand, was skewed in favour of quick development. As such, the needs of investors, who were ready to invest in any particular location, could be quickly met. Singapore, on the other hand, had adopted master planning from the outset due to land constraints. Prior to development of a piece of land, a plan has to be drawn up first to decide land use. Master-planning facilitates long-term and systemic use of land. It also fosters transparency and predictability, which are essential qualities in attracting non-governmental actors like private investors and developers.

During the initial years of SIP's development, the Suzhou Industrial Park Administrative Committee (or SIPAC which oversees the administration of the SIP) took over two choice plots of land next to the scenic Jinji Lake purportedly for government use and began construction work on it.[17] According to the master plan, the two plots of land were however not zoned for government use. In defending its action, one of the arguments put forth by SIPAC was that land-use rights for the two plots of land were not yet transferred to the Singapore-led joint venture company (JVC) responsible for developing the SIP.[18] There was thus no need to make a formal application to the JVC to grant permission for the two plots of land to be transferred to SIPAC for its own use.

---

[17] The author understands that SIPAC originally planned to build a government guesthouse, investment promotion facilities and housing for SIPAC officials and specialists on the two plots of land. Eventually, a luxurious hotel was built on the site originally planned for the government guesthouse.

[18] The JVC comprised a Singapore-led and a Chinese-led consortium of companies. From 1994 to end of 2000, the Singapore-led consortium held a majority ownership of 65% of the JVC,

However, from the perspective of the Singapore-led JVC, it was important to adhere to the master plan of the SIP since the objective of both sides was to develop a well-planned industrial township. Based on Singapore's practice, land value is not determined by its intrinsic value but rather it is derived from the purpose the land is being zoned for. If Singapore's practice is applied to the SIP, it would thus be inappropriate for SIPAC to take over the two plots of land and begin construction on them. At the very least, SIPAC should raise the matter formally with the JVC and jointly explore a way forward including negotiating an acceptable price to buy the land from the JVC.

The tussle between SIPAC and the Singapore-led JVC indicated the different practices and belief systems held by both sides, with each side insisting on its seemingly valid reasoning. Both sides could not find a resolution in the short run. It was only sometime later in 1999 that this was resolved as a package of issues after numerous rounds of discussion on both sides. This episode reveals the difficulties Singapore faced in implementing Singapore's software in the SIP during the early years. Nevertheless, the development of the SIP has adhered to the master plan and today, this is identified as one of its key competitive advantages. Industrial, commercial, residential, green belts, educational zones, incubation hubs are clearly delineated in the master plan. Looking back in hindsight, the difficulties encountered in implementation and transfer during the early years underscored the value of Singapore software.

To be sure, many of the difficulties Singapore encountered were associated with the SIP's physical development which required certain types of software that Singapore thought were mandatory and wanted to impart to China but were met with initial resistance. There is another dimension of software transfer that involved the provision of training to Chinese officials by the Singapore government in order to introduce them to Singapore's economic management and public administration experience. They would then be able to adapt and apply the lessons learnt from Singapore to the SIP. This training proceeded much more smoothly compared to the difficulties encountered in the physical development of the SIP.

From 1994 to 1996, the first two years of the project, Singapore focused on the macro-level aspects of software training with emphasis on knowledge acquisition, i.e. understanding Singapore's system of public administration.

---

while the Chinese-led consortium owned 35%. From 2001 onwards, ownership has reversed with the Chinese-led consortium assuming majority ownership of 65% while the Singapore-led consortium owning 35%. In 2005, with the entry of new equity shareholders, the Singapore-led consortium share was diluted from 35% to 28%.

Three key management systems were identified to help develop the overall administrative system of SIP, namely economic management system, urban management system and labour management system. The training courses were usually conducted in Singapore although seminars and briefing sessions were occasionally held on-site in Suzhou.

Over time, the focus of software training was realigned, shifting from macro-level training to micro-level issue-driven and problem-solving kind of training so as to be in tandem with the actual progress of the SIP. Different training programmes were conducted to equip Chinese officials with the technical know-how in administering various systems with an emphasis on adaptation, i.e. formulation and implementation of pro-business and transparent rules and regulations in SIP. Some of these training programmes covered the human resource system for civil servants, Central Provident Fund, finance and taxation, public housing, environment protection, customs administration, real estate management, public utilities management, public works management and technical capabilities development.

These micro-level training programmes or "small software" were geared towards achieving "big software" outcomes that included creating a pro-business environment, provision of one-stop service, and commitment to values of transparency and accountability so as to attract investors and developers to the SIP. Although the Singapore-led consortium in the JVC is no longer the majority owner of the project today, the Singapore government continues to provide software training through the Software Project Office (SPO) under the Ministry of Trade and Industry. This follows a commitment by Singapore that it will provide training for Chinese officials working on the SIP as long as they find it useful.[19] To date, the SPO has trained close to 3,000 officials in over 160 courses.[20]

In addition, Singapore was instrumental in the setting up of the Institute of Vocational Technology in 1997 to help train qualified skilled workers to meet the needs of companies in SIP. Prime Minister Goh Chok Tong raised the idea

---

[19] "Suzhou Handover in 2001", *The Straits Times*, 29 June 1999.

[20] "Singapore and China Commemorates 20th Anniversary of the Establishment of the China–Singapore Suzhou Industrial Park", Singapore's Ministry of Trade and Industry website, 1 June 2014, at <http://www.mti.gov.sg/NewsRoom/SiteAssets/Pages/Singapore-and-China-Commemorates-20th-Anniversary-of-the-Establishment-of-China-Singapore-Suzhou-Industrial-Park/SINGAPORE%20AND%20CHINA%20COMMEMORATES%020TH%20ANNIVERSARY%20OF%20THE%20ESTABLISHMENT%20OF%20CHINA-SINGAPORE%20SUZHOU%20INDUSTRIAL%20PARK.pdf> (accessed 31 March 2015).

for such an institute when he visited Suzhou in May 1997. After several rounds of discussion, the Jiangsu provincial government eventually gave its approval to set up the institute in December 1997. Singapore's Nanyang Polytechnic, with its experience in vocational training, was roped in to help set up the institute, which admitted its first batch of 72 students in September 1998.

The SIP today

SIP has advanced well beyond the teething problem phase of the early years to what is widely regarded as a successful industrial park today. It has performed well in both economic and non-economic indicators. Its remarkable achievements in the non-economic indicators can be attributed to the Singapore software that was transferred to the Chinese side. However, the Chinese side, including the Suzhou municipal government, the Chinese-led consortium and, in particular, the CPC SIP Working Committee and SIPAC, also deserves credit for building on the preliminary foundation and bringing the SIP to greater heights especially after the Chinese side became primarily responsible for the SIP since 2001. Some of the key economic and non-economic successes of the SIP are highlighted as follows.

By end-2014, SIP had attracted 5,276 foreign-invested projects including 92 Fortune 500 multinational corporations.[21] The total utilised capital of these foreign-invested projects amounted to US$26.7 billion out of a total contractual value of US$47 billion, which constituted more than half of US$90.7 billion in total investments that include projects by both foreign and domestic enterprises.[22]

In 2014, the gross domestic product contribution of the SIP was RMB200 billion, an increase of 5.3% from the previous year's RMB190 billion (Figure 1). The total value of SIP's imports and exports over the years generally displayed an upward trend except for two years. In 2014, its imports and exports amounted to US$80.3 billion, a slight dip from the previous year's US$80.5 billion. The dip can be attributed to the weak demand for Chinese products in its major export markets of the United States and Europe as well as China's efforts to rebalance its economy from export-oriented to more domestic consumption-driven. In 2009, it registered US$51.3 billion in imports and exports, a decline of 17.8% from the previous year. The decline in 2009 was due to the worldwide

---

[21] By end-2010, there were 84 Fortune 500 multinational corporations in SIP.

[22] Figures extracted from the China–Singapore Suzhou Industrial Park Development Company (CSSD).

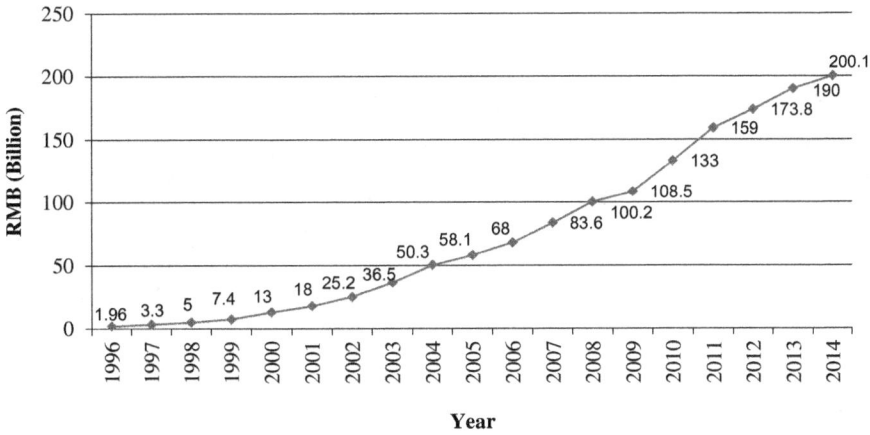

Figure 1 SIP's Contribution to Local GDP (1996–2014)
Source: Suzhou Industrial Park Administrative Committee (SIPAC).

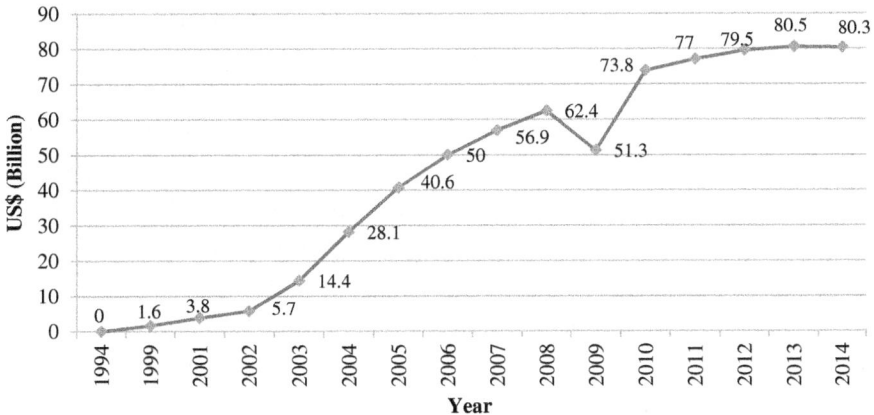

Figure 2 SIP's Total Value of Imports and Exports (1994–2014)
Source: SIPAC.

impact of the financial crisis that weakened import and export demands in general (Figure 2).

In terms of geographical distribution, as of end-2014, almost 50% or 47.4% of the foreign investment in SIP in value terms comes from Taiwan, Hong Kong and Macau. Among the three localities, Taiwan and Hong Kong make up the biggest contribution at 21.2% and 26.1%, respectively. This is followed by Europe (11.9%) and the Americas (11.2%). Within Asia, the next biggest group of investors is from Singapore (10%), followed by Japan (8.2%)

2014

South
Korea   Others   Americas
5.7%   5.6%   11.2%   Europe,
Japan 8.2%   11.9%

Singapore
10%
                Taiwan,
                Hong Kong
                & Macau,
                47.4%

2010

          South   Others   Americas
Japan   Korea, 6.07%   12.17%
7%   4.66%   Europe
Singapore   13.47%
9.35%
              Taiwan,
              Hong Kong &
              Macau,
              47.28%

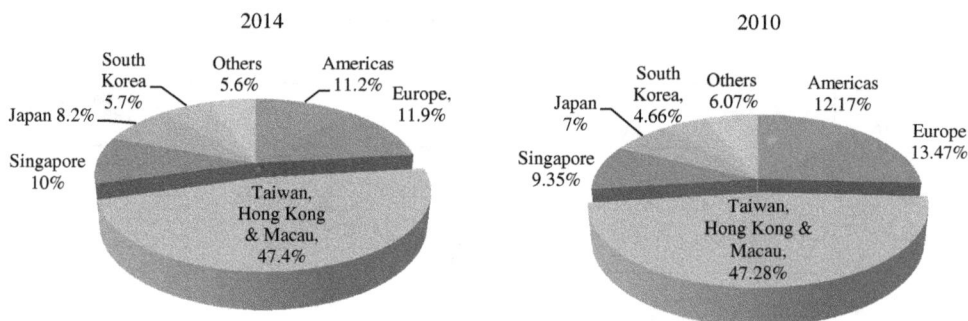

Figure 3 Geographical Distribution of Foreign Investors (2014 and 2010)
Source: SIPAC.

and South Korea (5.7%). Compared to 2010, there is generally a decrease in investments from Europe and the Americas and an increase in investments from Asia such as Japan, South Korea and Singapore (Figure 3). These figures reflect the relatively strong economic performance of countries in Asia compared to their counterparts in the Americas and Europe.

During the initial years of SIP's development, the Singapore government and the Singapore-led consortium made a conscious decision to market the SIP as a destination for international investors, beyond those from Asia. Singapore leveraged on its international network to actively market the SIP to investors in Europe and the Americas. This had helped to expand the pool of investors available to the SIP. More importantly, this approach reinforced the branding of the SIP as a park with international standards, thereby laying a strong foundation for further growth. In fact, at the time, there was a relatively stronger presence of investors from Europe and the Americas in addition to investors from Japan and Taiwan. Over time, although the balance has shifted in favour of investors in Asia, the SIP has retained its international orientation.[23]

In terms of sectoral distribution, the bulk of the foreign investments in the SIP in value terms are in manufacturing (79.6%), followed by properties (7.9%), leasing and business services (3.8%), and wholesale and retail (2.5%). Within the manufacturing sector, a large part of the foreign investment were injected into the high-end sectors such as computer, communication and other electronic equipment manufacturing (26%), general and precision equipment manufacturing (19%), electrical machinery and equipment manufacturing (11%) and transportation equipment manufacturing (6%). The electronic and

---

[23] For instance, investments from companies in Hong Kong has increased from single to double digits in percentage share.

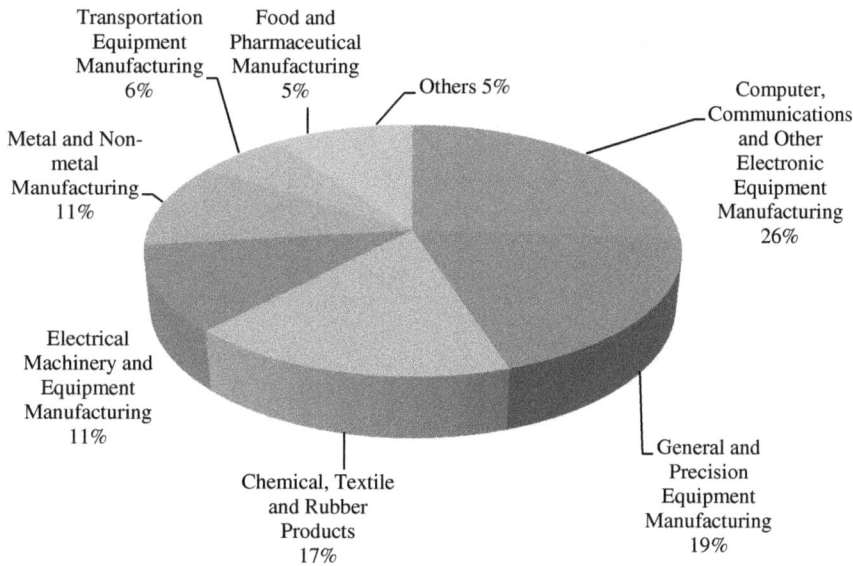

Figure 4 Sectoral Distribution of Foreign Investment in Manufacturing (as of August 2013)
Source: China–Singapore Suzhou Development Group Company (CSSD).

information technology and machinery manufacturing are the cornerstones of the SIP's industrial economy (Figure 4).

Apart from manufacturing, the SIP has also accorded great importance to the development of the food and beverage sector and the financial services and risk management sector. In addition, it has focused on developing high-tech and higher value-added service sectors over the past few years particularly in pharmaceutical and medical services, nanotechnology as well as cloud computing. Nanopolis was established in 2011 as a hub for nanotechnology development and commercialisation.[24] Other platforms that promote the biomedical services and research and development (R&D) sector include the Biobay and the Suzhou International Science Park (SISPARK), which were launched in June 2007 and April 2000, respectively.

---

[24] The areas of nanotechnology development and commercialisation include micro and nano-manufacturing (such as nanofabrication, printed electronics, instruments and devices), energy and environment (such as batteries, power electronics, water treatment, air purification, clean technology), nano materials (such as nano particles, nano structure materials, functional nano materials, nano composite materials), and nano biotechnology (such as targeted drug delivery, nano diagnostics, nano medical devices and nano bio-materials). See "Companies are the Actors, SIP's Nanopolis Builds the Theaters", SIPAC, 25 September 2014, at <http://www.sipac.gov.cn/english/news/201409/t20140929_296731.htm> (accessed 8 April 2015).

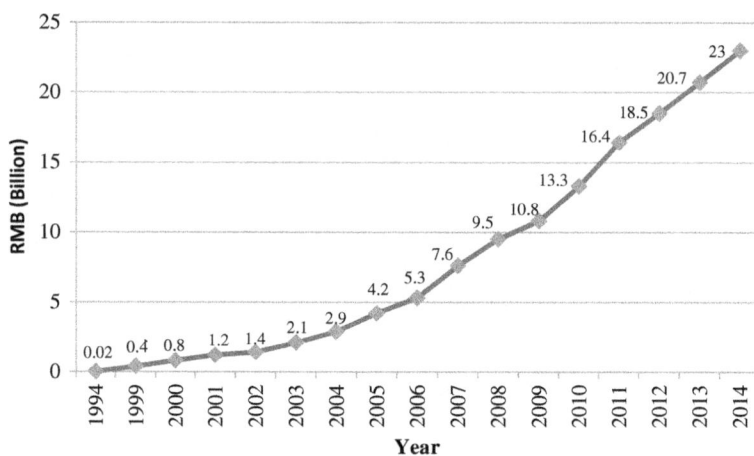

Figure 5 SIP Contribution to Fiscal Revenue (1994–2014)
Source: CSSD.

The SIP's contribution to fiscal revenue has grown over the years (Figure 5). Its fiscal revenue in 2014 was RMB23 billion, an increase of more than 11% over the 2013 figure of RMB20.7 billion. The fiscal revenue of RMB20.7 billion in 2013 contributed to 16% of Suzhou city's total fiscal revenue.

The JVC or the China–Singapore Suzhou Industrial Park Development Group Company (CSSD)[25] that spearheads the development of the SIP has been laying the groundwork for a public listing since 2004.[26] According to existing Chinese regulations, a company must be profitable for at least three consecutive years before it can qualify for a listing. CSSD has remained profitable since 2001, when the Chinese-led consortium took over majority ownership of the company (Figure 6). In 2003, in its third year of profit-taking, CSSD recouped its losses incurred in the previous years and paid out dividends to shareholders for the first time. A listing in the future will enable CSSD to raise the SIP's international profile and reaffirm the success of the SIP model.

Another testament to its success, the SIP model has been replicated in other parts of China. This "going-out" phase of the SIP can be categorised into two groups of geographical spread. The first geographical spread involves

---

[25] The China–Singapore Suzhou Industrial Park Development Group Company was renamed as such in June 2009, as part of its preparations for a listing. It was previously known as the China–Singapore Suzhou Industrial Park Development Company. Its acronym CSSD remains unchanged.

[26] "Suzhou Industrial Park to Face IPO Test", *The Straits Times*, 14 February 2011.

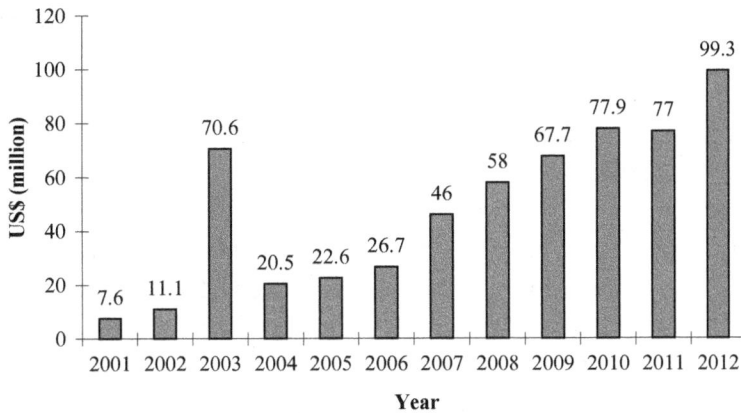

Figure 6 Profits of CSSD
Source: CSSD.

the sharing of the SIP experience with other localities in Jiangsu province where the SIP is located. For example, the SIP has shared its experience with the poorer and lesser-developed areas to the north of Jiangsu. Such projects are in line with the goals of the provincial authorities that encourage the richer and more developed areas in the south of Jiangsu to spur the growth and development of localities in the north. The Suzhou Suqian Industrial Park (which broke ground in Suqian in August 2007) and the Su-Tong Science and Technology Park (which broke ground in Nantong in May 2009) are examples of such projects. In addition, there are projects that are located in close proximity to the SIP such as the SIP-Xiangcheng Economic Development Zone, a collaboration forged in November 2011.

The second geographical spread involves the sharing of the SIP experience with other provinces outside Jiangsu. The Suzhou-Chuzhou Modern Industrial Park was first of such project to be undertaken outside Jiangsu. It broke ground in April 2012 in Chuzhou in Anhui province, an inland province whose growth has lagged behind China's coastal provinces. Another project that has SIP's imprint is the Horgos Economic Development Zone in Xinjiang that has good development potential as a gateway to Central Asia. The decision to collaborate on this development zone was made in October 2011.[27] The Horgos Economic Development Zone, located adjacent to Central Asia, is in an advantageous

---

[27] "Building Horgos Economic Development Zone with SIP Spirit", SIPAC website, 2 December 2011, at <http://www.sipac.gov.cn/english/news/201112/t20111202_128650. htm> (accessed 8 April 2015).

location to tap the economic opportunities arising from the Silk Road Economic Belt initiative announced by Chinese President Xi Jinping in Kazakhstan (that borders Xinjiang) in September 2013.

The achievements of SIP on the software front are equally commendable. Today, SIPAC prides itself on having a pro-business orientation, providing one-stop service, and offering transparent policies and regulations to investors. It is well aware of the importance of creating a stable and predictable environment in SIP and being responsive to investors' needs. For instance, on the home page of its website, SIPAC prominently displays a link that brings users to its "One Stop Service Center" website. This website contains relevant information and application forms for potential and existing investors (both local and foreign) on investing in the SIP, such as business application, capital increase, import-export, environmental protection, taxes, fire safety regulations and training needs. It also contains details and forms related to employment pass application for those working in SIP and for accompanying family members who intend to stay in the SIP.[28] The website provides a single contact number for investors to make telephone enquiries, as well as an online enquiry platform for investors. The online platform provides a detailed summary of the nature of enquiries, date and time of enquiries lodged, and date and time of responses to these enquiries. This website demonstrates SIPAC's commitment to provide a conducive environment for investors.

When an earthquake struck Fukushima, Japan in March 2011, SIPAC leaders and officials were quick to touch base with Japanese companies in SIP. The purpose was to better understand how these companies' production and import-export value chains would be affected by the crisis, and to come up with measures to help them tide over the difficult period. In his visit to Hitachi Display Devices (Suzhou) on 14 March 2011 for instance, the secretary of the CPC SIP Working Committee, Ma Minglong (the highest-ranking Party official in SIP that oversees the running of the park), reportedly told the Japanese management that "they could count on the local government for the help they need. He said the Chinese people wouldn't forget the support from the Japanese friends after Wenchuan was hit by a massive earthquake and this was a time to reciprocate…"[29]

Besides being pro-business, SIPAC also champions the policy of being "pro-people and pro-environment". On the environment front, the SIP was noticeably different from other industrial parks in China in terms of its greening

---

[28] "Suzhou Industrial Park One-Stop Service Center", SIPAC website, at <http://ossc.sipac.gov.cn/MainPage.jsp> (accessed 9 April 2015).

[29] "SIP officials Visit Japanese Companies and Promise Help", SIPAC press release, 14 March 2011.

efforts during its early years. In the 1990s, SIP was already known as a park with well-paved roads lined with trees and shrubs on both sides. SIPAC has since done much more to green and protect the environment. For instance, one of the most well-known lakes in SIP is the Jinji Lake which used to be a major freshwater fish farming area. This has been discontinued to reduce water pollution. Green areas, like the Red Maple Forest and Camphor Tree Park, now surround the lake and there are also green man-made islands in the lake such as the Taohua (or Peach Blossom) Island and Linglong Island.[30]

In fact, the Jinji Lake Scenic Area, as it is known today, has an area of 11.5 square kilometres and is made up of five functional zones: cultural convention and exhibition centre, fashion and shopping area, leisure and food area, central waterscape area and city-touring area.[31] Visitors to Jinji Lake can hop onto a bus that brings them round the lake on a 45-minute ride. It is reported that the attractions along Hubin Avenue receive an average of 50,000 visitors a day.[32] In July 2012, China's National Tourism Administration awarded a "5A" rating to Jinji Lake Scenic Area, the highest rating for scenic spots in China.[33]

Other large green belts in SIP include the Central Park (12.6 hectares), Baitang Botanical Gardens (47 hectares), Dongsha Lake Ecological Park (68 hectares), Fangzhou Park (11.4 hectares) and Zhongtang Park (seven hectares). There are also regular tree-planting efforts in SIP. In March 2015, 500 officials from SIPAC, SIP Working Committee, and government departments planted over 600 trees

---

[30] Over 50% of Taohua Island is covered by peach trees. There is a 40-metre high Ziyin Pavilion on the island where visitors can enjoy a panoramic view of Jinji Lake. Linglong Island is touted as an ecological island, providing a sanctuary for various types of birds.

[31] The cultural convention and exhibition centre is anchored by the Suzhou Culture and Arts Centre and the Suzhou International Expo Centre. The Harmony Time Square and Jiuguang Department Store are designated as fashion and shopping area. Ligongdi (a waterfront commercial street with restaurants and entertainment outlets) and Marina Cove (a garden/resort style shopping centre) are designated as the leisure and food area. The Ferris Wheel Amusement Park, Taohua Island, Moon Harbour (with restaurants and entertainment outlets) and Jinji Lake Water Tour fall under the central waterscape area. The music spring water curtain movie (an outdoor water fountain performance accompanied by laser, movie, music and fire effects) and Hubin Avenue (includes the Camphor Tree Park, Yacht Quay and City Square that extends for about two kilometres long) are designated as the city-touring area.

[32] "Jinji Lake Profile", SIPAC website, at <http://www.sipac.gov.cn/english/CommerceAndLife/Play/201011/t20101102_76484.htm> (accessed 9 April 2015).

[33] "Jinji Lake Scenic Area Upgraded to National 5A Tourist Attraction", SIPAC website, 6 July 2012, at <http://www.sipac.gov.cn/english/zhuanti/2012nztxhg/xgbd/201301/t20130130_197807.htm> (accessed 9 April 2015).

(including camphor, ginko and cherry tress) at Yangchenghu Peninsula in SIP.[34] Earlier in the same month, officials and staff from SIPAC and some local companies planted 282 trees (including osmanthus fragrans, crape myrtles and privets) in Dongsha Lake Ecological Park.[35] Regular tree-planting in SIP builds on the long-standing practice of beautifying and enhancing the environment for residents who live, work and play in SIP. It underscores the importance of man living in harmony with nature — a poignant reminder that many other parts of China face pollution problems that threaten health and the environment.

(From right) Wang Xiang, Standing Committee member of the CPC Suzhou Municipal Committee and secretary of CPC SIP Working Committee; Yang Zhiping, deputy secretary of the CPC SIP Working Committee and director of SIPAC; and Huang Jiyue, deputy secretary of the CPC SIP Working Committee and deputy director of SIPAC (partially hidden by tree). Photo credit: SIPAC.

At the same time, the SIP has made a conscious effort not to attract high-polluting industries to set up shop in the park. Apparently, from 1994 (when SIP started) till the end of 2014, the authorities have turned down 300 projects, amounting to US$2 billion, which posed potential hazards to the local

---

[34] "SIP Cadres Plant Over 600 Trees at Yangchenghu Peninsula", SIPAC website, 16 March 2015, at <http://www.sipac.gov.cn/english/news/201503/t20150316_345331.htm> (accessed 9 April 2015).

[35] "282 Trees Planted in Dongsha Lake Ecological Park", SIPAC website, 7 March 2015, at <http://www.sipac.gov.cn/english/news/201503/t20150307_344113.htm> (accessed 9 April 2015).

environment.[36] In addition, the waste generated and waste disposal by existing businesses are well regulated and managed. Due to its stringent environmental protection and safeguard measures, SIPAC has claimed that the standard carbon emission in SIP per RMB10,000 of GDP is one-third of the national average. Also, the rate of chemical oxygen demand (COD) and emission of sulphur dioxide (SO_2) in SIP is one-eighteenth and one-fortieth of the national average, respectively.[37]

The SIP is also known for its highly liveable environment. Residents generally enjoy living in SIP due to its beautiful and pleasant surroundings as well as its convenient access to amenities such as malls, recreational outlets, educational institutions, medical facilities and sports halls. Its proximity to the old historical town of Suzhou is an added bonus as residents in SIP benefit from a good living environment and immersion in the rich history of Suzhou.

To add vibrancy to living in SIP, there are various activities organised for residents throughout the year. For example, during important festivals like the Lunar New Year and Christmas, SIPAC would organise various events to jointly celebrate the festive seasons with enterprise representatives and residents in SIP. Other events include the Sixth Suzhou Jinji Lake International Half Marathon held in March 2015 that attracted the participation of 30,000 local and foreign runners (from over 40 countries). To appeal to a larger audience, the event was organised into different types of races: half marathon (21 kilometres), short marathon (14 kilometres), mini-marathon (4.5 kilometres) and family run (2.5 kilometres).[38] Other recreational activities like cycling, football, fishing,[39] table tennis[40] and

[36] "SIP Making Green Ecology a Key in Pursuing Sustainable Growth", SIPAC website, 12 December 2014, at <http://www.sipac.gov.cn/english/categoryreport/InfrastructureAnd Ecology/201412/t20141215_311533.htm> (accessed 9 April 2015).

[37] Ibid.

[38] "2015 Suzhou Jinji Lake International Halk Marathon Sees 30,000 Runners", SIPAC website, at http://www.sipac.gov.cn/english/news/201503/t20150330_347683.htm (accessed 9 April 2015).

[39] There are three designated areas along Jinji Lake that have been made available to anglers since January 2015. See "3 Angling Areas Now Available on Jinji Lake", SIPAC website, 20 January 2015, at http://www.sipac.gov.cn/english/news/201501/t20150121_337656.htm (accessed 9 April 2015).

[40] In November 2014, the SIP Foreign Enterprises Party Committee held the Fourth Table Tennis League Match at Suzhou Lake Sports Development Center that saw the participation of over 100 players from 28 teams of foreign enterprises. See "SIP Foreign Enterprises Party Committee Holds the 4th League Table Tennis Match", SIPAC website, 17 November 2014, at <http://www.sipac.gov.cn/english/ categoryreport/LifeAndCulture/201411/t20141117_ 304925.htm> (accessed 9 April 2015).

sailing are also held regularly.[41] SIP also hosted international events like the 2015 World Table Tennis Championships, held recently at the Suzhou International Expo Center from 26 April to 3 May 2015. Such international events, together with other regularly held activities, have enhanced the appeal of living in SIP.

The political impact of the SIP

A lesser-known but equally significant aspect of the SIP is its political impact, in addition to its success and progress that have been reviewed above. The political impact is still in play today and has a direct bearing on bilateral relations. There are two main aspects. The first aspect features the high-level bilateral cooperation framework that was initially set up to drive the SIP and later expanded to include other areas of bilateral cooperation. The second aspect concerns the Singapore brand name often associated with the success of the SIP.

The SIP encompasses a political rationale that has often been overlooked. The SIP was intended as a platform where leaders, ministers, officials and businessmen from both sides could convene to work jointly on a project. Such collaboration promotes interaction and mutual understanding, builds long-term relationships and strengthens bilateral ties.

To operationalise this rationale, both sides agreed on an institutional platform to engage with each other on the SIP at the start of the project in 1994. It comprised three levels (Figure 7). Steering at the top was a Joint Ministerial Council (JMC), headed by then Deputy Prime Minister Lee Hsien Loong and Vice Premier Li Lanqing. The role of the JMC was to set the overall direction and scope of the project, deploy necessary resources and review progress periodically. It brought together various ministries and agencies from both sides to facilitate the development of the SIP, including the officials from the Jiangsu government and Suzhou municipal government.

The Joint Working Committee (JWC), at the second level, oversaw the actual implementation of the SIP, and worked with the relevant ministries and agencies to carry out its task. The JWC reported directly to the JMC. A project office on each side responsible for identifying and coordinating areas of software transfer constituted the third level of the cooperation platform. The type

---

[41] For instance, in November 2014, the Fifth Lake Cup Regatta set sail on Jinji Lake with 28 boats and 140 sailors. See "28 Boats Set Sail for 3-Day Lake Cup Regatta in SIP", SIPAC website, 9 November 2014, at <http://www.sipac.gov.cn/english/zhuanti/20141110fcs/> (accessed 9 April 2015).

```
            ┌─────────────────────────┐
            │  Joint Ministerial Council │
            │      (JMC) on SIP         │
            └─────────────────────────┘
                        ▲
            ┌─────────────────────────┐
            │     Joint Working        │
            │  Committee (JWC) on      │
            │          SIP             │
            └─────────────────────────┘
                        ▲
            ┌─────────────────────────┐
            │       Software           │
            │    Project Office        │
            └─────────────────────────┘
```

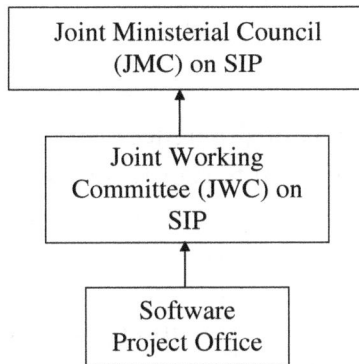

Figure 7   The Initial Bilateral Cooperation Platform
Source: Prepared by the author.

of software transferred has changed over time to meet the evolving requirements of the SIP as it progresses.

This initial bilateral cooperation framework has been upgraded over the years. There is currently a Joint Council for Bilateral Cooperation (JCBC) in place at the deputy prime minister level that oversees bilateral cooperation. In addition to the SIP, the Sino-Singapore Tianjin Eco-city, the second flagship project between Singapore and China, also comes under the purview of the JCBC. It is reasonable to argue that without the SIP, it would have been much more difficult for Singapore and China to embark on the Sino-Singapore Tianjin Eco-city. The collaboration on the industrial park and now the eco-city are concrete examples of both countries' constant efforts to stay relevant to each other and benefit from each other's growth. The success of these two flagship projects has strengthened and will continue to add substance to bilateral ties.

Augmenting the bilateral cooperation framework at the national level, Singapore has proceeded to establish bilateral cooperation mechanisms with seven other provinces in China. The network of engagement between Singapore and the Chinese provinces as well as between Singapore and Beijing have provided invaluable opportunities for leaders, ministers, officials and businessmen to meet regularly and work on areas of common interests, thus strengthening political and economic ties between the two countries. More importantly, the network has provided Singapore with an unprecedented level of access to the Chinese leadership at the central and local levels.

Besides lending significance to the JCBC framework, another important political impact of the SIP is the enhanced awareness of the Singapore brand name in China. More specifically, SIP's success today as evident in its software features of being pro-business, pro-environment and pro-people has vindicated the early unstinting efforts of Singapore in embarking on this project. In retrospect, the teething problems or differences encountered in the initial years reflected Singapore's commitment to transfer useful expertise or software to the Chinese side. The value of the expertise that Singapore transferred becomes increasingly more apparent as time passes. Today, the SIP has developed beyond its initial years with due credit to the leadership and hard work put in by the leaders and officials of the CPC SIP Working Committee, SIPAC, CSSD and the central and local government officials. Nevertheless, it would not have gone unnoticed to these leaders and officials that Singapore has played a key role in sowing the seeds of success early on.

In recognition of the role Singapore has played, China, especially the local government, the CPC SIP Working Committee, SIPAC and CSSD, continues to value Singapore's continuing involvement in the SIP. In particular, in its "going out" strategy to build mini-SIPs in other localities in China, the local authorities have publicly stated that the Chinese side is not "going out" alone. Rather, these ventures were undertaken on the basis of the successful experience of the Sino-Singapore collaboration on the SIP. In short, the Chinese side is leveraging on the Singapore brand name to explore opportunities elsewhere. To them, the Singapore component in CSSD is a significant feature in distinguishing SIP ventures from its other competitors.[42]

The response from the Chinese side towards the recent passing of Lee Kuan Yew on 23 March 2015 is a testament to the great importance it attaches to the Singapore connection. Yang Zhiping, deputy secretary of the CPC SIP Working Committee and director of SIPAC, who has been involved in the project since its early years, reportedly said that Lee Kuan Yew was the initiator of SIP. Yang recalled that Lee "visited Suzhou in 1992, and he chose Suzhou for experimenting and disseminating the experience of Singapore", and developed the "marshland on the shores of Jinji Lake". Yang said that Lee "gave us persistent instructions and support at every stage of development". Yang added that "in the future, SIP will follow the originally conceived goals and learn and adapt the successful experience of Singapore selectively to our practice, and translate the ideas of Mr. Lee Kuan Yew into reality. That is the best way to honor the memory of Mr. Lee".[43]

---

[42] At present, the Singapore-led consortium owns 28% of CSSD.
[43] "He Leaves Us a Legend: Lee Kuan Yew and Suzhou Industrial Park", SIPAC website, 24 March 2015, at <http://www.sipac.gov.cn/english/news/201503/t20150324_346755. htm> (accessed 10 April 2015).

Two days later, on 25 March, a photo exhibition titled "Lee Kuan Yew and Suzhou Industrial Park" was held at the SIP Archives Building. The exhibition was jointly put up by the SIP Office for Adapting Experience of Singapore (which is the software project office on the Suzhou side) and the Suzhou Singapore Club (founded in 1995 by officials and businessmen of Singapore stationed in SIP).[44]

On its part, the Singapore side has also recognised the importance of building on the success of the SIP. When Suzhou Mayor Zhou Naixiang visited Singapore in June 2014 to commemorate the 20th anniversary of the establishment of the SIP, he officiated the tree-planting ceremony of five *osmanthus fragrans* saplings at the Mediterranean Garden in Flower Dome at Gardens by the Bay — a first for a Chinese city to plant its city flower at Gardens by the Bay. The symbolic planting ceremony underscores the long-standing ties between Singapore and Suzhou. Singapore's Ministry of Trade and Industry (MTI) Deputy Secretary Lee Ark Boon, who represented MTI at the planting ceremony reportedly said that "Singapore and Suzhou have forged a strong friendship through twenty years of close collaboration and interaction at all levels. Today's planting ceremony reflects how the city life of Singapore and Suzhou has been enhanced by the sharing of our development experience. We will continue to build on this strong foundation of friendship and cooperation".[45]

It is noteworthy that both sides have since 1994 continued with the SIP software training programme, which was launched to provide relevant training for Chinese officials to enable them to better appreciate and implement Singapore's economic management and public administration software in the SIP. The training, conducted in Singapore, has persisted to this day with the majority of officials coming from the SIP and to a lesser extent from Suzhou. This training is another indicator of commitment and keenness of both parties to build on the success of the SIP.

Going forward, the Chinese side is keen to have continued support from the Singapore side to retain its share in CSSD and remain involved in SIP in view of the strong appeal of the Singapore brand name not only within but outside of China as well. On its part, the Singapore side also appears committed to this project as it offers a useful conduit for its leaders, ministers, officials and businessmen to interact and explore opportunities in tandem with China's growth.

---

[44] "Lee Kuan Yew Mourned in SIP Through Photo Exhibition", SIPAC website, 26 March 2015, at <http://www.sipac.gov.cn/english/news/201503/t20150326_347149.htm> (accessed 10 April 2015).

[45] "Singapore and China Commemorates 20th Anniversary of the Establishment of China–Singapore Suzhou Industrial Park", Ministry of Trade and Industry's Press Statement, 1 June 2014.

Concluding remarks

This chapter examines the SIP within the broader context of Sino-Singapore relations, centring on the argument that the project has laid an early and strong foundation for the development of relations between the two countries. The SIP is not the usual run-of-the-mill commercial project. In terms of its origins, the SIP was a government-to-government project conceptualised due to a confluence of political factors, namely Deng Xiaoping's specific mention of Singapore in his 1992 *Nanxun* speech and Singapore's intention to work on a hands-on project with China in line with its regionalisation strategy.

A defining feature of the SIP is Singapore's transfer of its economic management and public administration software. The value of software transfer was not immediately apparent but became increasingly obvious as years passed and especially after the Chinese side became primarily responsible for SIP's performance since 2001. The success of the SIP today can be attributed to the hard work of the leaders and officials in the Suzhou municipal government, CPC SIP Working Committee, SIPAC and CSSD as well as the robust foundation laid in the early years when Singapore steered its development.

Today, the SIP is outstanding not only in its economic performance but also, more importantly, in its non-economic strengths. The non-economic criteria includes embracing the mindset and practice of anticipating and being responsive to investors' needs, improving the environment and creating a quality living environment for residents. The SIP's achievement in the non-quantifiable aspects has hence differentiated SIP apart from other industrial parks in China.

Finally, the SIP has generated a far-reaching political impact, which still endures today. To drive the SIP project, a high-level bilateral cooperation framework was devised, which was subsequently upgraded to oversee all aspects of bilateral cooperation between the two countries. In addition, the fact that the SIP model has been replicated in other parts of China speaks for its success and reinforces the Singapore brand name. The Singapore brand name, a valuable asset that both Singapore and China are keen to leverage on and gain mileage while riding on China's growth opportunities, has greatly helped in facilitating the Chinese side to venture out of the SIP and the Singapore companies to strengthen their presence in China. Seen in this light, Singapore and China's commitment to ensure the SIP and other projects, including the Sino-Singapore Tianjin Eco-city project, remain on track and will be pivotal to strengthening of bilateral ties and the Singapore brand name.

Chapter 6

Tianjin Eco-city: A Low-Carbon Model in Singapore–China Cooperation

CHEN Gang

Singapore–China cooperation projects from the Suzhou Industrial Park to the Tianjin Eco-city have manifested China's shift from an export-oriented manufacturing base to a service-driven and low-carbon economy. Compared with the unilateral knowledge transfer from Singapore to China in the Suzhou Industrial Park project, the Singapore side has found its participation in the Tianjin Eco-city project to be an expertise-sharing and mutual-learning exercise as pollution and energy problems have pushed a rising China to lead the world in tapping renewable energy. It also marks Singapore's continued strive to stay relevant to China's rise by identifying a niche area for collaboration with China.

China embarks on Low-carbon Projects

Unequivocal scientific evidence shows that global climate is warming on a scale that is unprecedented in modern times, posing one of the most serious environmental threats to human development. China is probably the country that receives the most attention in East Asia and the world due to its dominant contribution to and worrying annual increase in global carbon emissions. Amidst various mitigation actions taken by the continental state against climate change, China may need to embark on regional low-carbon projects since local mitigation efforts can be more effectively managed due to regional industry make-up and local climate and socioeconomic factors. Influenced by the internationally popular concept of 'eco-city' that focuses on integrating sustainability into city planning, the Chinese government in recent years has paid increasing attention to the know-how of building cities that are in balance with nature. As the notions of 'eco-city' and 'garden city' are imported and China is still in the take-off stage of economic development, the country has to cooperate with other foreign partners in eco-city projects in the past few years, with the flagship China–Singapore Tianjin Eco-city Project as the most well-known and successful to date. While its goal of building environmentally friendly 'hardware' in the Tianjin Eco-city is on track, the two countries face the far more challenging tasks of developing the Eco-city's 'software' and 'heartware' that include the officials' right mind-set to adopt suitable policies, and residents' willingness to embrace recycling, environmental protection and other green habits.[1]

Eco-city as a new level of Singapore–China cooperation

Based on its indigenous experience with the construction of 'ecological garden cities' (*shengtai yuanlin chengshi*),[2] China has made efforts to plan and build its own eco-cities in some localities. The trajectory of Singapore–China project-based cooperation from the Suzhou Industrial Park (1994) to the Tianjin Eco-city (2008) has manifested China's shift in its economic strategy from building itself into an export-oriented manufacturing base to a service-driven and low-carbon economy. Compared with the unilateral transfer of knowledge from Singapore to China in the case of the Suzhou Industrial Park, the Singapore side has found its participation in the Eco-city project to a larger extent an expertise-sharing and mutual-learning experience when pollution and energy problems have pushed a rising China to lead the world in tapping renewable energy. At the strategic level, it marks Singapore's continued strive to stay relevant to China's rise by identifying a niche area for collaboration with China. In doing so, Singapore can leverage on China's growth. On China's part, the project enables the country to devise a model that balances the goals of

---

[1] For Tianjin Eco-city's challenges in developing its 'software' and 'heartware', please refer to speech by Singapore's Minister of National Development Khaw Boon Wan, "Green Minds with Green Hearts", 4 April 2014, <http://www.tianjinecocity.gov.sg/events/2014/20140404.htm> (accessed 20 April 2015).

[2] China's Ministry of Housing and Urban-Rural Development has standardised the assessment indexes for 'ecological garden cities', with a string of environmentally friendly cities like Qingdao, Yangzhou, Nanjing, Hangzhou, Weihai, Suzhou and Guilin already on the list. The per capita green land in an ecological garden city must reach at least 12 square metres with greenery coverage of over 45% and more than 300 'blue sky' days in a year. A 'blue sky' day is when the Air Pollution Index is equal to, or lower than, 100, which means the pollutant concentrations of SO_2, NO_2, PM_{10}, CO and O_3 in the atmosphere should not exceed 0.15, 0.12, 0.15, 10 and 0.2 milligramme/cubic metre respectively.

economic growth, environment protection and social harmony, one that is based on Singapore's own developmental experience which may be more realistic and attractive to China than other models. This collaboration is in line with the top leadership's call for a scientific concept of development enshrined in the constitution of the Chinese Communist Party. The project also dovetails with the implementation of China's regional development strategies.[3]

At the global level, living standards have been greatly uplifted due to rapid industrialisation and urbanisation in the past 50 years; this process, however, has also brought negative byproducts to the ecological system of our planet. Climate change, water and air pollution, ozone depletion, loss of bio-diversity, desertification and other environmental degradation are now so severe that they not only threaten the sustainable development of economies and people's health and life, but also pose an acute political challenge to global governance. Considering the increasing importance of today's cities and urban construction in determining the carbon and pollutant intensity of our modern life, building more environmentally friendly and sustainable cities has become a possible solution to intractable environmental problems faced by the international community. The relatively new concept of 'eco-city' has been envisioned and later put into practice by avant-garde architects and urban planners to create the best possible ecological footprint for city dwellers.

The city exists, like everything else, in an evolving universe, but it appears to have a special role in the evolution that may have a great deal to do with how we build and use it.[4] A successful city must balance economic, social and ecological needs from all sides. The notion of 'eco-city' or ecopolis is a big step forward in the long evolution of human urban construction. Such a city minimises the required consumption of energy, water and raw materials, and its waste discharge of air, solids and water pollutants. The year 2007 marked a watershed in human history when for the first time, half of the world's population was living in the cities.[5] As hubs of prosperity, cities have also been blamed for causing environmental degradation due to the high-carbon lifestyle and huge output of waste. It is therefore extremely important to understand that

---

[3] "First Meeting of the Sino-Singapore Tianjin Eco-City Joint Working Committee in Tianjin", press release by Singapore's Ministry of National Development, 31 January 2008.

[4] Richard Register, *Ecocities: Building Cities in Balance with Nature*, Berkeley, Berkeley Hills Books, 2002, p. 38.

[5] Cities Alliance, *Livable Cities: The Benefits of Urban Environmental Planning*, Washington D C, 2007, available at p. 1 <http://www.citiesalliance.org/doc/resources/cds/liveable/cover.pdf> (accessed 1 April 2015).

one of the most effective solutions to current environmental problems on a global scale lies in the way we plan and build our cities.

No single recipe for urban sustainability can be applied to all cities, but the various 'eco-city' schemes should share the three common goals of conservation, recycling and preservation of biodiversity. Designers of these cities would have to bear in mind that economic, social and environmental considerations are always interconnected and current urban development should not compromise the ability of future generations to meet their own needs.

It is important for 'eco-city' planners to manage environmental resources as strategic assets for the long-term interest of urban residents. Environmental resources such as clean air, fresh water, forest and open space are often taken for granted by city planners who do not pay enough attention to their efficient and sustainable utilisation. In an 'eco-city', clean air and drinking water sources that are crucial to human health would not be polluted in exchange for economic development. Biodiversity inside and near the city would be protected for maintaining the balance of nature and enhancing the resilience of ecosystems to environmental changes. Forests would be preserved because they not only are necessary watersheds and habitats, but also absorb huge amounts of greenhouse gases that cause global warming. More trees would be planted in the city area or the suburbs to purify the atmosphere and prevent the formation of an urban heat island. Other important environmental resources such as wetlands, coral reefs and mangroves could also be preserved in the process of urban expansion.

A typical eco-city should be a low-carbon city with improved public transport, and expanded pedestrian and cycling areas to reduce carbon emissions. To minimise the use of automobiles, the city would be compact and differentiated from the general urban pattern today — skyscrapers-centred cities with tens of thousands of acres of ground-scrapers sprawling all around. Instead, the blueprint should be a multi-centre one, with catering, education, medical care and shopping services made available to most residents. Dense subcentres and compact neighbourhood centres are situated fairly close to the major city hub. High-rise buildings are still encouraged in centre areas to save land, thus reducing long-distance commute by cars. Some of the outlying communities will be agricultural villages providing their own farm produces for the city hub and subcentres.

High density living, therefore, is a necessity for a sustainable city because it not only reduces per capita demand for occupied land, but also cuts per capita cost of supplying piped water, sewer systems, garbage collection, postal delivery and other public services. An eco-city must provide easy access to daily amenities via green travel modes like walking, cycling and taking public transport. New transportation hierarchy should be established with preference given to pedestrians, cyclists, subways, buses and finally private automobiles.

New energy-saving building materials should be widely used in the construction of an eco-city. To achieve low emissions, architects sometimes need to fit buildings with solar panels to produce electricity, which will be used for lighting, office equipment and air conditioning. Better ventilation strategies need to be worked out for reducing dependence on air-conditioning. Installation of blinds and details like the opacity of windows and the volume of airflow can be regulated throughout the building to conserve energy for heating and for balanced natural lighting.

An eco-city should strive to conserve water resources and interfere minimally with the intrinsic patterns of the water cycle in an ecological system. A compact city layout is necessary to reduce our footprint on the permeable soil, and efficient water recycling systems making full use of creeks and reservoirs should be established to regulate run-offs in the wet and dry seasons, and convert rain water into useful and drinkable fresh water resources. Urban aquifers should be protected from overuse or pollution, while the soil's permeability should be safeguarded to ensure the absorption of groundwater.

An eco-city should be a 'garden city' surrounded by green-belts and woodlands, with the preservation of local species and harmonious co-existence between humans and other creatures. Biodiversity increases the resilience of ecosystems to environmental changes. Rivers, lakes, wetlands and forest resources can be designated as protected areas to add to urban biodiversity as the city is built. If urban wastes are minimised and recycled, and the local people take responsibility to ensure that their daily activities do not endanger the existence of other species, the city itself can become a botanic garden where urbanism does not lead to humanity's confrontation with other animals and plants. An eco-city could also take the form of arcologies that take less land, less energy to operate and less connecting materials such as pipes and wires. In an arcology, major social, economic and civic activities are available within short distances, and farm production is located just outside the city gates. Individual buildings, communities and the city as a whole are maintained with great efficiency and little wastages.

Location is the key

Tianjin, designated by the central government as the economic centre of North China, has the ambition and potential to become a low-carbon model city in China. Japan's Trade Minister Masayuki Naoshima said after an APEC (Asia-Pacific Economic Cooperation) ministerial meeting in June 2010 that Tianjin should be chosen as APEC's first low-carbon city to test new technologies including smart grids and renewable-power generation as part of efforts to reduce dependence on fossil fuels.

It seems to be mission impossible for a manufacturing powerhouse with double-digit growth rates to lead the building of a low-carbon and renewable economy; however, according to the Tianjin Municipal Master Plan (2005–2020), one of Tianjin's strategic goals is to build itself into a liveable city with good ecological environment. Orientated as China's third growth pole after Shanghai and Shenzhen, Tianjin differs from its counterparts in its special focus on environmental protection and energy conservation. Such green commitment is closely related to China's long-term ambition of improving energy efficiency and restructuring its economy in a low-carbon direction. On the eve of the Copenhagen Climate Summit in 2009, China for the first time declared that it was targeting a hefty 40–45% cut in carbon intensity, i.e. carbon dioxide emissions per dollar of gross domestic product (GDP), by 2020. This goal is not only intended to improve its image, but also to tackle China's serious energy shortage problem caused by growing demand, inefficient use and limited energy reserves. In the context of sustainable development, as a pilot city for a new round of reform and further opening-up, Tianjin is expected by the central government to function as a not only business hub and international port, but also model city for environmental protection and a low-carbon economy.

Tianjin's Binhai New Area invested RMB14 billion (US$2.06 billion) in 2011 and 2012 to build a low-carbon industrial cluster and develop renewable energy. The Binhai New Area is all set to ban energy-guzzling and heavily polluting enterprises in the New Area, and has asked the local administrative regions to set emission-cutting targets for individual companies and projects. The Binhai New Area is committed to making the Tianjin Economic-Technological Development Area (TEDA) and Dagang district into an ecological industrial park, as well as the development of solar energy, methane and geothermal energy.

Tianjin Dashentang Wind Farm, the first wind farm under construction in Tianjin, started equipment installation in February 2010. It lies south to Sajintuo village of Hangu in the Binhai New Area and is four kilometres from the east of Dashentang village. Its installed capacity is 26 MW with an investment of RMB370 million. The wind farm can provide clean and reliable green power of 52,130,000 kilowatt-hours each year for the development and construction of the Binhai New Area and for over 50,000 households with a household consumption power of 87 kWh a month. Each year, the wind farm is expected to save an equivalent of 19,000 tons of standard coal, 30,400 tons of water, 6,000 tons of carbon dioxide, 88 tons of nitrogen oxide, 10.4 tons of smoke dust and 39.2 tons of sulphur dioxide.

The Asian Development Bank (ADB) approved a $135 million loan to help China build a 250-megawatt coal-fired integrated gasification combined cycle (IGCC) plant in Tianjin city that can generate up to 1,470 gigawatt-hours of electricity a year. To reduce greenhouse gas emissions and acid rain, China has launched a clean coal power generation programme, GreenGen, with the Tianjin project as the cornerstone of the first phase. ADB provided $1.25 million in technical assistance for the second and third phases of the programme which resulted in a scaled-up IGCC plant fitted with carbon capture and storage technology in 2013. As the IGCC technology reduces greenhouse gas emissions, the project can meet certified emission reductions requirements under the Clean Development Mechanism set by the Kyoto Protocol. The United States' United Solar Ovonic, a subsidiary of Energy Conversion Devices, and Tianjin Jinneng Investment Company, set up a joint venture (JV) in Tianjin to convert US-made solar cells into solar modules for the Chinese market. United Solar Ovonic does about 75% of the manufacturing in Michigan and then rolls it up and ships it to Tianjin for completion and cutting into proper sizes.

Ideas and norms of eco-city planning

To achieve urban development projects with integrated sustainable solutions across all sectors, eco-city guidelines and objectives have to be woven into local requirements.[6] In view of the complexity of city construction today, urban planners need to promote cooperation in a multidisciplinary planning team as well as among all stakeholders. An eco-city should be understood as a single integrated system (holistic approach) and not as a combination or result of many sectoral developments planned in isolation.[7] The idea of integrated planning is the basis for sustainable urbanism, which requires repeated and ongoing processes of analysis and a multidisciplinary approach to sustainability. In eco-city planning, sectors related to the metabolic and environmental functions of the city (transport, energy and material flows and socio-economic aspects), which conventional planning considers as subsidiary to urban structure, are considered

---

[6] Philine Gaffron, Ge Huismans and Franz Skala, *Ecocity Book II: How to Make It Happen*, Vienna, Facultas Verlags- und Buchhandels AG, 2008, p. 37.

[7] Philine Gaffron, Ge Huismans and Franz Skala, *Ecocity Book II: How to Make It Happen*, Vienna, Facultas Verlags- und Buchhandels AG, 2008, p. 38.

at the same level of importance. Extensive participation is an important part of knowledge-based eco-city planning because the more stakeholders are involved in the decision making, the more they will contribute to the bottom-up planning process.

With active participation of different sectors and relevant stakeholders, the whole process of eco-city planning and construction is usually focused on such key areas as urban structure, transportation, energy and other resource efficiency and socio-economic aspects. The main principles of sustainable urban development, i.e. minimising the use of land, energy and materials and minimising the impairment of natural environment, should always be followed throughout the construction process.

1. *Urban structure*

The efficient use of land resource is a basic requirement of eco-city planning. Eco-city planners need to pay sufficient attention to the spatial level of quarters and the neighbourhood. It is necessary to optimise the density of settlements in relation to the potentially contradictory requirements of transportation (higher density of origins and destinations), solar architecture (depending on the climate: either avoiding shading between buildings or using it for passive cooling) and quality of life issues (e.g. open spaces for social functions and personal comfort).[8] Instead of detached, single-family houses with large gardens, compact building structures, such as multi-storey residential, commercial or mixed-use buildings, should be considered.[9] Habitats for plants and animals must be created or conserved in urban contexts, with enough open space and green areas maintained in the form of gardens, parks, street trees, green roofs, green facades and natural water features.

2. *Transportation*

The use of public transport and green modes of travel should be given priority in eco-city planning. A variety of tools that involve policies on car parking, car access and car ownership should be used to reduce travel by private cars. Economic tools including road tolls for lorries and private cars as well as subsidies for rail transport can be adopted to encourage people to choose low-carbon transport. Eco-city designers should give preference to arrangements that

---

[8] Philine Gaffron, Ge Huismans and Franz Skala, *Ecocity Book II: How to Make It Happen*, p. 25.
[9] Philine Gaffron, Ge Huismans and Franz Skala, *Ecocity Book II: How to Make It Happen*, p. 22.

reduce the need for transport, measures that encourage travel at low speed, usage of public transport and mass transit, and limiting usage of car transport. The compact and multi-centric layout of an eco-city should allow most travel to take place on foot, by bike and by public transport. For private car owners, special tax incentives could be introduced to encourage them to buy hybrid vehicles that use energy more efficiently. Alternatives however must be good enough to reduce the need for a car, otherwise the transport inconvenience that may result from such alternatives may provoke public dissatisfaction or even sharp criticisms.

3. *Energy and resource efficiency*

The use of energy and other resources efficiently and sustainably is a key part of an eco-city project. Measures could be taken to minimise the energy demand of the built urban structure and energy losses of buildings. The use of fossil fuel for air-conditioning and other electricity supply should be limited while a variety of renewable energy is to be used widely. Urban architectures should include solar systems to capitalise on clean energy from the sun, giving preferences to environmentally friendly and sustainable produced materials. Advanced devices could also be adopted to treat wastewater for recirculation in the water cycle without negative impacts and the collection and purification of rainwater will help city dwellers use natural resources more efficiently. Solid waste could be recycled or reused, with special devices introduced to use landfill gases as a kind of new energy.

4. *Social infrastructure and economic viability*

Besides environmental protection, for the eco-city to be an attractive and prosperous place, it has to provide a satisfactory social and economic infrastructure for a better quality of life. One important element is easy access to day-to-day facilities. Kindergarten and elementary schools should be within walking distance or take a maximum of 30 minutes to reach by public transport, so should other schools, clinics and hospitals. Leisure and recreation facilities such as cinemas, theatres and fitness centres ought also to be within walking distance or easily accessible by public transport.

These conveniences may come at a cost. Economic viability is thus important. To achieve economic sustainability a plurality of investors including owner-inhabitants, real estate companies and professional developers may need to be involved right from the start. A public-private partnership is desirous for eco-cities.[10] Co-operation of all sectors on eco-city projects makes it possible to divide the risks among partners, attain public, social and societal goals with reduced funding from public sources and raise the return on investment of related private investments.[11] Short-term investments and returns should not be the only index for measuring the profitability of an eco-city project whose long-term success depends on whether it helps to create a unique city context with significant reduction of pollution, ensure minimum use of fossil fuels and other resources, improve people's health, attain high quality of life, minimise car accidents and provide more convenience for social activities.

5. *Monitoring and evaluation mechanisms*

Certain monitoring and evaluation mechanisms, and procedures must be in place to ensure that the urban development process serves the goals of conserving resources, reducing pollution, increasing greening spaces and improving people's residential life. Such evaluation is also important for getting valuable empirical information that can be used as a reference for other eco-cities and future improvement. One indispensable feature of the eco-city is public participation; a good monitoring system depends on not only the technical ways of data-collecting on energy saving, emission reduction and water consumption, but also well-designed social feedback mechanisms that assimilate public opinions and assessments. Continuous evaluation with the participation of all relevant stakeholders is essential for maintaining the vitality of the eco-city, which needs to rely on qualitative and quantitative tools to assess whether the proposed environmental, economic and social objectives have been met. A set of indicators associated with urban structure, transport, energy, material flows and socio-economy need to be developed to monitor urban maintenance and management. Appropriate adaptations and adjustments have to be made from time to time in response to the latest evaluation result.

Cooperative development of the Tianjin Eco-City

The Sino-Singapore Tianjin Eco-city was mooted by Singapore's Senior Minister Goh Chok Tong and agreed to in-principle by Chinese Premier Wen Jiabao when they met in Beijing in April 2007.[12] The project was regarded as mutually

---

[10] Philine Gaffron, Ge Huismans and Franz Skala, *Ecocity Book II: How to Make It Happen*, p. 36.

[11] Philine Gaffron, Ge Huismans and Franz Skala, *Ecocity Book II: How to Make It Happen*, p. 36.

[12] "Singapore, China to Jointly Develop an 'Eco-City'", *The Straits Times*, 26 April 2007.

beneficial since Singapore and China could jointly share their experience and expertise and achieve a demonstration effect that went beyond the confines of the project itself. Both sides had moved briskly to implement the idea.

The distinctive features of the Sino-Singapore Tianjin Eco-city can be viewed at two levels. The first is at the broad strategic level where the framework of cooperation that oversees the implementation of the project will be examined. The framework is lacking in most other eco-city projects. The second is at the operational level where the features directly related to the project will be highlighted. These features may be common to other eco-city projects, differing only possibly on the extent of these features and the targets set. The focus on the key features is not to suggest the success or failure of a project. Rather, it is to highlight some of the major differences between this and other projects.

Framework of cooperation

The Sino-Singapore Tianjin Eco-city project is not an ordinary commercial undertaking. In most other eco-city projects, the government's involvement is either minimal or even non-existent. The usual practice is to let the private sector take the lead with the government creating the right conditions for the project to succeed. In contrast, for the Sino-Singapore Tianjin Eco-city project, the Singapore and Chinese governments have not only attempted to create the right conditions for the project to take off but also brought it under an official supervisory mechanism.

In fact, the project has been set within the framework of bilateral cooperation between the two countries. In this sense, the two governments regard the project's development as indicative of the substantive relations between the two countries. The success or failure of the project would strengthen bilateral ties or negatively impact on bilateral relations. It is reasonable to assert that neither the Chinese nor Singapore government would want to draw such a linkage if it was not confident that the project would have a fair chance of succeeding.

The two sides set up a mechanism to oversee the development of the project. The mechanism can be divided into two main levels (Figure 1). The highest and first level is the Joint Steering Committee (JSC) comprising heads of the relevant ministries and government agencies from both countries and the Tianjin municipal government. Co-chaired by a deputy prime minister (DPM) from Singapore and a vice premier from China, the JSC examines all major or policy issues related to the development of the eco-city.[13] The JSC itself reports to the

---

[13] Wang Qishan's predecessor for the JSC was Madam Wu Yi who stepped down as vice premier in March 2008.

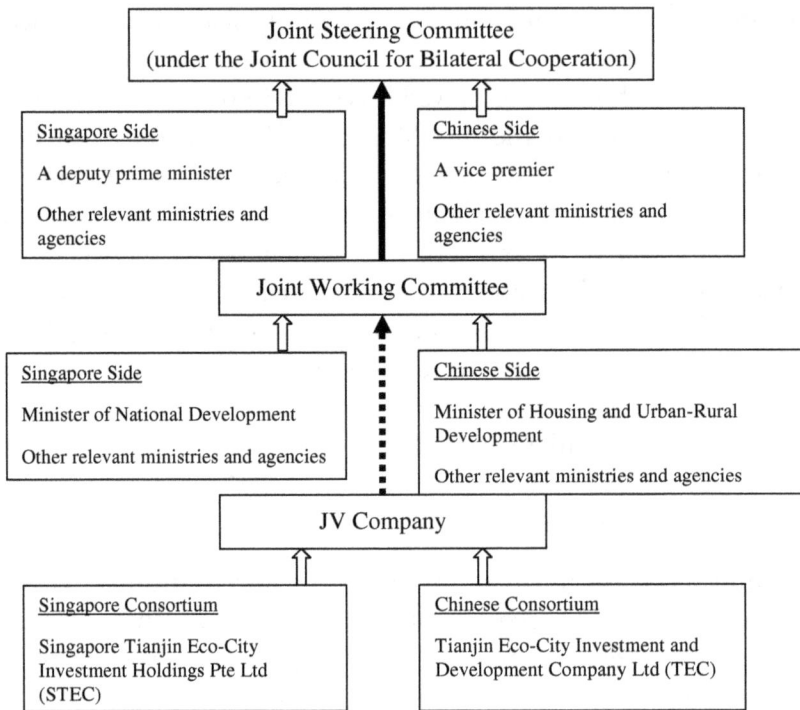

Figure 1 Overview of Supervisory Mechanism
Source: Created by the author.

Joint Council for Bilateral Cooperation (JCBC) that oversees all aspects of cooperation between Singapore and China.[14]

Under the JSC, the relevant ministries and agencies on the Singapore side include the Ministry of National Development, Ministry of Environment and Water Resources, Ministry of Foreign Affairs, Ministry of Trade and Industry, Building and Construction Authority, International Enterprise Singapore, Jurong Town Corporation, National Parks Board, Public Utilities Board, Urban Redevelopment Authority, Housing and Development Board and the National Environment Agency. On the Chinese side, the relevant ministries and agencies include the Ministry of Housing and Urban-Rural Development, Ministry of Environmental Protection, Ministry of Land and Resources, Ministry of Foreign Affairs and other relevant agencies.

The JSC held its inaugural meeting in Tianjin in September 2008. At that meeting, Singapore's Deputy Prime Minister Wong Kan Seng and Chinese Vice Premier Wang Qishan noted that the development of the eco-city had

---

[14]The JCBC was established in 2003.

made 'rapid and good progress' since the idea was mooted about one-and-a-half years ago. Most significantly, the meeting agreed that the key areas of work ahead would not only include the physical and infrastructural development of the eco-city but also cover the formulation of policies in line with the vision of the eco-city and the principle of the three harmonies (i.e. harmony between man and man, between man and the environment, and between man and economic activities) to complement and support the project's development.[15]

The second level of the supervisory mechanism is the Joint Working Committee (JWC). The bold upward pointing arrow line in Figure 1 indicates that the JWC reports its key deliberations directly to the JSC. Co-chaired by Singapore's minister for National Development and China's minister for Housing and Rural-Urban Development, the JWC addresses operational issues related to the development of the eco-city.

The JWC has addressed issues such as KPIs (key performance indicators) to guide the planning and construction of the eco-city, the Master Plan for the entire 30 square kilometres, the detailed plan for the three square kilometres start-up area; the work schedules and key milestones of the project; and the roles, powers and responsibilities of the Eco-City Administrative Committee that will administer the eco-city. The JWC also draws upon the resources and expertise of the relevant ministries and government agencies on both sides to carry out its tasks.

The aforementioned supervisory mechanism was formalised with the signing of the 'Framework Agreement on the Development of an Eco-City in the PRC' in November 2007.[16] The agreement was signed by Singapore's Prime Minister Lee Hsien Loong and Chinese Premier Wen Jiabao at the Istana, the official residence of the president, during the visit of Premier Wen to Singapore in November 2007. In addition to the Framework Agreement, a Supplementary Agreement was also signed at the same time between Minister Mah Bow Tan and Minister Wang Guangtao (former minister of Housing and Rural-Urban Development) to facilitate and support the joint development of the eco-city in accordance with the Framework Agreement. These agreements underscore the active role played by the governments on both sides to ensure the success of the project.

---

[15] "Inaugural Sino-Singapore Tianjin Eco-city Joint Steering Council Meeting", press release by Singapore's Ministry of National Development, 3 September 2008.

[16] "Agreements to Develop Eco-city in China Signed", press release by Singapore's Ministry of National Development, 18 November 2007.

Besides the official supervisory mechanism, there is the commercial component that comprises the JV company. The rationale of having a JV company is
to ensure that the eco-city will be guided by sound commercial principles in
its development. This will ensure its financial sustainability. Operationally, the
JV company exists as an independent entity. Nevertheless, the JV company
indirectly reports the progress or issues that cannot be resolved at their level to
the JWC which in turn reviews or addresses them. In this way, the JWC can
give the project an added push when needed. This indirect relationship
between the JV company and the JWC is denoted in Figure 1 by the bold
upward pointing dotted line.

Known as the Sino-Singapore Tianjin Eco-City Investment and Development
Company, the JV company has an initial registered capital of RMB4 billion
(US$583 million) with equal contribution from the Singapore consortium and
the Chinese consortium.[17] The Singapore consortium, the Singapore Tianjin
Eco-City Investment Holdings (STEC), is currently wholly owned by Keppel
Corporation which is seeking international institutional investors to co-invest
in the STEC. Already, the Qatar Investment Authority has signed a
Memorandum of Understanding (MOU) with Keppel Corporation to partici-
pate as an equity investor in the project by taking up a 10% stake in the STEC.[18]

The Chinese consortium, the Tianjin Eco-City Investment and Development
Company, is led by the Tianjin TEDA Investment Holding Company, which is
wholly owned by the Tianjin municipal government. The company has spearheaded the development of the TEDA since 1984. It is also involved in various
sectors such as property, finance, transport and energy in the TBNA (Tianjin
Binhai New Area) (with a total land area of 2,270 square kilometres) where both
TEDA and the Sino-Singapore Tianjin Eco-city are located.[19] The Tianjin TEDA
Investment Holding Company therefore brings to the JV company not only valuable experience and expertise but also a strong network for conducting business.

The Sino-Singapore Tianjin Eco-city aims to be environmentally friendly,
socially harmonious and economically sustainable. It is located at the Coastal

---

[17] Under the JV agreement signed on 1 July 2008, the Chinese consortium will transfer land for
the development of the eco-city to the JV company as its contribution in kind to the registered
capital of the JV company. The Singapore consortium's contribution to the registered capital
will be in the form of cash.

[18] "Joint Venture to Jointly Develop Eco-City in Tianjin, The People's Republic of China", press
release by Keppel Corporation, 1 July 2008.

[19] See website of Tianjin TEDA Investment Holding Company, available at <http://www.teda.
com.cn/shouye/index.asp> (accessed 2 January 2014).

Leisure and Tourism Zone of the TBNA. Three square kilometres of the start-up area were completed in 2013. The entire development is expected to be completed in 10 to 15 years' time, with a projected population of 350,000 residents.[20]

A major feature of the eco-city lies in its conversion to good use of an otherwise unproductive land, balancing ecological rehabilitation with urban development. The eco-city will be built on a 30-sq kilometre site consisting largely of non-arable land, including salt farms and vacant land. There will be a central core (known as the eco-core) of conserved ecological wetlands and rehabilitated water bodies including a wastewater pond currently being used as an effluent discharge ground. The areas surrounding the eco-core will be divided into four main districts, each to be served by an urban sub-centre. Each district will have a mixture of residential, commercial, industrial, cultural and recreational land.

The second key feature of the eco-city is the focus on maximising convenience for residents by locating the necessary services and facilities nearby. The basic building block of the eco-city is the eco-cell that integrates different land uses within a modular 400 metres by 400 metres grid. Education institutions, commercial areas, workplaces and recreational areas are distributed inside these eco-cells which are in turn sited within walking or cycling distance of residential areas. Together, the eco-cells form neighbourhoods, districts and eventually urban centres.

The main mode of transport will be a light rail line running through the eco-city, but the construction work has been delayed.[21] It will be complemented by cycling paths and green connectors. There will also be a secondary network of buses or trams. The goal is to make commuting via public transport and non-motorised means so convenient that residents will gradually rely less on or even stop the use of fossil-fuelled vehicles. Certain incentives may also be introduced to achieve this goal.[22] The approach takes into account current realities of individual preferences of owning private cars as a status symbol.

---

[20] "Sino-Singapore Tianjin Eco-City Draft Master Plan Unveiled", press release by Singapore's Ministry of National Development, 17 April 2008.

[21] "Growing pains for Tianjin Eco-City", *The Straits Times*, 13 October 2013, available at <http://www.straitstimes.com/the-big-story/asia-report/china/story/growing-pains-tianjin-eco-city-20131013> accessed 4 June 2015.

[22] "Zhongxin hezi gongsi chengli, Tianjin shengtaicheng cong guihua jinru shizhan" (Sino-Singapore Joint Venture Company Established, Tianjin Eco-City Moves from Master Planning into Real Combat), *Lianhe Zaobao*, 2 July 2008.

The third distinguishing feature of the eco-city is its strong message of social harmony or more specifically, efforts to meet the needs of ordinary folks. The eco-city has positioned itself as a model of harmonious living where people from all walks of life, regardless of their income or social status, can come together. This is akin to Singapore's concept of neighbourhood communities where different ethnic groups, professions and religions can co-exist as a vibrant and cohesive entity. In particular, about 20% of the residential areas in the eco-city will be set aside for public, subsidised housing.[23] To meet this goal, Singapore and China aim to leverage on their experience of providing public housing and devise the most feasible way forward.[24] It remains to be seen how this will be operationalised.

About 2,000 villagers of affected developments of the eco-city were resettled to avoid incidence of protest. Elsewhere in China, there have been umpteen instances of resettlement cases gone awry, leading to affected residents protesting against developers and local authorities. Given the sensitivity of resettlement cases, the Singapore and Chinese sides have paid particular attention to addressing the concerns and needs of the would-be affected residents. The 2,000 villagers who had been relocated were provided with jobs and housing in the eco-city.

A final attractive feature of the eco-city is the emphasis on adopting the best practices from both the Singapore and Chinese sides. The collaboration can be described as a partnership rather than the predominance of one over the other on how things should be done. By jointly contributing, the parties involved would have greater vested interest to see their ideas come to fruition. For instance, the green area per person in the eco-city was set at 12 square metres by 2013, which has been achieved to date.[25] In terms of water quality, the target is to make all water in the eco-city portable. All buildings in the eco-city will

---

[23] "Zhongxin Tianjin shengtaicheng zongti fangan chulu, 2020 nian jiangda 35 wanren" (Sino-Singapore Tianjin Eco-City Master Plan is released, in year 2020 the population will reach 350,000), *First Financial Daily* (Shanghai), 7 May 2008.

[24] "Tianjin shengtaicheng jiangjian gongwu ge jieceng renmin neng hexie gongchu" (Tianjin eco-city will build public housing, various social groups can live harmoniously), *Lianhe Zaobao*, 17 April 2008. See also "HDB-style living in Tianjin eco-city", *The Straits Times*, 17 April 2008.

[25] Yiting Sun, "China's future city", MIT Technology Review, 18 November 2014, available at <http://www.tianjineco-city.com/en/NewsContent.aspx?news_id=13866&column_id=10350> accessed 5 June 2015.

conform to green building standards that will marry Singapore's green mark with China's green standards.[26]

Low-carbon and social aspects of Tianjin Eco-City

On 1 December 2009, Sino-Singapore Tianjin Investment and Development Company (SSTEC), master-developer of the Singapore Tianjin Eco-city, inked an MOU with Samsung C&T Corporation to create the first-of-its-kind green central business district (CBD), also known as the Eco-CBD, in the China–Singapore Tianjin Eco-city. This Eco-CBD aims to integrate economic, social and community activities sustainably, and demonstrate that environmental conservation and urbanisation can progress in tandem with economic activities.

On 30 December 2009, the SSTEC started to develop a 130-hectare Eco-Industrial Park (EIP) in the Singapore Tianjin Eco-city. Positioned as a premier eco manufacturing base for eco investors in the Bohai Rim area, the EIP will be home to light clean industries from green business clusters including clean energy, green building, green transport, clean water, clean waste management and clean environment. Estimated to cost RMB4 billion to develop, the park is expected to generate 10,000 jobs when completed.

In May 2010, the SSTEC signed three industrial land deals involving more than RMB1 billion in investments in the Eco Business Park (EBP) and the Eco Industrial Park. SSTEC also announced strategic collaborations with three companies in the green technology field. Tianjin House Construction Development Group Co Ltd announced its investment of RMB300 million to develop low-carbon and energy-efficient green buildings, while Keppel DHCS Pte Ltd planned to develop and operate a district heating and cooling system in the EBP. SSTEC signed an MOU with the Hitachi Group to serve as its strategic technology partner for test-bedding and development of eco solutions in the areas of home energy management systems and electric vehicle charging solutions, building energy management systems, community energy management

---

[26]On transportation, the target is to achieve at least 90% of residents commuting on foot, using public transport or cycling when travelling within the eco-city by 2020. Another target is to have 100% barrier-free access for residents in the eco-city. In terms of economic contribution, the target is to have at least 50 R & D scientists and engineers per 10,000 workforce in the eco-city by 2020. A total of 26 KPIs (22 quantitative and four qualitative ones) have been agreed to by both sides. They can be found at <http://www.tianjinecocity.gov.sg/KPI.htm#21> (accessed 1 January 2013).

systems, smart grid and water management solutions. SSTEC also inked a strategic partnership with Singapore Technologies Electronics Limited (ST Electronics) for the development of green solutions for intelligent building management and energy saving systems, intelligent transport management systems, e-learning solutions and training and simulation systems for the Eco-city.[27]

These eco-efforts bore fruit when Wan Tuo Residential Project (First Phase) in the Start-Up Area of the Sino-Singapore Tianjin Eco-city clinched the third class award of the 2011 National Green Building Innovation Award organised by China's Ministry of Housing and Urban-Rural Development. The project was ranked 11 out of a total of 16 nationwide projects.

Investments began to pour in when the Pan Asian Water Manufacturing (Tianjin) Co Ltd (PAW) became the first investor in the Tianjin Eco-city Eco-Industrial Park on 29 March 2011. A groundbreaking ceremony was held for the construction of PAW's China headquarters and its key manufacturing base in the EIP. With this base, PAW will consolidate its existing manufacturing operations in China. The base will also serve as PAW's global logistics and warehousing hub, R&D centre and control centre for brand building and marketing of Duvalco products. The total investment is RMB100 million.

On the same day, the topping out for Phase I of the Ready-Built Factories (RBFs) in the EIP took place. SSTEC will invest RMB220 million for the construction of RBF Phase I with a built-up area of 63,800 square metres to cater for a range of high value, low-carbon footprint cleantech production and other value-added operations. This green industrial space will provide manu-facturing companies with a cost effective and convenient platform to jump-start their business in the Eco-city.

The Tianjin Eco-city project differs from the Suzhou Industrial Park project in important ways. The first difference lies in the nature of cooperation. The Suzhou Industrial Park is a model of knowledge transfer, from Singapore to China, while the Chinese side is more or less an equal partner in the Tianjin Eco-city project. The working relationship has therefore shifted from knowledge transfer to knowledge sharing. The second difference has to do with the nature of the project. If the Suzhou Industrial Park is more of an economic project, Tianjin Eco-city is more than an economic project. Its social dimensions are also very important. Both governments have emphasised this point, a reason why

---

[27] "Tianjin Eco-City Attracts 6 New Investments in Manufacturing and R&D, with a Total Investment Amount of RMB1 billion", available at <http://www.tianjineco-city.com/en/news_center/press_release/1117.aspx> (accessed 1 May 2012).

social harmony is one of the 'three harmonies' underpinning the planning and development of the Tianjin Eco-city.

One of the plans for 2009 was to produce a social policy framework for the Eco-city. Two research institutes were involved. Major work was done by the Shanghai-based Huaxia Research Institute. This institute is well known in China for its research on community development and management. It worked closely with the Bureau of Legal Affairs of the Eco-city Administrative Committee, which is responsible for social policy making. On the Singapore side, the East Asian Institute of the National University of Singapore was invited by the Ministry of National Development to play a supporting role in the process.

Developing a social policy framework touches upon the institutional aspect of building an eco-city. Over the years, China has already put in place a set of policies. Tianjin Eco-city has to work within this framework. For instance, China's social security system is very different from Singapore's Central Provident Fund (CPF) system. It is not possible to model Tianjin Eco-city's social security system after Singapore's CPF system.

Within the constraint of the broad policy framework, the Chinese team felt that there is still much room to learn from Singapore's experiences in social development. Both countries place priority on GDP growth. However, the social consequences of high economic growth are very different in the two countries. Singapore has achieved a high level of economic development at relatively low social costs. Society has been remarkably stable as its economy develops. By comparison, China has difficulties balancing its economic and social development. As its economy develops, society seems less stable, as evidenced by rising social protests and social grievances. Against this backdrop, the Chinese team had a strong interest in Singapore's experiences in social development.

A key foundation of Singapore's racial and social harmony lies in its Housing and Development Board (HDB) system. The HDB system not only is a public housing programme, but also plays important political and social functions beyond providing public housing. It serves the political function of rooting Singaporeans in Singapore by giving them a stake in the country. The HDB system is also the basis for community development, political communication, social integration and public transport development. Seen in this light, the HDB is a core institution that makes Singapore a stable and harmonious society as it is today.

The HDB system was well received by the Chinese side who visited Singapore and saw how the HDB system works. Gradually both teams concurred on the importance of the HDB as a public housing programme and as a foundation for a stable and harmonious Singapore. The finalised policy proposal, completed in late 2009, placed a great deal of emphasis on making local residents 'stake-holders' of Tianjin Eco-city.

The Chinese side is also interested in Singapore's experiences in education and health care. The Singapore system emphasises both high quality and high efficiency in these two fields. As a percentage of GDP, China's spending on health care is considerably higher than that of Singapore. However, Singapore has done better in almost every health indicator. China is now reforming its public hospitals and Tianjin officials have shown strong interest in Singapore's experience in restructuring and managing its public hospitals. Tianjin Eco-city is also cooperating with Singapore in the area of education.

Even on the basis of knowledge sharing, Singapore still has much to offer to the Chinese side. Incorporating Singapore's experience into the Eco-city is an ongoing process, depending on many factors such as China's general policy framework, the willingness of the Chinese side to learn from Singapore and the ability of Singapore to market its experiences to China.

Conclusion

Over the years, the two governments of China and Singapore have been instrumental in identifying new projects to stay relevant to each other's development needs, providing various platforms for political and economic engagement and proactively addressing any issues that arise. Suzhou Industrial Park and Tianjin Eco-city underscore the determination of the two countries to add substance to their relationship. In coping with future challenges, the officials running the Eco-city must embrace the right mind-set to adopt suitable environmental and social policies. Equally important, the residents, too, need to be champions of green living who embrace recycling, environmental protection and other green habits.[28]

The seven other bilateral cooperative mechanisms, though less well-known than the two flagship projects, are equally important in promoting political and economic interactions at the provincial levels. These bilateral cooperative bodies between Singapore and China's provincial governments have helped to further strengthen the foundation of the bilateral relationship.

---

[28] Speech by Singapore's Minister of National Development Khaw Boon Wan, "Green Minds with Green Hearts", 4 April 2014, <http://www.tianjinecocity.gov.sg/events/2014/20140404.htm> (accessed 20 April 2015).

While differences may arise from time to time in carrying out various projects, both sides have accumulated experiences in managing the differences. By working through differences together, both sides can foster better mutual understanding and this will create a more realistic basis for future cooperation. How to retain Singapore's relevance to China will be a key factor shaping future bilateral relationship. Seen in this light, the Tianjin Eco-city project is very important. If successful, it will show that Singapore's experience in social development and management is relevant and valuable to China.

Chapter 7

Sharing Singapore's Successful Development Experience

Singbridge

Singbridge is actively involved in developing the Sino-Singapore Guangzhou Knowledge City and Sino-Singapore Jilin Food Zone among its other projects in China. Unlike the Suzhou Industrial Park and the Tianjin Eco-city which are government-to-government projects, the Guangzhou Knowledge City and Jilin Food Zone are driven by the private sector with strong government support. They represent a different but equally important model of cooperation between Singapore and China that further demonstrates Singapore's continuing efforts to stay relevant to China's growth and to derive mutual benefits by collaborating in areas of mutual interest.

Overview

Singbridge invests in, develops and manages integrated cities and sustainable urban solutions internationally by leveraging on Singapore's successful development experience. It capitalises on the global trends of rapid and large-scale urbanisation, environmental improvement and economic development to create new growth platforms for Singapore and its companies. In this role, Singbridge contributes to ongoing efforts to make Singapore relevant to other countries and provides avenues for Singapore to continue to grow and prosper.

In sharing Singapore's experience, Singbridge adopts an integrated and holistic approach in developing sustainable cities that encompasses the best practices in urban planning, economic development, environmental protection, social development and public policy. Each project is conceptualised and tailored to meet the strategic objectives of the host government as well as to benefit the local community.

Singbridge is the co-master developer and investor in the Sino-Singapore Guangzhou Knowledge City (SSGKC) project with its Chinese counterpart, the Guangzhou Development District Administrative Committee. The SSGKC is being developed into a unique, vibrant and sustainable city which is highly attractive to talent and skilled manpower and knowledge-based industries. Apart from the SSGKC, Singbridge also invests in various large-scale integrated projects such as the Sino-Singapore Tianjin Eco-city, Singapore-Sichuan Hi-tech Innovation Park, Raffles City Chongqing, and the latest project in the form of the Sino-Singapore Jilin Food Zone (SSJFZ).

This chapter focuses on Singbridge's two key projects, i.e. the SSGKC and the SSJFZ. It highlights interesting areas such as the origins, key features and plans behind these projects, as well as the challenges faced in implementing them. The purpose is to provide readers with an understanding of a different model of Singapore–China cooperation. Unlike the Suzhou Industrial Park and the Tianjin Eco-city which are considered government-to-government projects, the SSGKC and the SSJFZ are led by the private sector with strong government support. For instance, the SSGKC falls under the purview of the Singapore-Guangdong Collaboration Council that meets once a year. The Jilin Food Zone is reviewed annually by a joint steering committee that involves Temasek (that owns Singbridge) and the Jilin provincial government. While they are not flagship projects per se, they are in our view equally important projects that Singapore is implementing with the individual provinces of Guangdong and Jilin.

One of the key challenges in SSGKC lies in showing the way forward in building a knowledge-based economy in an environment that had depended on manufacturing as the main economic driver for decades. Another key challenge is to implement in the SSGKC a whole-of-government approach to overcome the existing fragmented bureaucratic interests. As for the SSJFZ, two critical pillars will need to be in place to ensure its success. They are the maintenance of a foot-and-mouth disease-free zone and the implementation of an integrated food safety system of international standards. The challenges can be viewed in terms of obstacles that stand in the way of bilateral collaboration. The other approach, which is more proactive and pragmatic, is to regard the challenges as opportunities for both the Singapore and Chinese parties to work together to build even stronger ties. In many ways, the success of the two projects will help to strengthen the presence of Singapore companies in China and in turn reinforce the bilateral relationship.

Sino-Singapore Guangzhou Knowledge City (SSGKC)
A new chapter in Singapore–China collaboration

In September 2008, in the wake of the global financial crisis, then Guangdong Party Secretary Wang Yang led a 400-member delegation to visit Singapore and met Prime Minister Lee Hsien Loong, Senior Minister Goh Chok Tong, and the late Mr Lee Kuan Yew, who was Minister Mentor. Both sides were in favour of an iconic cooperation project between Guangdong and Singapore that would serve as a model for Guangdong's economic transformation. It was also agreed that the project would be a platform through which Singapore's expertise in urban planning and social management could be adapted to help Guangdong address the various social challenges arising from rapid urbanisation. This marked the beginning of a new chapter of collaboration between Singapore and Guangdong.

Prime Minister Lee Hsien Loong met with Guangdong Party Secretary Wang Yang in Singapore on 16 September 2008. This was Wang Yang's first visit to Singapore since his appointment as Guangdong's party secretary in 2007. Photo credit: Guangzhou Development District Administrative Committee.

In an interview with the media during his 2008 visit to Singapore, Wang Yang reportedly said that "...Guangdong now would like to leverage on the successful experience of Singapore, and integrate it with the actual conditions in Guangdong, thereby forging a way that is suitable for Guangdong, so that it can become a modern city like Singapore."[1]

Separately, Wang Yang remarked in a conversation he had with a Singapore minister during the same visit that a key challenge facing Guangdong was to restructure its economy as its labour costs were higher than that of other regions in China. He had told his officials in Guangdong's leading cities like Shenzhen and Guangzhou that "Singapore has been independent since 1965. Its economy until today is still more vibrant than the economy in Guangdong....So if you don't know how to restructure the economy, go and learn from Singapore."[2]

Location of SSGKC

The SSGKC broke ground on 30 June 2010 as the next iconic project of Singapore–China cooperation after the Suzhou Industrial Park and Tianjin Eco-city. Positioned as a unique, vibrant and sustainable city that is highly attractive to both talents and knowledge-based industries, SSGKC covers an area of 123 square kilometres and will provide a "live, work, learn and play" environment to an expected live-in population of 500,000 over the next 20 years.

This large-scale city development project is located in the north-east of Guangzhou city, between the second and third ring roads, at the core of the Pearl River Delta region. It sits 35 kilometres, or about a half-hour drive, from the Guangzhou city centre and is 25 kilometres from Guangzhou Baiyun International Airport. The location falls within southern China's extensive transportation network with links to other economic hubs such as Shenzhen and Hong Kong.

The Guangzhou Metro lines 14 and 21 and the dedicated Knowledge City Line, when operational in 2017, will shorten travel time for mass transit between downtown Guangzhou and SSGKC to 15 minutes. These lines are currently under construction and seven of the nine stations of the Knowledge City Line will be in the Knowledge City itself. Road networks such as the Guanghe

---

[1] "Wang Yang: 'Guangdong jiaoban Xinjiapo' yanxu Deng Xiaoping yiyuan" (Wang Yang: 'Guangdong to Compete with Singapore' and Continue with Deng Xiaoping's Last Wish), *Lianhe zaobao*, 1 September 2008.

[2] "Guangdong Studies Singapore's Economy", *The Straits Times*, 10 October 2008.

Expressway have also reduced the travel time from the SSGKC to Guangzhou Baiyun International Airport to 30 minutes from one hour previously. The Huadu-Dongguan Expressway is expected to be operational in 2017, thereby further reducing the travel time from the SSGKC to Guangzhou Baiyun International Airport to 20 minutes. The Guangzhou-Dongguan-Shenzhen inter-city rail will also reduce travel time between the SSGKC and major cities in the Pearl River Delta region to one hour from the current two hours.

The joint-venture company

The Sino-Singapore Guangzhou Knowledge City Investment and Development Co., Ltd (GKC Co) is a 50-50 joint-venture company established by Guangzhou Development District Administrative Committee (GDDAC) and Singbridge as the master developer of the SSGKC. GKC Co is responsible for developing the Start-Up Area (SUA) as the first phase, and subsequently the rest of the 123 square kilometres in stages.

Guangzhou Development District (GDD) is one of China's most competitive development zones and has been named the national model development zone. GDD is the gateway to the eastward development of Guangzhou City and lies exactly at the heart of the Pearl River Delta. Singbridge, as a wholly owned subsidiary of Singapore's Temasek Holdings, invests in, develops and manages integrated cities and sustainable urban solutions internationally through leveraging on Singapore's successful developmental experience.

In addition to development of residential, commercial and business parks land, GKC Co is also tasked to engage in investment promotion, industry development and "software" transfer. GKC Co works closely with the GDDAC to ensure that land development is in line with the overall economic and social objectives of the local government.

The green urban space

The Concept Master Plan of SSGKC and the Urban Design Plan for the SUA, developed by renowned architect-planner Dr Liu Thai-Ker, have set new standards in terms of urban planning and design.

Development is planned in an integrated manner comprising hi-tech business parks, residential, commercial, recreational and public amenities, including neighbourhood centres. Green connectors and water bodies form a network through the entire city, with large green belts dividing it into the Northern, Central and Southern Areas.

These green belts integrate with the existing rich natural ecology and link up to the surrounding Maofeng and Fuhe mountains. A comprehensive water networks of reservoirs, Pinggang River, Fenghuang River and Liusha River also flow through the city. Two major water landscapes, Jiulong Lake and the Fenghuang Lake, serve to enhance SSGKC's green ecological and living environment.

The initial development phase began at the Southern SUA of about 6.27 square kilometres to be developed over a period of five to eight years to support a total population of 78,000 and provide 38,000 job opportunities. The SUA adopts a Transport-Oriented Development (TOD) model, whereby development intensities around major transportation nodes are the highest and land uses like residential, industrial park, commercial, government, amenities and green space are intermixed within the Southern SUA. The Southern SUA will set the standards in construction, urban management, business and investment and the goal is to replicate its successes for the rest of SSGKC.

The 6.27-square kilometre Southern SUA of the SSGKC undergoing construction to serve as a pilot area that could be replicated for the rest of the project. Photo credit: SSGKC, 2014.

Land use allocation is relatively evenly distributed with one-third of the land zoned for residential purpose, one-third assigned for industrial land and the remaining one-third set aside for administration, municipal, amenities, road and green space. The future-ready infrastructure construction comes with provisions that accommodate future smart and eco-related initiatives (e.g. fibre optics and smart grid systems), and similar to the Tianjin Eco-city, the SSGKC also features 100% potable water from the tap. In addition, the abundance of water features in southern part of China allows for a wide range of waterfront lifestyle options, while the provision of a dense network of green transportation pathways encourages walking and cycling within the city, thereby promoting eco-friendly commute.

The neighbourhood centre (NC), a familiar Singapore concept, is also incorporated in the SSGKC, with five NCs being planned for development within the SUA itself. Centrally located within residential districts, the NCs form a core around which schools, sporting facilities, recreational outlets and other amenities will be developed to meet the needs of the SUA residents. Some of the services provided by the NCs include integrated neighbourhood child-care centres, supermarkets, beauty salons, food courts, and government and health-care services. Through the NCs, residents can enjoy accessibility to common services, thus reducing the need for extended commute which, in turn, reduces transportation pressure and resources.

Guangdong's new economic paradigm

The vulnerability of Guangdong's predominantly manufacturing-based industries was most evident during the 2007 global financial crisis which triggered global economic malaise and weakened global consumption for goods and

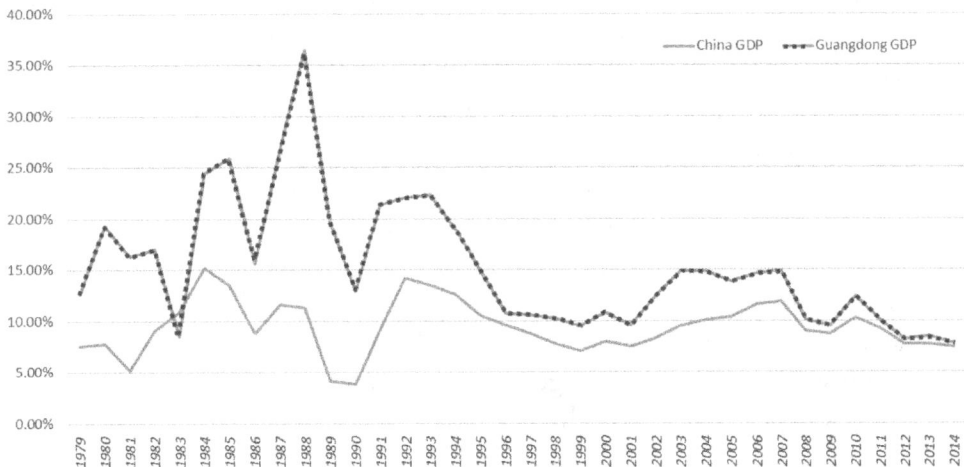

Figure 1 Guangdong's Gross Domestic Product (GDP) Compared to the Rest of China (1979–2014)

Note: The "crests" and "troughs" of Guangdong's GDP were more pronounced compared with the rest of China, reflecting weak resilience of its economy against events such as the global financial crisis in 2007/08.

Source: Data from National Bureau of Statistics of China.

services. During this difficult period, foreign investments into Guangdong declined significantly and a number of the smaller, less competitive companies were forced to close down. Existing factories in Guangdong reduced production as a result of shrinking overseas demand. The then Guangdong Party Secretary Wang Yang recognised the need to upgrade Guangdong's economy from an industry-based to a knowledge-based one to ensure greater economic resilience.

To expedite the upgrading process, a few key measures were taken. The Knowledge City Administrative Committee (KCAC) was granted municipal-level authority, which encompasses legal provisions in many areas. With the given authority, many investment-related approvals could be settled at KCAC's level without going through the Guangzhou municipal government, including implementation and development in the areas of talent development, industry promotion, technology and finance. In addition, the strategy for economic upgrading had also prescribed the formation of six pillar industry clusters and the development of operational headquarters economy as key components of the knowledge-based economy. The "six-plus-one" components of the knowledge-based economy — which include next-generation information and communication technology (ICT); biotechnology and pharmaceuticals; new energy and clean technology; culture and creative services; science and education services; new-generation materials; and the operational headquarters economy — are aimed at generating higher value-added employment opportunities for residents in Guangzhou.

In building a knowledge-based economy, SSGKC leverages Singapore's international networks to tap potential investors in technology- and knowledge-intensive economies such as the United States, Germany, Israel, Japan, South Korea and Singapore. In addition, GKC Co also facilitated trainings, seminars and workshops in order to share with the local governments Singapore's experience in economic growth and restructuring. However, as district-level governments currently have limited authority to change systems and policies issued by higher-levels of the Chinese government, much work is needed to adapt Singapore's experience to the local context, such as Singapore's whole-of-government approach to resolve issues and reduce red tape.

GKC Co also works with governments and chambers of commerce to build business network platforms in SSGKC to catalyse the growth of the "six-plus-one" key pillar industries. Besides, the company is exploring opportunities with the United Kingdom, Israel, Singapore and the European Union to consider establishing representative offices in SSGKC as local outposts to better understand the business climate in the south China region. Enterprises from these respective countries are able to tap into such resources when they decide to venture into China; and it is also envisaged that these representative offices can act as conduits for local Chinese companies to better understand the overseas market.

To better appreciate Guangdong's new economic paradigm, it is important to acknowledge that China today is different from China in the 1990s. More Chinese are now well-travelled and getting educated overseas. Moreover, they have greater access to information, and are also increasingly innovative and creative and more environmentally conscious. With economic growth and increased international awareness, the objective of the Singapore–China collaboration has shifted from "showing them [the Chinese] how it is done" to "let us learn from each other". The key challenge in SSGKC is to implement economic restructuring in an environment that has depended on manufacturing as its main economic driver since 1978. This challenge is compounded by the difficulty to replicate in Guangzhou Singapore's whole-of-government approach, which is one of Singapore's key factors of success. This new economic paradigm for Guangdong is therefore still a work in progress. While the goal is clear, the Chinese and Singapore sides would need to jointly work together to develop a path towards it.

Key industrial parks

The development of SSGKC's "six-plus-one" key pillar industries will require business parks and commercial space to be readily available. Several projects, with different market positioning, are currently under development. Ascendas OneHub GKC Business Park, a joint venture with Singapore's Ascendas Group, was the first project to be developed in SSGKC. Most significantly, the priority accorded to this project reflects Singapore's fundamental belief that a city must first have a vibrant economy that can provide employment opportunities to residents in order to be regarded as successful. At the same time, the local government's strong support of the project underscored its resolve in implementing economic restructuring. The following section provides an overview of the projects which the local government and GKC Co collaborate on in a concerted effort to promote economic upgrading.

Ascendas OneHub GKC Business Park

Ascendas OneHub GKC is developed by Singapore's Ascendas Group with a total investment of RMB2.3 billion. The business park has a planned area of 30 hectares and a build-up area of 600,000 square metres.

The park seeks to attract leading enterprises in the industries of next-generation ICT, culture and creative sectors, services outsourcing, energy-saving and environmental protection, Fortune 500 enterprises, transnational corporations and independent innovation enterprises with advanced technology. This next-generation, multifunctional business space caters to the park's community seeking a vibrant one-stop location to work, live and enjoy recreation.

The Phase 1A of the Ascendas OneHub Business Park nearing completion with tenants expecting to move in by end of 2015. Photo credit: Ascendas OneHub GKC.

Intellectual Property Rights Utilisation and Protection Hub (IP Hub)

The planned state-level IP Hub in SSGKC covers 49 hectares and will be located in the Southern SUA. Singapore's Jurong International will undertake the overall design of the site that accommodates Guangdong Patent Examination Cooperation Center of the State Intellectual Property Office (SIPO) and Guangdong Intellectual Property Services Park. Leveraging Singapore's and other developed countries' experience, SSGKC aims to develop an integrated IP Hub that focuses on IP trading, evaluation, IP pledges, information services, agency services, training and financing, catering not only to southern China, but also the rest of China.

Guangzhou Dongfang International Healthcare Valley

Occupying a planned area of two square kilometres (200 hectares) in SSGKC, the Dongfang International Healthcare Valley will provide an ideal cooperation platform between existing medical-care resources in Guangzhou and high-end medical research institutes from Singapore, the United States and Taiwan. The project envisions an international health-care services hub covering research and development (R&D), prevention, medical treatment and rehabilitation services. The first phase of the project occupies a land area of 17 hectares that includes institutions such as Sun Yat-sen University-affiliated South China Tumor Hospital, Guangzhou Taihe Cancer Hospital, Guangzhou Royal Cancer Hospital and two proton therapy centres, and it is now known as the most advanced tumour treatment and rehabilitation centre in south China. Dongfang International Healthcare Valley is therefore poised to attract world-class medical research and services institutions, promote high-end medical care and pharmaceutical industries, and offer customised, international and comprehensive medical-care services to patients.

Global Education and Innovation Hub

To better serve the knowledge-based industries, the Global Education and Innovation Hub aims to partner with enterprises to launch a collaboration platform that provides education, training, research and other innovative services. The hub will host specialised colleges, high-end training institutes, incubators and R&D centres to step up efforts to nurture science talents to drive the knowledge-based economy and build a first-class international education integrating innovation platform.

Currently, Singapore's Nanyang Technological University (NTU) and Southern Industrial Technology Research Institute of Zhejiang University have set up a representative office in SSGKC. Separately, NTU, Technological University of Munich and South China University of Technology have signed a collaboration agreement to establish a joint research institute in SSGKC. SSGKC is also exploring collaborations with other reputable local and foreign universities such as Peking University, Tsinghua University, Sun Yat-sen University, Beihang University, National University of Singapore and University of Warwick, and research institutions from Singapore like the Agency for Science, Technology and Research (A*STAR), NUS Enterprise, etc.

Guangzhou Greenland City

Covering a planned area of 31 hectares, the E-Innovation Valley is an integrated retail, commercial, business and residential cluster, which includes operational headquarters, smart R&D industries, international health care and a vibrant community. A 150-metre high-rise commercial office, eco workplaces, apartments, waterfront commercial retail districts, five-star hotels and high-end residential housing are among the major developments that will build and support an integrated sustainable community.

Academician Innovation Park

Leveraging the existing academic talents in Guangzhou Development District and SSGKC, the Academician Innovation Park aims to nurture academicians and top scholars with expertise to translate important scientific and technological achievements into commercial ventures. The first phase of development of the Academician Innovation Park will occupy five hectares of designated total land area of 13 hectares, with facilities to support academicians and their research teams.

Smart Technology Park

The 183-hectare Smart Technology Park, which aims to become a model for smart technology and high-end smart equipment park, will focus on the development in the areas of high-end smart equipment, 3D (three-dimensional) printing technology and industrial robotics, as well as smart robotics for the inspection of high-voltage transmission lines. The park has brought in companies like ABB's Robotics Application Center, Guangzhou OTIS Research and Development Center, Guangzhou Feirui Robot Technology R&D Center and Guangzhou Yueyan Robot Automation Equipment Company.

City development strategy

SSGKC endeavours to embody smart, eco and learning features into the city as part of a comprehensive city development strategy. The smart, eco and learning features define three broad areas of development that give SSGKC a distinctive theme and attract innovative knowledge-based industries to use SSGKC as a living laboratory to pilot new ideas and concepts for the betterment of the city and improve quality of life for residents. GKC Co is working closely with the local government to catalyse the materialisation of these three major areas in the strategy.

Eco City

SSGKC will integrate essential eco-friendly attributes such as energy efficiency, water efficiency and other sustainability solutions in urban planning as a comprehensive approach towards sustainable development. For instance, all buildings in SSGKC will comply with Green Building Standards, and the transportation system will include the use of electric and hybrid vehicles. As part of its efforts to become a premier hub with green features and solutions, SSGKC will adopt several Eco city-related technologies and solutions, and engage in relevant R&D of new ideas and products for commercialisation.

To improve the quality of life and boost growth of green economy, SSGKC is committed to applying ecological technology to develop an environment where man and nature can coexist in harmony. Making green features commercially viable will ensure their long-term sustainability.

Smart City

The Smart City focus area encompasses components such as sustainable economic growth, high quality of life and effective management of natural resources, which can be achieved through the integration of urban management systems and information and telecommunication technologies. In 2013, SSGKC was selected as one of the state-level smart city pilot sites to provide a test bed for leading-edge technologies. SSGKC aims to employ next-generation ICT, cloud computing, and the internet of things to develop a world-class city where residents can live and work in a safe, efficient and resource-friendly environment. The government administration will also leverage ICT to optimise the delivery of services to residents and enterprises.

Learning City

The Learning City focus area sets out the vision to provide all residents of SSGKC access to high-quality education and information resources. SSGKC will utilise new technologies and innovative teaching methodologies to nurture a literate and well-informed community that will embrace lifelong learning. The city endeavours to attract the participation of world-class universities and institutions and adopt Singapore's hardware and software in learning.

SSGKC has since benefited greatly from the Singapore–China collaboration platform which allows access to resources offered by Singapore agencies. For example, Singapore's Building and Construction Authority (International) has helped develop a set of Green Building Standards for SSGKC; the Infocomm Development Authority of Singapore (International) has helped develop the Smart City Master Plan; and Nanyang Technological University is working closely with South China University of Technology and Technical University of Munich to develop a joint research institute in SSGKC.

Close collaboration among GKC Co, GDDAC and Singapore and international partners is imperative in the continuing effort to shape and develop the three focus areas of the city.

Software collaboration

A large majority of the city development initiatives planned for SSGKC are "hardware"-related programmes. The softer aspects that take the form of "software collaboration" are equally important, which in the case of SSGKC involves the sharing of Singapore's experiences in areas such as social development and city management. By working on various projects, Singapore's systems and processes are adapted, optimised and integrated to meet the objectives and evolving needs of the SSGKC and Guangzhou towards achieving a globally competitive knowledge-based economy.

"Software" covers many areas such as methodologies, policies and processes pertaining to intellectual property, planning and management of infrastructure, environmental protection, economic development, social management, township development, public administration, and others. These "software", in combining the strengths of both China and Singapore, will differentiate SSGKC from other Chinese cities.

As evident in the various initiatives outlined below, the support and conviction of the local government is integral to the success of software collaboration. To this end, GKC Co has run a highly successful and well-endorsed "Inbound & Outbound" Training Programme. From 2011 to 2014, a total of 2,187 officials and enterprise representatives have participated in training sessions in intellectual property, social management, green building, etc. SSGKC has also created other platforms such as the annual Sino-Singapore Knowledge Forum which is jointly organised by GKC Co and GDDAC with the support of both the Guangzhou municipal government and Singapore-Guangdong Collaboration Council. The forum convenes experts to discuss current issues and challenges facing Guangdong and even China today, such as economic development experiences, brand competitiveness and intellectual property rights protection. These initiatives help bolster SSGKC as an important platform for software collaboration between Singapore and China.

The Annual Sino-Singapore Knowledge Forum is a major event in GKC Co's inbound training initiatives. The event in 2014, which was in its second instalment, featured luminaries in the field of intellectual property from China, Singapore and the United States. Photo credit: SSGKC.

Conclusion

SSGKC is a work in progress. Its future success will hinge on the concerted efforts of many different parties forging towards a common goal. GKC Co, being a commercial entity, has to constantly fine-tune its role as the master-developer and that of an overseer to help the local government steer its economic restructuring and social management. On its part, the local government has to persevere to ensure the success of the city in the face of a complex bureaucracy with a multitude of interests. The SSKGC has clearly exemplified Singapore and Singaporeans' mindset to constantly stay ahead of the curve and think of areas to create value for ourselves, in order to remain relevant to a continually growing and globalised China.

Sino-Singapore Jilin Food Zone (SSJFZ)

China's urgent need for food safety

According to the World Health Organization, unsafe food is linked to the deaths of an estimated two million people annually.[3] Changes in consumer habits, including travel, inevitably result in an increase in the number of people buying and eating food prepared in public places. Globalisation has further triggered growing consumer demand for a wider variety of foods, resulting in an increasingly complex and longer global food chain. These trends are especially prevalent in China, given its state of rapid urbanisation in recent years. Combined with existing lapses in China's complex food preparation and regulation systems, food safety issues in China have drawn both domestic and global attention and at times, criticisms. In an effort to help improve food safety in China, the idea of a SSJFZ was conceptualised to focus on the production of quality and safe food.

In recent years, food scandals have increasingly become a major concern of Chinese consumers. In 2013, a McKinsey research found that Chinese residents are more concerned about food safety than health care, unemployment and even crime.[4] According to a 2011 study, more than 94 million people become ill from bacterial food-borne diseases in China every year—with approximately 3.4 million hospitalisations and more than 8,500 deaths.[5]

Food safety concerns in China are real. They not only involve local food companies, but also international food companies with presence in China. Most recently, Husi Food Co., Ltd, a Chinese meat factory owned by OSI Group of Aurora, Illinois, was accused of selling out-of-date and tainted meat to clients including McDonald's, Starbucks, KFC and Pizza Hut chains.

China has approximately 500,000 food production and processing companies, and approximately 70% of them have a staff strength of fewer than 10 employees.[6] Such highly fragmented food chain networks make it extremely difficult for authorities to control and implement food safety policies. As even

---

[3] "World Health Day 2015: Food Safety", *World Health Organization*, 7 April 2015, at <http://www.who.int/campaigns/world-health-day/2015/event/en/> (accessed 20 May 2015).

[4] "It's a Shame to Let a China Food Scandal Go to Waste", *South China Morning Post*, 11 August 2014, at <http://www.scmp.com/comment/blogs/article/1571442/its-shame-let-china-food-scandal-go-waste> (accessed 20 May 2015).

[5] Mao Xuedan, Hu Junfeng and Liu Xiumei, "Epidemiological Burden of Bacterial Foodborne Diseases in China-Preliminary Study", *Chinese Journal of Food Hygiene*, 24 June 2011.

[6] "It's a Shame to Let a China Food Scandal Go to Waste", *South China Morning Post*, 11 August 2014.

major international renowned companies such as Pizza Hut and McDonald's were embroiled in food scandals, it is little wonder why Chinese consumers' confidence in local produce has been further affected.

The need to improve food safety levels in China is a common theme that cuts across all social strata. The Chinese government has taken stronger actions and measures to ensure safer food. Increasingly, it recognises the need to have greater harmonisation among various authorities that monitor different stages of the food value chain. Both Chinese President Xi Jinping and Chinese Premier Li Keqiang had stated on a number of occasions that food safety should be a top priority. The Chinese government has also included food safety in its 12th Five-Year Plan for Social and Economic Development.

Why Jilin?

Site selection is an utmost important criterion for a project that emphasises animal health and food safety. The ideal location must be agriculturally suitable for crop plantation and rearing of animals, and should also be situated in an unpolluted environment with natural barriers to control and prevent disease outbreaks. The present site in Yongji county was selected based on these considerations.

Yongji county, in Jilin city of Jilin province, is located in the central area of north-east China, which is rich in natural and mineral resources. The province has 27,000 species of wild plants, 9,000 kinds of medicinal herbs and 165 types of discovered minerals. Ginseng, sables and deer antlers, well known in both China and overseas as the "three north-eastern treasures", are specialties of Jilin province.[7]

Jilin, because of its fertile soil, has been called one of the "golden corn belts" of the world. The province has more than 55,000 square kilometres of arable land, accounting for 4.3% of China's total arable land area. The arable land area per capita in Jilin is 134% higher than the country's average. The province is also China's largest granary, with its grain output accounting for 5.5% of the country's total output.[8]

The SSJFZ is strategically located between Changchun city and Jilin city — the two major cities of Jilin province. Both cities combined ensure a steady

---

[7] "Introduction to Jilin Province", *China Knowledge*, at <http://www.chinaknowledge.com/Business/Provincedetails.aspx?subchap=9&content=45#Introduction> (accessed 20 May 2015).
[8] "Agriculture in Jilin", *China Knowledge*, at <http://www.chinaknowledge.com/Business/Provincedetails.aspx?subchap=9&content=45#Agriculture> (accessed 20 May 2015).

supply of talent and manpower for the food zone, and also serve as a huge market base that covers close to 45% of Jilin province's total population and more than 60% of the province's GDP.

A unique proposition: The SSJFZ

Collaborating with Singapore, whose name is synonymous with quality, reliability and efficiency, to develop a food zone was an obvious choice for Jilin. The transfer of Singapore's experience in food safety measures and traceability systems into the food zone will not only help to ensure high safety standards and quality food production but also, more importantly, raise the confidence of Chinese consumers of locally produced food due to the good Singapore brand name.

Through the development of modern agriculture and food processing, the SSJFZ aims to become an advanced, sustainable, replicable and scaleable model zone for safe and quality food. The SSJFZ, being the first bilateral cooperation of an agricultural nature for both sides, will be developed based on an enterprise-led, government-supported model to ensure commercial viability. The project also has a first-mover advantage as it is one of the first international large-scale agricultural projects in China.

Covering half of the Yongji county of Jilin city at 1,450 square kilometres, the Jilin Food Zone comprises of a 57-square kilometre core area. The core area will encompass several functions of the SSJFZ, such as food processing zone, logistics zone, residential zone, recreational zone, office and research and development centre and a nature zone. The master plan for the core area was designed by Singapore's Jurong International.

In September 2012, Singbridge and the Jilin city government signed an investment and cooperation agreement at the Great Hall of the People in Beijing, witnessed by Singapore Prime Minister Lee Hsien Loong and then Chinese Premier Wen Jiabao. The agreement helped put in place a framework to develop the SSJFZ for the next 15 to 20 years.

The Sino-Singapore Jilin Food Zone Management and Development Co., Ltd, a joint-venture company between Singbridge and Jilin city government was established in September 2013 to oversee and manage the food zone development. In contrast to many other Sino-Singapore projects where both Chinese and Singapore shareholders hold equal shares, the Jilin city government holds 60% of the Jilin Food Zone management company's stake while Singbridge holds 40%. This unique shareholding structure reflects the high level of commitment from the Chinese partners to ensure the success of the SSJFZ.

The signing ceremony of the investment and cooperation agreement at the Great Hall of the People in Beijing on 9 June 2012. Photo credit: SSJFZ.

Although still in its early stages of development, the SSJFZ has received much attention and support from both countries. In addition to leveraging Jilin province's rich resources and the Singapore brand name in marketing food products, establishing and maintaining a foot-and-mouth disease-free zone and implementing an integrated food safety system of international standards are the twin pillars critical to the success of the food zone.

The twin pillars fundamental to the success of Jilin food zone
Foot-and-mouth Disease-free Zone (DFZ)

In August 2012, Yongji county was accredited by China's Ministry of Agriculture as a foot-and-mouth disease-free zone (DFZ), one of the only two foot-and-mouth disease-free zones in China conforming to the international standards of the World Organisation for Animal Health (OIE).[9]

This development is significant to the building of a safe food zone in China, as foot-and-mouth disease is a highly contagious viral disease of livestock that affects cloven-hoofed animals (e.g. pigs, cows, goats and sheep). Yongji county, with its surrounding natural barriers of mountain ranges and rivers, is ideal for

---

[9] The other foot-and-mouth disease-free zone is located in Hainan province.

the prevention of a foot-and-mouth disease incursion, hence ensuring a steady supply of safe food.

To secure the DFZ status, the local government had put in place various sets of hardware and software enablers to achieve accreditation of the status. These include the setting up of laboratories, animal quarantine stations and sanitary control checkpoints; and the implementation of laws and regulations, management practices and inspection and quarantine policies.

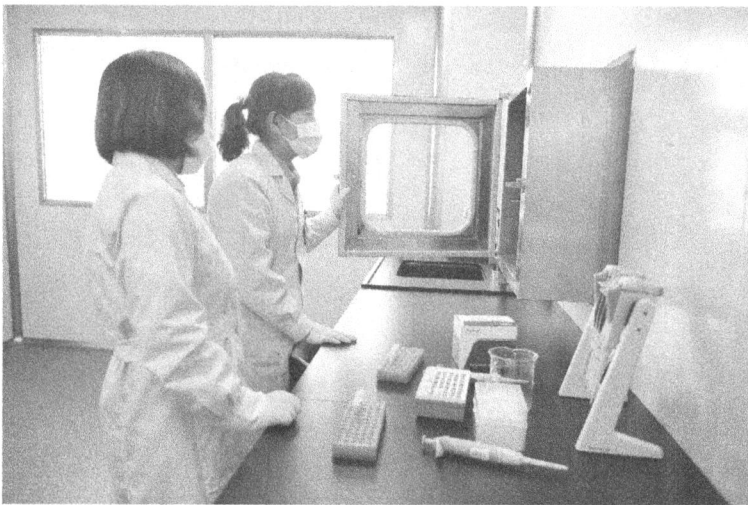

Laboratory testing in the DFZ. Photo credit: SSJFZ.

The endorsement of the SSJFZ by the Agri-Food and Veterinary Authority of Singapore has enhanced Jilin Food Zone's status as a credible and internationally recognised disease-free zone. Despite the current focus on foot-and-mouth disease, the principles behind maintaining the DFZ is also applicable in the prevention and control of other common severe diseases, and over time, relevant procedures will be developed to cover all species of animals reared in the DFZ.

Integrated food safety system

With the help of Agrifood Technologies Pte Ltd, the consultancy arm of Singapore's Agri-Food & Veterinary Authority, the local government in Jilin is in the process of setting up an integrated food safety system to ensure consistent standards and implementation of food safety practices and policies, thereby allowing the production of safe food. This involves a complete value chain control from "farm to table" to ensure traceability and security of food production.

The Jilin Food Zone Food and Drug Administration was set up in 2014 to serve as a one-stop single agency overseeing the standards, controls, inspection, sampling, testing, certification, labelling and traceability of food production and processing within the SSJFZ. This increases efficiency and convenience by cutting down on unnecessary procedures.

The Sino-Singapore Jilin Food Zone Management and Development Co., Ltd will be working closely with the local government in the implementation of the food safety system. Once the implementation is complete, Jilin Food Zone's Integrated Food Safety System has the potential to be a model system that can be replicated in other parts of China.

Government support: The Singapore brand

Unlike the Suzhou Industrial Park and Tianjin Eco-city which are both government-to-government projects, the SSJFZ is a commercially-driven project. Notwithstanding its commercial nature, the project is on the agenda of the Joint Council for Bilateral Cooperation headed by the deputy prime ministers of both Singapore and China, given its scale and significance.

Living up to the name as the "Singapore Inc.", besides Singbridge's stake in the management company of the SSJFZ, many other Singapore organisations and corporations are also involved in the building of the food zone. Jurong International, from the commercial side, was commissioned to draw up the Food Zone Core Area Master Plan. Keppel T&T will be jointly developing an international logistics park with the Jilin city government to address all logistical needs within the food zone, including warehousing and cold chain facilities, trading centre, wholesale retail centre, and simple processing and packaging. SATS Ltd is a direct investor in the integrated pig farm project that aims to produce one million porkers annually when completed.

Governmental support is premised on an overarching memorandum between Singapore's Ministry of National Development and China's Ministry of Agriculture that lays out specific objectives to be executed by Singapore's Agri-Food & Veterinary Authority and Agrifood Technologies Pte Ltd, both of which are involved in partnerships with the local government in the establishment and maintenance of the SSJFZ's DFZ status and the integrated food safety system, as well as the establishment of a green lane for food exports into Singapore.

Work commencement ceremony of the SSJFZ International Logistics Park on 29 October 2012. Photo credit: SSJFZ.

To further cement the existing close relationship at strategic and working levels, an annual joint steering committee meeting between Temasek and the Jilin provincial government serves as an official platform to help drive the development of the food zone and exchange views for deliberation and resolution.

With the strong support of the Singapore government and organisations involved in the SSJFZ, together with the commitment of the Chinese counter-parts, it is expected that Chinese consumers will have access to a safe source of food supply from the food zone in the near future.

The future of the SSJFZ

Chinese Vice Premier Li Keqiang remarked at the first plenary meeting of the food safety commission under the State Council in 2010 that "food is essential, and safety should be a top priority for food. Food safety is closely related to people's life and health and economic development and social harmony".[10]

---

[10] "China Vows New Food Safety Campaign", *China Daily*, 10 February 2010, at <http://www.chinadaily.com.cn/china/2010npc/2010-02/10/content_9462104.htm> (accessed 15 June 2015).

Construction of the Jilin Food Zone Food Processing Zone as of 2014. Photo credit: SSJFZ.

Establishing a food zone of this magnitude is a long, tedious but essential process. At present, China feeds around 20% of the world's population, with 9% of the world's land and 6% of its water.[11] The food industry in China comprises hundreds of thousands of large businesses and millions of small ones. Ensuring the safety of all food grown, produced and consumed in China is therefore a complex and uphill task.

Overcoming the apparent rising incidents of food safety scandals may be challenging. However, shifting mindset and increased awareness of food safety of both consumers and producers are an inexorable and growing force that can be leveraged upon for commercial success. Together with the cooperation from the Singapore and Chinese governments and organisations, the SSJFZ has the potential to become a scaleable and replicable model food zone that produces safe and quality food for the populations of China, Singapore and beyond.

---

[11] World Health Organization, "Food Safety — World Health Day 2015", at <http://www.wpro. who.int/china/mediacentre/factsheets/food_safety_whd2015/en/> (accessed 20 May 2015).

Chapter 8

Growing Educational Exchanges between Singapore and China

ZHAO Litao

Educational links are an important part of the bilateral relations between Singapore and China. Starting from a low base, educational exchanges and collaborations have moved beyond language training and broadened in scope. China is a major source country of international students in Singapore. Meanwhile, the number of Singaporeans studying in Chinese universities has grown rapidly in recent years. Singapore is also well known for its leadership training programmes tailored to Chinese officials. Whether the two countries can maintain the momentum of collaboration depends on how both sides can stay relevant to each other in a changing context where there is free open choice of regional and global players for partnership.

Introduction

Historians have documented a long history of people exchanges between China and present-day Southeast Asia. The Chinese trade in the *Nanhai* (known later as the *Nanyang*) region dates back to as early as the second century BC.[1] Nevertheless, the main force that shaped Southeast Asia in the modern era was European colonialism, which transformed subsistence farming into cash crops and plantations, integrated the

---

[1] Wang Gungwu, *The Nanhai Trade: Early Chinese Trade in the South China Sea*, Singapore, Times Media Private Limited, 2003.

region into the world, and gave rise to a new "coolie" trade in the 19th century.[2] Singapore emerged as a British trading port in 1819, and gained self-rule in 1959 and independence in 1965.

Against this background, the history of educational exchange between China and Singapore is rather short. Educational links certainly existed before Singapore gained independence. However, if educational exchange is narrowly understood as the exchange of students or professional personnel for the purpose of further education or research collaboration, there is little need to look too far back. In fact, even in the 1990s, educational exchanges between Singapore and China remained limited by today's standards.

Much of the changes occurred in the 2000s. The two governments signed the memorandum of understanding (MOU) on educational exchanges and cooperation in 1999, paving the way for institutionalised mechanisms of forging educational links at various levels. From China's perspective, Singapore is a Chinese-majority society with a good development model and robust educational system. From Singapore's perspective, China is important not just in cultural terms, but more so in economic and geopolitical terms. Both sides recognise the benefits of forging closer ties. To varying extents, other stakeholders — from universities, schools to students — share the same view.

From a broader perspective, both countries have made plans to ride the tide of the internationalisation of education. The consensus in Singapore in the late 1990s was to develop into an international education hub, making the education industry an engine of economic growth, capability development and talent attraction for Singapore. China is a latecomer in the global competition for international students, yet it has been quickly catching up with some of the major destination countries. The ideal of using higher education as a soft power tool further fuelled the efforts to attract foreign students to China since the mid-2000s. Growing educational exchanges between Singapore and China have been facilitated by their respective plans to tap on the internationalisation of education.

As the two countries made great efforts to forge closer political and economic ties in the last two decades, cooperation in the field of education also moved in tandem. Starting from a low base, educational exchanges and collaborations have moved beyond language training and become much broader and deeper in scope. Chinese leaders since Deng Xiaoping have appreciated

---

[2] Brenda S A Yeoh and Lin Weiqiang, "Chinese Migration to Singapore: Discourses and Discontents in a Globalizing Nation-State", *Asian and Pacific Migration Journal*, vol. 22, no. 1, 2013, pp. 31–54.

Singapore as an economically vibrant and socially harmonious city-state that has much to offer in industrial upgrading, urban planning and establishing good governance through knowledge transfer and sharing. On the other hand, as China rises to become an economic superpower, Singapore sees the value and need to have a better understanding of China, culturally, economically and politically. The conviction that both sides have much to gain from each other has led to closer educational links since the early 2000s. Down the road, the challenge is whether Singapore and China will continue to stay relevant to each other.

Building institutional mechanisms

Little has been written on educational exchanges between Singapore and China before the 1990s. To a large extent, the Cold War had polarised the two countries into two different worlds of competing ideologies. Deng Xiaoping's visit to Singapore in 1978 bore great significance in forging trust and relationship at the leadership level. Both sides had since made regular official exchange visits and focused on strengthening bilateral economic ties. Institutional mechanisms to facilitate educational exchanges and collaborations were however still lacking. One of the few initiatives was an agreement on language training by Singapore to offer 35 scholarships to train English language teachers for Chinese universities from 1988 onward.[3] The selected Chinese candidates would receive 10 months of training at Singapore's National Institute of Education (NIE). Up to five trainees from the cohort each year would be selected to pursue a master's programme that had to be completed within one year.

Singapore and China established formal diplomatic relations in October 1990. According to the information provided by the Chinese Embassy in Singapore, starting from 1992, Singapore began to offer scholarships annually to about 200 students from a number of reputable Chinese universities.[4] This scholarship scheme was later known as SM3 (Senior Middle 3). From 1995 onward, the scholarship scheme was expanded. The new schemes — SM1 and SM2 — were established to recruit students from China at the level of Senior

---

[3] See <http://www.edusg.org.cn/publish/portal50/tab3383/info66458.htm> (accessed 12 February 2015).

[4] See <http://www.edusg.org.cn/publish/portal50/tab3383/info66458.htm> (accessed 12 February 2015).

Middle 1 and Senior Middle 2. The number of SM1 and SM2 scholars ranged between 300 and 500 annually in the 1990s.

The year of 1999 marked a milestone in the history of educational exchanges between Singapore and China. Teo Chee Hean, then Minister of Education of Singapore, led a delegation to China in June 1999 and the two governments signed a memorandum of understanding on exchanges and cooperation in the field of education. The MOU formalised mechanisms, pre-existing and new, to forge closer educational ties between the two countries.

At the official level, both sides agreed to have annual exchanges of delegations in the field of education to strengthen links and mutual understanding. In terms of student exchange, both sides agreed to exchange 10 students, including undergraduates, postgraduates and students enrolled in continuing education, on a one-year scholarship. This was largely symbolic compared to the number of scholarships each government offered to international students.

In terms of teacher and language teaching exchanges, Singapore would continue to offer 35 scholarships to train English language teachers of higher institutions for China. The China side appointed China Scholarship Council to nominate candidates to Singapore, while the Singapore side assigned the National Institute of Education to select and train the teachers. On the other hand, China had agreed to assist Singapore in the teaching of Chinese language by offering three scholarships a year to Chinese Language teachers from Singapore to attend training courses of six-week duration in China. In addition, the China side would assist Singapore to recruit up to 60 teachers from China to teach Chinese language in Singapore schools.

In terms of academic exchange and cooperation, both sides affirmed the need to encourage direct exchanges and cooperation between their universities, including exchange of lecturers and professors to give lectures, and organising conferences and seminars.[5]

The 1999 MOU has played an important role in building institutional mechanisms for forging educational ties between Singapore and China, thus allowing both sides to meet regularly and discuss areas where educational links could be built and strengthened. In 2000, both sides established an education office in their respective embassy based in each other's country. In short, the 1999 MOU has paved the way for broader and deeper educational relations between Singapore and China.

---

[5] See <http://wcm.fmprc.gov.cn/pub/eng/wjb/zzjg/yzs/gjlb/2777/2778/t16196.htm> (accessed 12 February 2015).

Expanding and deepening educational exchanges

Educational exchanges between Singapore and China entered a new stage at the turn of the new century. Compared to the 1990s, the 2000s witnessed broader and deeper educational links between the two countries in different forms and at various levels.

Studying in Singapore/studying in China

A major form of educational link is education-related migration from China to Singapore and vice versa. Globally, China has been a major source of international students. In 2012, nearly 400,000 Chinese students went overseas, and an overwhelming majority — 374,500 of them — were privately funded. For many countries including the United Kingdom, Germany, France, Japan, South Korea, Australia and New Zealand, China is the top source country of international students.[6] Singapore's top source of international students is also from China. Singapore, despite its small size, has attracted a sizeable number of students from China. The exact number is not available. A report by the *Straits Times* in 2008 put the figure at around 36,000.[7] A study done by Chinese scholars estimated that about 50,000 Chinese students were studying in Singapore in 2012, making up nearly 56% of international students in the country.[8] According to the same study, Singapore was the top seventh destination country for Chinese students studying abroad, after the United States, Australia, Japan, the United Kingdom, Canada and South Korea.

Among the 50,000 Chinese students in Singapore, over 10,000 were in higher education institutions, including universities and polytechnics, and over 10,000 were in public secondary and primary schools, while the remaining were in private schools.[9] Online information provided by China's Ministry of Foreign Affairs has shown that there were nearly 14,000 Chinese students in

---

[6] Wang Huiyao and Lü Miao, *Zhongguo liuxue fazhan baogao 2013 No. 2* (*Annual Report on Chinese Students Studying Abroad 2013, No. 2*), Beijing, Social Sciences Academic Press, 2013.
[7] "Tough Life for 'Study Mamas'", *The Straits Times*, 28 September 2008.
[8] Wang Huiyao and Lü Miao, *Zhongguo liuxue fazhan baogao 2013 No. 2* (*Annual Report on Chinese Students Studying Abroad 2013, No. 2*).
[9] Ministry of Education Research Team on Chinese Students Studying Abroad, "Zhongguo zai Taiguo, Xiniiapo, Malaixiya sanguo liuxue renyuan qingkuang diaoyan" (Research on Chinese Students in Thailand, Singapore and Malaysia), *Shijie jiaoyu xinxi* (*World Education Information*), no. 2, 2012, pp. 65–70.

Singapore's higher education institutions in 2013.[10] A sizeable number of Chinese students can be found at every educational level, from kindergarten to primary, secondary and tertiary, making Singapore uniquely different from other destination countries.

The reasons for Chinese students' choice to study in Singapore are likely to vary across educational levels. According to a survey on college/university graduates pursuing postgraduate education in Singapore conducted by MyCOS, the most trusted brand in higher education consulting and assessment in China, 46.7% of the respondents were primarily attracted by the quality of education, 23.3% by the affordability of education, 6.7% by the convenience of immigration, and 6.7% rated open environment and easy application procedure as the top reasons.[11] Another research, conducted by China Education Online, identified up to 10 competitive advantages that attribute Singapore as the first choice of destination for Chinese students keen to study abroad, including "world-class universities with high education quality assurance", "safe environment", "Western education system", "bilingual education", "lower tuition fee and living cost" compared to the United Kingdom, Australia and the United States, "IELTS and TOEFL are not necessarily required", "the best pathway to pursue further study in the West", "high possibility to get visa", "good job prospects in Singapore" and "Singapore's welcoming immigration policies".[12]

While the number of Chinese students going abroad, including those heading to Singapore, has been growing rapidly, the number of international students bound for China is also on the rise. Within a decade, China has moved from an insignificant player to become a major destination for international students. The total number of international students increased nearly sixfold from 52,000 in 2000 to about 293,000 in 2011 (Figure 1). China is now one of the world's top 10 major destination countries and the only developing country on the list. To become the top destination country in Asia, it plans to increase the total number of foreign students to 500,000 by 2020.

Self-financed students are the main driver of growth, totalling 267,000 in 2011 and thereby accounting for 91% of international students in China's

---

[10] See <http://wcm.fmprc.gov.cn/pub/chn/gxh/cgb/zcgmzysx/yz/1206_35/1206x1/t6013. htm> (accessed 12 February 2015).

[11] Cited in Wang Huiyao and Lü Miao, *Zhongguo liuxue fazhan baogao 2013, No. 2* (*Annual Report on Chinese Students Studying Abroad 2013, No. 2*).

[12] Cited in Saw Swee-Hock and Ge Yun, "Enhancing Educational Collaborations between China and Singapore", *Advancing Singapore–China Economic Relations,* ed. Saw Swee-Hock and John Wong, Singapore, World Scientific, pp. 264–288 .

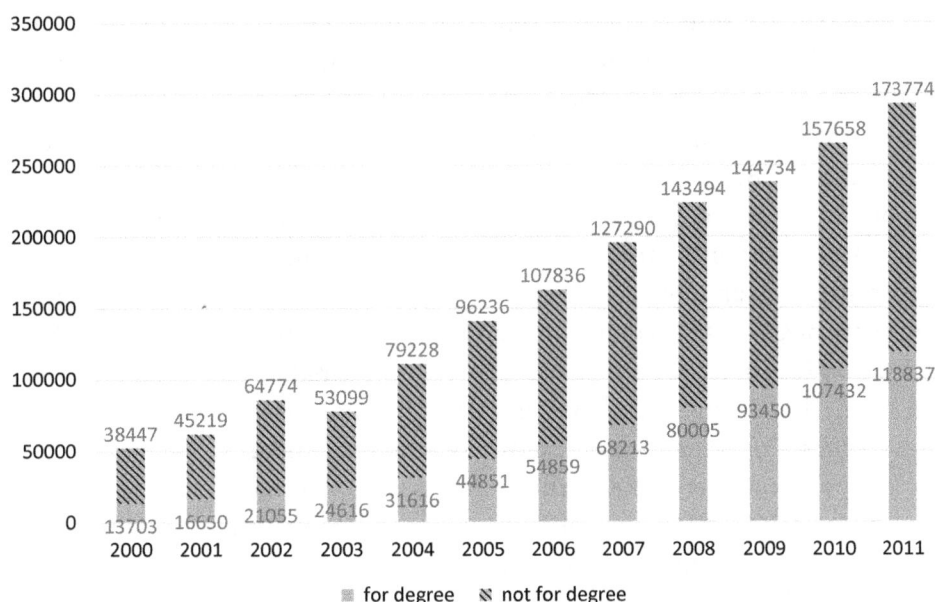

Figure 1 Number of International Students in China's Higher Education Institutions
Source: *China Education Yearbook*, Beijing, Zhongguo da bai ke quan shu chubanshe, various years.

higher education institutions.[13] China's economic rise, particularly its role in the regional and global production network, has increased the economic payoffs of receiving higher education in China. Students on short-term training made up the majority at over 60% of international students throughout the 2000s. Most of them studied Chinese language. Over time, however, the share of degree students has also been on the rise, and the popular courses are medicine, economics, management, sciences and engineering.[14] More than two-thirds of international students come from Asia. The largest source countries are all China's neighbours, with the exception of the United States. South Korea is by far the largest source country, totalling 62,957 in 2011. The United States is ranked a remote second (19,668), followed by Japan (16,808), Thailand (13,177), Vietnam (13,018), Russia (12,481), Indonesia (9,539), India (9,014), Kazakhstan (7,874) and Pakistan (7,406).[15]

---

[13] See *Zhongguo jiaoyu nianjian 2012* (*China Education Yearbook 2012*), Beijing, Zhongguo da bai ke quan shu chubanshe, 2012.

[14] Zhao Litao, "China Attracting International Students", *EAI Background Brief no. 680*, 2011, East Asian Institute, National University of Singapore (unpublished).

[15] See *Zhongguo jiaoyu nianjian 2012* (*China Education Yearbook 2012*).

Singapore as a source country started from a very low base. In 2002, there were only 583 students from Singapore. However, the number has increased rapidly. As data provided by the Chinese Embassy in Singapore has shown, the number of Singaporean students in China's higher education institutions increased to 1,480 in 2007, 2,155 in 2008, and 3,198 in 2009.[16] In 2013, the number had reached 5,290.[17] Reflecting the general pattern, the majority of Singaporean students are on short-term programmes in Chinese language. Degree students are concentrated in a dozen of universities, such as Nanjing University of Chinese Medicine, Fudan University, Tsinghua University, Peking University, Central China Normal University, Shanghai Jiao Tong University, and so on. The recent years have also seen Singaporean students spreading out from Chinese language to other fields. For instance, Fudan University admitted 12 Singapore students in 2005, all in language programmes. In 2010, the enrolment expanded to 44. Some of the students chose to study law, journalism, medicine, business administration, or international relations.[18]

Compared to students from other countries, Singaporean students are found to be more adaptive, partly because of the edge they have in learning and grasping Chinese culture and language. As for the motivation to study in China, some Singaporean students cited good job prospects as part of their considerations, which also include avoiding direct competition to gain admission into Singapore's local universities, and capitalising on their bilingualism since China becomes a popular investment location for Singapore firms and multinational corporations.[19]

Student exchange programmes

Another major form of educational links is the student exchange programmes. Exchange programmes exist at different levels between Singapore and China — from university students to secondary and primary students — and are aimed to enhance mutual understanding.

---

[16] See <http://www.csc.edu.cn/laihua/newsdetail.aspx?cid=121&id=500> (accessed 12 February 2015).

[17] See <http://wcm.fmprc.gov.cn/pub/chn/gxh/cgb/zcgmzysx/yz/1206_35/1206x1/t6013.htm> (accessed 12 February 2015).

[18] See <http://www.csc.edu.cn/laihua/newsdetail.aspx?cid=121&id=500> (accessed 12 February 2015).

[19] See <http://www.csc.edu.cn/laihua/newsdetail.aspx?cid=121&id=500> (accessed 12 February 2015).

At the tertiary level, Singapore and China signed a memorandum of understanding on undergraduate exchange programme in May 2002. Both sides agreed to exchange up to 50 university students annually and to enlist the help of the All-China Youth Federation and the National Youth Council of Singapore to run the visit programme. The programme in Singapore would be co-organised by the Ministry of Manpower, Ministry of Trade and Industry, National University of Singapore and Nanyang Technological University.[20]

The First Sino-Singapore Undergraduate Exchange Programme started in Singapore on 30 November 2003. A total of 43 university students from Tsinghua University, Beijing Foreign Studies University, Beijing Language and Culture University, and Beijing University of Posts and Telecommunications came to Singapore for the inaugural exchange programme. During their two-week stay in Singapore, they visited several government agencies, companies and education institutions, including the Ministry of Education, Jurong Town Corporation, National University of Singapore and Nanyang Technological University. They were introduced to Singapore's key education and economic policies, and participated in dialogue sessions with Singapore politicians and senior government officials.[21] The annual Sino-Singapore Undergraduate Exchange Programme still continues today (see photo).

In addition to the Sino-Singapore Undergraduate Exchange Programme, some universities have set up the twinning programme to facilitate student exchanges. One such example is the student exchange programme established between Singapore University of Technology and Design (SUTD) and the International Design Institute (IDI) of Zhejiang University. This 15-week exchange programme allows SUTD students to "experience the various elements of design, ranging from the aesthetic and artistic aspects to technological and architectural aspects. A series of hands-on projects will be offered to students revolving around the central theme of Design and Technology". During the exchange, "students will attend classes held at various workshops, and will also be exposed to the working environment in Cixi and Hangzhou cities through internship opportunities".[22]

---

[20] See <http://www.moe.gov.sg/media/press/2003/pr20031128.htm> (accessed 12 February 2015).

[21] See <http://news.sina.com.cn/o/2003-12-02/10011234329s.shtml> (accessed 12 February 2015).

[22] See <http://www.sutd.edu.sg/alp_2013.aspx> (accessed 12 February 2015).

The 11th Sino-Singapore Undergraduate Exchange Programme 2014: Chinese Heritage Centre at Nanyang Technological University

Source: Reproduced with permission from Office of Global Education and Mobility, Nanyang Technological University, at <http://global.ntu.edu.sg/GMP/gemdiscoverer/Special%20Programmes/Pages/Sino-SingaporeUndergraduateExchange(SSUE).aspx> (accessed 12 February 2015).

At the secondary and primary levels, the twinning programme is the most popular form of educational exchanges between Singapore and China. In 2004, Singapore's Ministry of Education established the School Twinning Fund (STF) to support its schools' twinning programmes with Chinese schools. In 2005, the STF was expanded to support Singapore schools to forge ties with foreign partner schools in China and other countries. In 2008, the STF was replaced with the Internationalisation Fund (IF), giving schools greater discretion over the administration of the IF. From the perspective of the Ministry of Education, "having an overseas experience is now an integral part of the learning experience in our schools and post-secondary educational institutions".[23] The Singapore government has set targets for proportion of students at each level of education — 10% for primary, 25% for Institute of Technical Education (ITE), 33% for secondary, junior college and polytechnic, and 50% for university — to have at least one overseas immersion trip during their time in school.

Recognising that Singapore students "need to be receptive to looking for opportunities in new markets outside Singapore while being mindful of the complexities and opportunities in the region",[24] Singapore's Ministry of Education launched the Bicultural Studies Programme (Chinese), or BSP(C), with specific focus on China in 2005. The BSP(C) is a four-year programme that starts from Secondary 3 to junior college. The idea for the BSP(C) was first mooted in June 2004 by then Senior Minister Lee Kuan Yew, who "felt the need to go beyond bilingualism to nurture a group of highly able Singaporeans with an interest in and capacity to engage China in future".[25] The BSP(C) is offered in four schools: River Valley High School, Hwa Chong Institution, Nanyang Girls' High School and Dunman High School. Students enrolled in the programme need to go through a more intensive Chinese curriculum and significant period of immersion in China.

The immersion trip to China is the most attractive part of the BSP(C). Destinations are often cities where partner schools are located, or cities that have historical value and economic ties with Singapore. The immersion trips range from two to five weeks, involving classroom lessons, home stays, site visits and meetings with Singaporeans in the host city.[26]

Singapore also supports schoolteachers and school management through observational and networking trips to other countries. China has been "a hotspot for study trips and learning journeys at policy-making level". As explained by an education official, "China is a rising economy with a long history and a rich culture. Engaging China allows our students to better appreciate Chinese language, culture and values, and enables them to plug into the new worlds.

---

[23] See <http://www.moe.gov.sg/teachers-digest/2008/pdf/contact_oct08.pdf> (accessed 12 February 2015).

[24] See <http://www.moe.gov.sg/teachers-digest/2008/pdf/contact_oct08.pdf> (accessed 12 February 2015).

[25] See <http://www.moe.gov.sg/media/press/2004/pr20040903.htm> (accessed 12 February 2015).

[26] See <http://www.moe.gov.sg/teachers-digest/2008/pdf/contact_oct08.pdf> (accessed 12 February 2015).

Our students and educators need to keep abreast of the latest developments in the world as China evolves quickly and introduces many reforms, including education ones."[27]

In April 2009, Singapore and China signed a revised government-to-government memorandum of understanding on education cooperation. Through the new memorandum, the two countries agreed to bolster cooperation in areas such as school twinning programmes, school-leader and teacher exchanges and professional sharing conferences and seminars.[28]

Leadership training programmes

Encouraged by both governments, leadership training programmes form an important part of educational cooperation between Singapore and China. At the government level, the Ministry of Foreign Affairs in both countries have set up training programmes for their diplomats in the past decades.[29]

Perhaps the best known leadership training programme is the one conducted in Chinese at the Nanyang Technological University (NTU), widely known as the "Mayors' Class". NTU began to provide training to Chinese officials in as early as 1992. In 1998, it launched the Master of Science in Managerial Economics (MME) programme targeting high-potential mainland Chinese mayors and senior executives of large state-owned enterprises. The success of the MME programme prompted NTU to launch the Master of Public Administration (MPA) programme in 2005, targeting senior government officials who are groomed to be the next generation of leaders. The two programmes have trained over 1,000 Chinese officials to date. In addition, NTU offers short-term executive training programmes in public administration, economic management, urban planning, human resource management and community management.[30] In total, NTU has provided training to about 13,000 Chinese officials since 1992.[31]

---

[27] See <http://www.moe.gov.sg/teachers-digest/2008/pdf/contact_oct08.pdf> (accessed 12 February 2015).

[28] See <http://www.moe.gov.sg/media/press/2009/04/singapore-and-peoples-republic.php> (accessed 12 February 2015).

[29] Saw Swee-Hock and Ge Yun, "Enhancing Educational Collaborations between China and Singapore", pp. 264–288.

[30] See <http://www.ncpa.ntu.edu.sg/Eng/Programmes/GraduateProgrammes/Pages/Home.aspx> (accessed 12 February 2015).

[31] See <http://news.xinhuanet.com/world/2013-07/10/c_124984185.htm> (accessed 12 February 2015).

There is growing competition among local institutions that offer training programmes to Chinese officials in recent years. The Lee Kuan Yew School of Public Policy at the National University of Singapore (NUS) started its first Chinese-language programme — the Master in Public Administration and Management (MPAM) in 2010. Tailor-made for senior Chinese officials and business leaders, the MPAM curriculum integrates public administration and business management education. It also includes study visits to regional countries and the United States, as well as attachments with Singapore government organisations, statutory boards and government-linked firms. In addition to the MPAM programme, the Lee Kuan Yew School of Public Policy also offers short-term executive training programme conducted in Chinese. Speaking at the inaugural opening ceremony of the MPAM programme on 17 April 2010, Li Yuanchao, then head of the Central Organization Department of the Chinese Communist Party, acknowledged that "out of all the destinations where we send our leading officials to receive training, Singapore is the top choice, because Singapore is the most sincere in helping China develop, due to our long-standing warm relationship."[32]

Singapore's Civil Service College is also an important player in forging educational ties between government officials of the two countries. It has been hosting study delegations from China's Central Party School since 2002. The annual programme is organised under the framework of the Singapore Cooperation Programme, which was formally established in 1992 under the Ministry of Foreign Affairs to share its development experience and expertise with developing countries. The long-term engagement between the Civil Service College, Singapore's leading training institution for the public service, and the Central Party School, China's leading training institution for Party cadres and government leaders, "provide[s] valuable opportunities" for both sides to "exchange views and ideas on how government can be more effective in serving the people" and to "develop closer ties between officials from China and Singapore".[33] In Singapore, Chinese delegates "learn about Singapore's principles of governance, and study Singapore's experience in areas such as urban planning, human resource management, and maintaining social harmony and social security". They are also given "a first-hand look at the

---

[32] "Singapore is Tops for Training of Senior Chinese Officials", *The Straits Times*, 18 April 2010.
[33] See <https://www.cscollege.gov.sg/About%20Us/newsroom/2010/Pages/CIVIL-SERVICE-COLLEGE-HOSTS-STUDY-GROUP-FROM-CHINAS-CENTRAL-PARTY-SCHOOL.aspx> (accessed 12 February 2015).

implementation of policies at the agency level" through learning journeys to government agencies.[34]

To facilitate coordination of training programmes among Singapore institutions, International Enterprise Singapore launched the Singapore Talent Development Alliance (TDA) in January 2013. The members of Singapore TDA are made up of seven key players from the public and private sectors: Civil Service College, ITE Education Services, Nanyang Polytechnic, Nanyang Technological University, National University of Singapore, NTUC LearningHub and Singapore Management University. This is the first-ever partnership between public and private education and training institutions in Singapore that convenes members of Singapore TDA to plan and work together to provide a holistic suite of courses to meet China's education and training needs. The Civil Service College would tap into its expertise on public administration, policy and governance; ITE Education Services are to focus on consultancy and training services in technical and vocational education and training; Nanyang Polytechnic could offer courses on management and capability development of technical and vocational education and training institutions; Nanyang Technological University would specialise in public administration, economic management and urban development; National University of Singapore would take advantage of its strength in public policy and governance, sustainability planning and management, and corporate and financial governance; NTUC LearningHub is expected to focus on employability and technical skills; and Singapore Management University would share its expertise on banking, health-care management and management of public-private partnership.[35]

From Singapore's perspective, "education and training have always been a key area of collaboration between Singapore and China. The Singapore brand of education and training is synonymous with quality and professionalism, and is well-received in the market". Through the new platform, "each member of the Singapore TDA can provide better value-add to their Chinese partners, thereby gaining them access to a greater pool of opportunities". The formation of the alliance "will position our players strategically to tap into the increasing

---

[34] See <https://www.cscollege.gov.sg/About%20Us/newsroom/2010/Pages/CIVIL-SERVICE-COLLEGE-HOSTS-STUDY-GROUP-FROM-CHINAS-CENTRAL-PARTY-SCHOOL.aspx> (accessed 12 February 2015).

[35] See <http://www.iesingapore.gov.sg/Media-Centre/Media-Releases/2013/1/IE-Singapore-Launches-Singapore-Talent-Development-Alliance-for-education-and-training-players> (accessed 12 February 2015).

demand for in-market training" and "further differentiate our players in the competitive market consisting of both local and foreign providers".[36]

Recognising China as Singapore's largest trading partner and investment destination, Singapore not only hosts study groups from China but also sends its officials to China. The Civil Service College, for instance, has organised nine Overseas Study Visit Programmes to China as of April 2015. The purpose of this programme is to provide Singapore's public officers with "exposure to China's developments and culture through first-hand experiences and direct encounters with key government officials and industry leaders".[37]

Some other institutions run similar training programmes. The Centre for Liveable Cities — established in 2008 under the Ministry of National Development — provides a five-day high-level programme for mayors from around the world through its Temasek Foundation Leaders in Urban Governance Programme, and a three-week programme for local high-potential urban leaders from various sectors through its Leaders in Urban Governance Programme. The centre also works with the Ministry of Foreign Affairs to provide urban governance training under its technical cooperation programmes such as the City Executive Leaders Programme. Through these programmes, the Centre for Liveable Cities helps to forge ties between officials and agencies of Singapore and China, particularly in the area of urban governance, by hosting study groups from China and even receiving Chinese officials for a three-month attachment in Singapore.[38] On the other hand, the centre also organises study trips to China for Singapore's high potential public officers.

University initiatives and collaborations

University initiatives and collaborations between Singapore and China have increased in recent years. In many cases, these initiatives and collaborations are made possible because of the close political and economic ties forged between Singapore and the different levels of government in China that already constitute and reinforce the existing strong relationship between them.

---

[36] See <http://www.iesingapore.gov.sg/Media-Centre/Media-Releases/2013/1/IE-Singapore-Launches-Singapore-Talent-Development-Alliance-for-education-and-training-players> (accessed 12 February 2015).

[37] See <https://www.cscollege.gov.sg/programmes/pages/display%20programme.aspx?pid=2836> (accessed 12 February 2015).

[38] See <http://www.clc.gov.sg/Training/trainingprogrammes.htm> (accessed 12 February 2015).

In 2010, Xi Jinping, then vice president of China, and Singapore Prime Minister Lee Hsien Loong witnessed the signing of two agreements to broaden and deepen cooperation in research and education. National University of Singapore signed an agreement with the Suzhou Industrial Park Administrative Committee to establish a research institute in the park. Meanwhile, Nanyang Technological University (NTU) sealed a memorandum of understanding with the Tianjin Municipal Education Commission and Sino-Singapore Tianjin Eco-city Administrative Committee to set up a college in Tianjin Eco-city. The trend is clear in terms of the selection of location and Chinese partners. Suzhou Industrial Park is the first government-to-government flagship project between Singapore and China and Tianjin Eco-city is the second such project.

The NTU Tianjin College is intended to provide high-quality research on clean technologies and digital animation, which fit squarely with the strategic interests of Tianjin Eco-city. The college will also serve as a base for NTU students to gain immersive experience in China. Internships will be offered in places such as Tianjin's Binhai New District, one of the most dynamic areas in China. Moreover, the college will facilitate tie-ups with Chinese venture capitalists and entrepreneurs, providing opportunities for start-ups to commercialise their technologies.[39]

In September 2013, NTU signed an agreement on research collaboration with Tianjin University (TJU), one of the two top universities in Tianjin. Both sides agreed to leverage their strengths and establish three virtual centres in the areas of environmental science and engineering, new media and business case writing. The three virtual centres are the first step towards the establishment of the NTU-TJU joint research institute.[40]

Inaugurated in 2010, the NUS (Suzhou) Research Institute (NUSRI) was officially opened on 29 May 2013. NUSRI was the first overseas research institute established by a Singapore university. It has a research focus on integrated sustainability. Similar to NTU Tianjin College, NUSRI is also expected to facilitate tie-ups with investors and technology entrepreneurs to commercialise new technologies.

In 2014, NUS signed an agreement with Suzhou Industrial Park Administrative Committee to establish three new centres at NUSRI. The Lee

---

[39] "NUS, NTU to Open Research Institutes in China", *The Straits Times*, 16 November 2010.
[40] See <http://www.tju.edu.cn/english/News/Focus/201310/t20131015_179885.htm> (accessed 12 February 2015).

Kuan Yew School of Public Policy Suzhou Centre will offer advanced public administration degree programmes and short-term executive programmes on topical issues such as social governance, urbanisation, environmental and water management, and sustainable development. It will also serve as a bridge for the Lee Kuan Yew School of Public Policy students to immerse themselves in China for a better understanding of China's development and public policy. In addition, the centre will conduct studies on innovations of China's local governments and non-governmental organisations.[41]

The Institute of Real Estate Studies (IRES) Global Logistic Properties Research Centre will "plan and organise thought leadership activities to provide policymakers and industry leaders in China with a platform to analyse and strategise issues in urbanisation, logistics and related sectors".[42] The third centre, the NUS Business School's China Business Centre, is the first China business-focused centre set up by a Singapore university. It seeks to "contribute to the globalisation and transformation of China-related businesses by deepening the understanding of China's business environment", and "focus on three main areas: advancing research in management challenges in China; developing leaders with deep China insights through high-quality China-focused business education; and building on NUS Business School's expertise on China and comprehensive network of Chinese alumni and business connections to provide thought leadership on China business".[43] NUSRI will also host the new Singapore–China (Suzhou) Innovation Centre. The centre will focus on international technology exchange and commercialisation, seek to become a preferred launch pad for international tech start-ups into the China market, and set up a platform for training and exchange in best practices in intellectual property and technology management knowhow from around the world.[44]

---

[41] See <http://lkyspp.nus.edu.sg/wp-content/uploads/2014/10/Media-Release-LKY-School-to-Launch-New-Education-Centre-in-Suzhou-China.pdf> (accessed 12 February 2015).

[42] See <http://news.nus.edu.sg/highlights/8258-nusri-sets-up-three-new-centres> (accessed 16 February 2015).

[43] See <http://bschool.nus.edu.sg/tabid/1575/NewsID/835/Default.aspx?view=news> (accessed 16 February 2015).

[44] See <http://www.nusri.cn/ent/singapore-china-suzhou-innovation-centre> (accessed 16 February 2015).

Since its inception in 2010, NUSRI has launched over 30 research projects, and secured about RMB27 million (S$5.6 million) in research funding.[45] In 2014, it filed 10 patent applications.[46] Through integration of academic resources within NUS, and with the support of local government in Suzhou, NUSRI is off to a good start.

The partnership between Singapore University of Technology and Design (SUTD), Singapore's fourth public university, and Zhejiang University, one of the most prestigious universities in China, represents another model of collaboration. By design, SUTD hopes to harness the best practices and values of the East and the West. For this purpose, it partners with the Massachusetts Institute of Technology based in the United States and Zhejiang University based in China. It signed an agreement with Zhejiang University in 2010 to collaborate in a wide range of activities covering education, student exchanges, joint design competitions and research.

In the area of curriculum development, Zhejiang University will offer five electives, taught in English by its faculty, on business culture and entrepreneurship in China; the role of technology and design on growth of modern China in the 21st century; the history of Chinese urban development and planning; the sustainability of ancient Chinese architectural design in the modern world; and culture formation and innovative product design. In terms of student exchanges, SUTD will send up to 100 students per year to Zhejiang University. These students can choose either to take up courses at Zhejiang University or undertake internships at one of the many leading companies that collaborate with Zhejiang University, such as Alibaba.com and Apple (China). Zhejiang University will also send up to 50 students annually over to study alongside SUTD students. In terms of collaborative research, the areas identified by the two universities include transportation, clean energy, the environment, health care, and so on.[47]

University initiatives and collaborations can take diverse forms other than those mentioned above. Some are driven or encouraged by the government, while others are initiated by the Chinese or Singapore partner for mutual benefits. For instance, NTU partnered with Shandong University to set up

---

[45] See <http://news.nus.edu.sg/highlights/8258-nusri-sets-up-three-new-centres> (accessed 16 February 2015).

[46] See <http://www.nusri.cn/res/nusri-filed-10-patent-applications-in-2014> (accessed 16 February 2015).

[47] See <http://www.sutd.edu.sg/newsdetails.aspx?news_sid=20110124MzgaRz5s84aO> (accessed 16 February 2015).

NTU Confucius Institute in 2005, one of the earliest Confucius Institutes in the world.[48] Overseen by China's Office of Chinese Language Council International (Hanban), Confucius Institutes are an initiative of the Chinese government in seeking to increase China's "soft power". Meanwhile, there are also programmes and initiatives driven by a shared desire to tap into the education and training market. For instance, the Antai College of Economics and Management of Shanghai Jiao Tong University collaborated with NTU's Nanyang Business School to launch a new Master of Business Administration programme in 2014. The collaboration between the two universities started much earlier in 2002 when Shanghai Jiao Tong University decided to move its graduate programme launched in 1993 to Singapore in NTU, where it set up Shanghai Jiao Tong University Singapore Graduate School.[49] The relocation has made NTU the university that hosts the first, and so far the only, overseas graduate school of any Chinese university.

Sustaining the momentum

To a large extent, the growing educational exchanges and collaborations between Singapore and China are part of the global trend that accelerated in the 1990s and particularly in the 2000s. Studying in overseas universities is a phenomenon that may be as old as the universities themselves. Having a sizeable international student body in universities is, however, a relatively new phenomenon. The current wave of the "internationalisation" of higher education is unprecedented in human history, not only in terms of the scale of international student mobility but also in terms of the legitimating discourse and the impact such discourse has on government policies. By the 1990s, a powerful discourse had emerged arguing that the flow of capital, goods and services should be more frequent around the globe, and that a freer flow is good for the world economy and society. This discourse has far-reaching impacts on higher education. The belief that "the more international a university is — in terms of students, faculty, curriculum, research, agreements, and network memberships — the better its reputation" has made universities much more open to foreign students and faculty.[50]

---

[48] See <http://english.hanban.org/confuciousinstitutes/node_10684.htm> (accessed 16 February 2015).

[49] See <http://edu.qq.com/a/20141215/028272.htm> (accessed 16 February 2015).

[50] Jane Knight, "Five Myths about Internationalization", *International Higher Education*, no. 62, Winter 2011, p. 14.

Indeed, many rating agencies have acted on such beliefs and myths and used the percentage of foreign faculty and students as one of the proxies for education quality when ranking universities worldwide. Increasingly, national governments and universities look to recruit more foreign faculty and students in the quest for world-class status.

Both Singapore and China have proactively responded to this global trend. In the case of Singapore, the government launched an ambitious "Global Schoolhouse" project in the early 2000s to build Singapore into a global educational hub.[51] The plan was to attract an additional 100,000 international students and 100,000 international corporate executives for training in 10 years' time, on top of 50,000 international students already studying in Singapore's public and private education institutions.[52] Recognising that Singapore possesses several competitive advantages in the global competition for international students and talents, including its strategic geographical location, reputation for educational excellence, a vibrant business hub, and a safe and cosmopolitan environment, the "Global Schoolhouse" project highlighted education as an engine of economic growth, as well as its functions of talent attraction and capability development.

In the case of China, a big change occurred in the 2000s. The total enrolment of foreign students studying in China increased fivefold from 52,150 in 2000 to 265,090 in 2008. The rapid growth changed China's position in the international higher education market. Its global share was insignificant at 0.7% in 2000. By 2008, the share had increased to 2.4%, making China the only developing country with a global share higher than 2%.[53] In less than a decade, as noted by the United Nations Educational, Scientific and Cultural Organisation (UNESCO), China has emerged as a new popular destination for international students.[54]

In 2003, China's Ministry of Education announced the 2003–2007 Action Plan for Revitalizing Education. To attract international students, the plan

---

[51] Ravinder Sidhu, "Building a Global Schoolhouse: International Education in Singapore", *Australian Journal of Education*, vol. 49, no. 1, 2005, pp. 46–65; and Yang Peidong, "Privilege, Prejudice, Predicament: 'PRC Scholars' in Singapore", *Frontiers of Education in China*, vol. 9, no. 3, 2014, pp. 350–376.

[52] See <https://www.mti.gov.sg/ResearchRoom/Documents/app.mti.gov.sg/data/pages/507/doc/DSE_recommend.pdf> (accessed 16 February 2015).

[53] Zhao Litao, "China's Higher Education as a Soft Power?", *EAI Background Brief no. 659*, 2011, East Asian Institute, National University of Singapore (unpublished).

[54] UNESCO Institute for Statistics, *Global Education Digest 2009*, p. 43.

pledged to "expand the enrolment, raise educational levels, improve the quality, and regularise the management". In 2004, as a follow-up to the action plan, the Ministry of Education devised a five-year plan for attracting international students. The most recent commitment to the internationalisation of China's higher education is specified in the Outline for Education Reform and Development in the Medium and Long Term (2010–2020). The outline has identified the further opening-up of China's higher education as one of the few priority areas. Apart from measures such as attracting more world-class scholars, importing quality textbooks, and increasing the percentage of foreigners in the university faculties, China plans to make greater efforts towards mutual recognition of academic credentials and degrees and joint conferment of academic degrees between Chinese and foreign higher education institutions, give more support to student exchange programmes, and provide more central and local government scholarships to international students. The target is to double the total number of international students to 500,000 by 2020.

Singapore and China have embraced the internationalisation of education since the 2000s. There have been growing student mobility, educational exchanges and research collaborations between Singapore and many countries; the same is true for China. Growing student mobility, educational exchanges and research collaborations between Singapore and China are part of this larger trend.

Nevertheless, global trend alone — i.e. the growing internationalisation of education — cannot explain the pace and scale of the rapidly broadening and deepening educational relations between Singapore and China. As noted by some scholars, Singapore provides nearly 1,000 pre-tertiary scholarships and over 1,000 undergraduate scholarships to attract international students annually.[55] Recipients of such scholarships — or "scholars" — primarily come from developing Asian countries such as India and members of the Association of Southeast Asian Nations (ASEAN), but "most notably of all, from the People's Republic of China (PRC)".[56] Indeed, there are specific scholarship schemes for PRC students. At the pre-tertiary level, the SM1 scheme offers bond-free scholarships to PRC students recruited to study in Singapore's schools and junior colleges from secondary three to the Advanced level, or commonly known as "A" Level. At the tertiary level, the SM2 scheme recruits

[55] Brenda SA Yeoh and Lin Weiqiang, "Chinese Migration to Singapore", pp. 31–54.
[56] Yang Peidong, "Privilege, Prejudice, Predicament", pp. 350–376.

second-year high school students from top schools in China while the SM3 scheme recruits students from a number of reputable Chinese universities.[57]

The special or even unique aspects of educational links between Singapore and China can be attributed to several factors. One of the factors, noted by some scholars, is the need to maintain multiculturalism based on four "founding races" — Chinese, Malay, Indian and Others — in Singapore, or the CMIO model in acronym. Over the years, diverging fertility trends are perceived as a threat to the model. The strong growth of PRC migrants, including students, is (implicitly) seen as a way to maintain the balance of the CMIO model.[58] On the other hand, many PRC officials, educators and students recognise that Singapore is the only country other than China where ethnic Chinese make up the majority of the population. The perceived language and cultural affinity make them inclined to choose Singapore as the destination for studying abroad or as a partner in forging educational links.

There are also more important attributing factors. The broadening and deepening political and economic ties are an important driving force behind the growing educational links between Singapore and China. The Joint Council for Bilateral Cooperation (JCBC), launched by then Singapore Prime Minister Goh Chok Tong and Chinese Premier Wen Jiabao in November 2003, functions as a high-level institutional mechanism to forge formal and personal ties and identify areas of collaboration. Under the JCBC framework structure are seven bilateral cooperation councils between Singapore and provincial governments.[59] These institutional mechanisms at the central and provincial levels have provided a useful platform to review not only political and economic ties but also educational exchanges and collaborations. Many of the university initiatives and collaborations between Singapore and Tianjin, or between Singapore and Suzhou, are facilitated by such institutional mechanisms.

Each of the two government-to-government flagship projects, Suzhou Industrial Park and Tianjin Eco-city, has an education component. The location of NUSRI in Suzhou, the first overseas research institute by a Singapore university, would not be possible without the groundwork already laid by the Sino-Singapore Suzhou Industrial Park. By the same token, NTU Tianjin College is feasible mainly because of the Sino-Singapore Tianjin Eco-city.

---

[57] Brenda SA Yeoh and Lin Weiqiang, "Chinese Migration to Singapore", pp. 31–54.

[58] Brenda SA Yeoh and Lin Weiqiang, "Chinese Migration to Singapore", pp. 31–54.

[59] John Wong and Catherine Chong, "The Political Economy of Singapore's Unique Relations with China", in *Advancing Singapore–China Economic Relations*, ed. Saw Swee-Hock and John Wong, Singapore, World Scientific, 2014, pp. 31–61.

The rise of China is another critical factor behind the establishment of the government-to-government flagship projects and the councils for bilateral cooperation between Singapore and China's central and provincial governments. From Singapore's perspective, China's economic rise, at an unprecedented pace and scale, is an opportunity not to be missed by Singapore. Singapore's participation in China's rise can bring benefits to Singapore. From China's perspective, Singapore is the epitome of good development model. A partnership with Singapore can help propel China's economic and social development. Both sides are convinced of the mutual benefits of cooperation and collaboration.

China's rise is indeed a key factor behind the growing educational exchanges and collaborations between the two countries. Recognising that China's rise can benefit Singapore, the Singapore government has emphasised the need for schools and universities to increase student awareness of China's rise through immersion trips, and lent support to initiatives that aim to prepare students for participation in China's development. It becomes pertinent to initiate exchanges and collaborations with Chinese universities because knowledge about China's business environment and market demands is essential for start-ups and for commercialisation of technologies. China's rise means a much larger education and training market for Singapore's education and training institutions, and also growing research resources for Singapore's research institutes and researchers based in China. In various ways, Singapore's education institutions are more willing to forge ties with Chinese partners because of China's emergence.

From China's perspective, Singapore has much to offer in terms of knowledge transfer and sharing. While that was the case in the 1990s, it remains the case today. From industrial park to eco-city and social management/governance, Singapore has been able to keep pace with China's changing needs. Taken from a long-term perspective, the rise of China and Singapore's ability to participate in China's rise have broadened and deepened political, economic and educational ties between the two countries.

The increasing educational exchanges and links between Singapore and China are not without complications, however. The growing presence of PRC nationals, including students, in Singapore "has not spelled their automatic acceptance, but has instead incited fresh social tensions and stereotypical associations".[60] There are complaints that some PRC students are using Singapore's reputed, English-medium education system as a springboard for more popular destinations, particularly the United States, without fulfilling

---

[60] Brenda SA Yeoh and Lin Weiqiang, "Chinese Migration to Singapore", pp. 31–54.

their service obligations in Singapore.[61] Furthermore, some "immersion" trips to Singapore, organised by commercial travel agencies, were quite disturbing and disruptive to the teaching and learning of the receiving schools. Under the pressure from students and teachers, Singapore government schools openly declared that they have refused to be a tour site hosting such "immersion" trips.[62] On the other hand, the sociocultural experiences of PRC "scholars" in Singapore are also complicated. The feeling of "privilege" is often a mixed feeling of "prejudice", as they "encounter certain local discourses of discrimination and exclusion", and of "predicament", as they "sometimes experience complex and conflicted feelings about being made Singapore's 'foreign talent'".[63]

Conclusion

Singapore and China have forged closer educational links at various levels and in different forms since the 2000s. Educational exchanges and collaborations have broadened and deepened to an extent that was unforeseeable in the 1980s or even the 1990s. While the global trend of growing internationalisation of education constitutes a conducive factor, the key factor is the unique political relationship forged by the top leadership of both sides that has paved the way for closer and mutually beneficial economic and educational links. Whether the two countries can maintain the momentum of collaboration down the road depends on how both sides can stay relevant to each other in a changing context where there is free open choice of regional and global players for partnership.

---

[61] Brenda SA Yeoh and Lin Weiqiang, "Chinese Migration to Singapore", pp. 31–54.

[62] See <http://www.scedugroup.com/news_show.php?tid=22&aid=59> (accessed 16 February 2015).

[63] Yang Peidong, "Privilege, Prejudice, Predicament", pp. 350–376.

Chapter 9

The Chinese Community: *Huashe* and its Contributions

LIM Tai Wei

This is a narrative, constructed chronologically and historically, on "soft" contributions by the Chinese community in Singapore from 1965 to 2015. "Soft" contributions encompass the intangibles such as culture, arts, education and identity formation. The Chinese community made extraordinary achievements in "hard" tangible contributions, particularly in the areas of economic development, investments, political events, diplomatic achievements, etc., which have been researched extensively. Together, the "soft" and "hard" aspects of Chinese contributions compose an eclectic picture of a dynamically-evolving *huashe* or Chinese community and their contributions to Singapore. Education, economy, arts and culture, afterlife traditions and food culture are the five themes covered in this historical survey of the Chinese community in Singapore.

Introduction

There are three salient points to take note when analysing the Chinese community (*huashe*) in Singapore. First, Singapore is a multicultural society and the primordial identity of Chinese ethnicity is subsumed under a broader identity of being Singaporean in the post-1965 generation. Second, Singapore is a migrant society, and the tapestry of the Chinese community in Singapore is therefore multilayered and has experienced successive waves of Chinese migration, with the older settlers and their offspring undergoing indigenisation and finally nativisation into local ways and lifestyles. Third, indigenisation of successive generations of Chinese Singaporeans means the exciting development of a cosmopolitan, nativised and hybridised culture that we now recognise as Singaporean. The discussion in this chapter is situated in the context of new migrants, local ethnic Chinese whose forefathers were migrants and most important of all, being Singaporeans. It is also a story of their contributions.

This chapter is a chronological and historical narrative of the period from 1965 to 2015, corresponding to the thematic focus of this book to celebrate Singapore's 50 years of independence. The author highlights the "soft" contributions made by the Chinese community — in other words, the intangibles such as culture, arts, education and identity formation. The author also juxtaposes the discussion with the "hard" tangible aspects of the Chinese community's contributions to Singapore in areas like economic development, investments, political events, diplomatic achievements, etc. Together, the "soft" and "hard" aspects of Chinese contributions present an eclectic picture of a dynamically-evolving *huashe* or Chinese community and their contributions to Singapore. This chapter is by no means comprehensive but offers a glimpse of the contributions made by an important segment of Singapore's society. Following the historical synopsis is a presentation of the historical survey of the Chinese community in Singapore in five identified themes: education, economy, arts and culture, traditions related to ancestral worship and food culture. These themes were selected to introduce an eclectic view of the community life of the Chinese community. They also highlight the continuities and discontinuities in traditions, customs and lifestyles of this community over the years with successive influx of migrants since the 19th century.

Historical background

This section, derived from the author's observation fieldwork on 28 January 2015 at the Nanyang Technological University Chinese Heritage Centre's (CHC) exhibition, entitled "Chinese More or Less — An Exhibition on Overseas Chinese Identity", will provide some essential backgrounder on the Chinese community in Singapore. The evolution of the Chinese community in Singapore is visually captured in this exhibition. The Chinese community with its waves of migrants had evolved into a society with various socio-economic groups. The first few waves of Chinese migration to Singapore included large numbers of labourers from China, known as "coolies". They arrived in waves from the second half of the 19th century to the Great Depression era.[1] Many of them lived in less desirable conditions in the colony. This is how Singapore's

---

[1] National Library Board, Singapore Infopedia, "Chinese Coolies", 2004, at <http://eresources. nlb.gov.sg/infopedia/articles/SIP_87_2004-12-15.html> (accessed 29 January 2015).

Urban Redevelopment Authority (URA) describes the living conditions of pre-war (World War II) Chinese settlers:

> As the population continued to grow, overcrowding, congestion and pollution became major problems. The area's residents had to share small cubicles with little sanitation, sagging walls, damp floors and rat infestations. Secret societies, gang crimes and prostitution and opium dens thrived.[2]

Single women from the Guangdong province also came to work in Singapore as *amahs* and *ma jie*s (female childcare providers, maids and general helpers) and they were sworn to single sisterhood, renouncing their rights to get married. The commentary at the CHC exhibition stated that their mass migration was the result of a slump in silk filatures in China. When these early pioneers arrived in Singapore, they established self-help organisations, secret societies and Chinese associations to lend support to each other. The parochial nature of these organisations can be seen in the way dialect groups gathered around their own kind in the new strange adopted lands of *Nanyang* (the "South Seas").

The Singapore Hainan Hwee Kuan. An example of native place-based Chinese associations that provided services for their fellow countrymen. Photo credit: Lim Tai Wei.

---

[2] Urban Redevelopment Authority (URA), "About Chinatown (includes Maxwell No. 38 and 89 Neil Road)", at <http://www.ura.gov.sg/uol/conservation/conservation-xml.aspx?id=CNTWN> (accessed 12 February 2015).

The stakeholder class

Prominent Chinese leaders in Singapore emerged in the late 19th century, having spotted economic opportunities as hardworking and visionary individuals. Some of them were featured in portraits at the CHC exhibition, including Lim Nee Soon (1879–1936), a local rubber and pineapple plantation owner, who later represented the Teochew community in Singapore. Another example of a pioneering *towkay* (tycoon or "big boss") elite was Tan Kah Kee (1874–1961) who was a Singapore-based rubber trader and philanthropist and a symbol of the *huaqiao* (or overseas Chinese) identity in Singapore as well as China.[3] Their pioneering contributions in building up their business empires were the "hard" tangible results evident in pre-independent Singapore's economic development. With wealth came political activism. For example, the shophouse at 51 Armenian Street, a stone's throw from the Peranakan Museum today or formerly Tao Nan School, was originally the site of the United Chinese Library opened by Dr Sun Yat-sen on 8 August 1910 to disseminate revolutionary ideas. Singapore became the site of fund-raising activities for many young Republican revolutionaries planning to overthrow the Qing dynasty regime.

With accumulated wealth, some wealthy Chinese community elites began to build ancestral properties in China, e.g. "Tiger Balm King" Aw Boon Haw's mansion in hometown Yongding, Fujian. From ties that bind to a cosmopolitan outlook on community life, the exhibition showed the gradual cosmopolitanisation of Chinese in Singapore as depicted in a photograph that featured a Chinese woman in European wear and high heels in the early 1900s (the source of this photo is National Archives of Singapore). Indeed, ladies led the fashion world and the exhibition also featured Rosalind Foo, a fashionable socialite in the Chinese Ladies' Association, who had a hand in planning charitable events in Singapore in 1954 (source: the Loke Wan Tho Collection, Cathay Organisation Holdings Ltd). This elite celebrity crowd probably represented the most successful and conspicuous members of the Chinese community.

Aside from Chinese high society and wealthy elite members who still maintain ties with Chinese culture or their hometown but have stakes in the success of Singapore, the earliest and most integrated segment of the Chinese community in Singapore are probably the Straits-born Chinese or the Peranakans. The Peranakans are a group of nativised Chinese within the Chinese community who have intermarried with locals or adopted the Southeast Asian culture and lifestyle. The following caption, recorded from the author's fieldwork in the

---

[3] To read more about Tan Kah Kee, see this seminal volume by Janet Salaff, Raymond Ch'u and Fred Ward, *The Memoirs of Tan Kah Kee*, Singapore, Singapore University Press, 1995.

Peranakan Museum in Singapore, elucidates the origins of the Baba, Straits Chinese or Peranakan community:

> The Baba community in Malacca can be traced back to at least the 17th century, when the city was under the colonial rule of the Portuguese and later the Dutch. When the British founded new colonies in Penang and Singapore at the turn of the 19th century, they invited the Malaccan Baba community to move to these vibrant new trading entrepots. These three communities became a wider Peranakan community known as the Straits Chinese or Straits-born Chinese.

A number of Peranakans navigated seamlessly between the Straits-born community and the Chinese community at large, including the Chinese entrepreneur elites. A prominent member of this community is Dr Lim Boon Keng (1869–1957), the first Chinese Queen's scholar from colonial Singapore. He was unusual as a Peranakan, being well-versed in Chinese cultural nuances, especially since the Straits-born Chinese generally have a cosmopolitan lifestyle and outlook that integrated and fused selected elements of the East and the West, including British, Malay and Chinese sources of influences. Some Peranakan houses, in a similar vein, manifest cosmopolitan design fusion of Chinese, Asian and European influences. A caption at the CHC's "Chinese More or Less" exhibition has aptly addressed the Baba identity as one "… which expressed itself in speech (Malay), food (Chinese and Malay mix), dress (of Malay inspiration) and material culture (Chinese architecture and household utensils given a local inflection)".

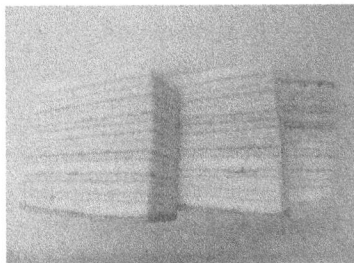

(Left) Typical tile designs that have come to be known as Peranakan-style in origins. These tiles are embedded in an old building dating back to 1925. Photo credit: Photo collection of Lim Tai Wei.

(Middle) *Kueh Lapis*, a confectionery that is associated with the Chinese Peranakans in Singapore or the Indonesian Chinese community. Photo credit: Photo collection of Lim Tai Wei.

(Right) The *otah* confectionery associated with Peranakan snack and dessert culture. Photo credit: Photo collection of Lim Tai Wei.

The author recommends readers who are interested to learn more about Chinese migration to read the important works written by Professor Wang Gungwu.[4] Professor Wang, chairman of East Asian Institute at the National University of Singapore, is the world's leading authority on overseas Chinese migration. Huang Jianli's important article on Professor Wang's contribution is probably the most informative summation of Wang's work in this area. Wang was born in Indonesia (then known as the Dutch East Indies before independence), raised in Malaysia (then known as Malaya before independence) and educated in Singapore for his tertiary studies so he is very much the symbol of overseas Chinese migration with an affinity for studying China:

> I did not set out to study the Chinese overseas. My interest was always in Chinese history. This is partly because I started life as a Chinese sojourner, a *huaqiao* [华侨], someone temporarily resident abroad. If circumstances permitted it, such a person would look foremost to China. I was no exception.[5]

Wang's seminal work on the Nanhai (South Seas) trade is considered to be the starting point of an entire subfield of research and teaching on Chinese migration. Huang puts it succinctly:

> In retrospect, this short but incisive account of Chinese abroad may be regarded as the defining moment of a "take-off" when Wang crafted a new sub-field of research and teaching within the broader framework of China studies, one which was centered on Chinese migration and settlements abroad.[6]

Wang's contribution to the field is immense and the space allocated in this articles does not do justice to the wide-ranging contributions he has made to the field. Hence, the author selectively mentions some of Wang's contributions. First, Wang, well-versed in the Chinese classics, set about defining the terminologies precisely that soon became important in overseas Chinese studies, including but not limited to "Nanyang Chinese", "Overseas Chinese" and

---

[4] For Wang Gungwu's seminal book on Chinese migration, see Wang Gungwu, *The Nanhai Trade: The Early History of Chinese Trade in the South China Sea*, Singapore, Times Academic Press, 1998.

[5] Huang Jianli, "Conceptualizing Chinese Migration and Chinese Overseas: The Contribution of Wang Gungwu", *Journal of Chinese Overseas*, vol. 6, 2010, p. 2, at <http://blogs.baruch.cuny.edu/hisaas4900/files/2014/01/Huang-on-Wang.pdf> (12 February 2015).

[6] Huang Jianli, "Conceptualizing Chinese Migration and Chinese Overseas", p. 3.

"*huaqiao*", using the principle of what Huang coins as the "rectification of names" (or *zheng ming*).[7] The year 1984 marked another milestone in Wang's contribution to the subfield. Huang noted that Wang had highlighted four Chinese waves of migration, beginning with the "*huashang*" (华商)/trader, made up of merchants and artisans; the "*huagong*" (华工)/coolie, including those who departed China from the 1850s to 1920s; the "*huaqiao*"/sojourner, who were nationalistically associated with the Chinese Republican revolution; and the "*huayi*" (华裔)/descent or re-migrant or the post-1950s movement of ethnic Chinese from one foreign country to another (all three categories except the fourth were used to analyse Singapore's Chinese community).[8] As Chinese migration to the rest of the world continued unabated, Singapore underwent a paradigm shift in 1963 when it became independent as part of Malaysia and in 1965 as a sovereign nation. An important political figure came into the picture when studying modern Singapore — that is, Singapore's first Prime Minister Lee Kuan Yew. Lee and his team had produced tangible and visible "hard" results of political activism in building modern Singapore's economy. It was a multiracial effort by the state-building pioneer generation, including the *huashe* which worked in tandem with others towards common goals.

Post-independence

Modern Singapore's founding father Lee Kuan Yew transformed Singapore from a colonial outpost with poor socio-economic conditions and underdeveloped infrastructure into a modern city after gaining independence (Singapore is celebrating its 50th year of independence at the time of writing). The transformation of Singapore under the leadership of Lee Kuan Yew, along with his old-guard political colleagues, had also changed the shape and form of the Chinese community in this newly-independent country. In post-independence Singapore from 1965 onwards, the introduction of modern freight transportation made the traditional role of Chinese "coolies" obsolete and they moved on to work as artisans, retail assistants and domestic helpers.[9] This marks a significant transformation from brute labour to semi-skilled and service industry jobs as Singapore embarked on industrialisation under the leadership of the then Prime Minister Lee's team.

---

[7] Huang Jianli, "Conceptualizing Chinese Migration and Chinese Overseas", p. 4.
[8] Huang Jianli, "Conceptualizing Chinese Migration and Chinese Overseas", pp. 8–9.
[9] National Library Board, Singapore Infopedia, "Chinese Coolies".

Nearly one and a half decades after independence, given the diversity of Chinese dialect groups in Singapore including those discussed earlier, the far-sighted government instituted the Speak Mandarin Campaign 1979 to create a lingua franca platform and enhance a sense of community among the different Chinese groups.[10] Younger generations of Singaporeans were able to speak Mandarin with each other and also interact with other Mandarin speakers in Taiwan and post-1979 China. This also fostered Singapore's business ties, migration and cultural exchanges in Mandarin with these locations. Mandarin became a unifier of the dialect groups within the Chinese community and enabled them to develop a common linguistic platform for communication and through interactions, develop a common mindset in understanding the vital issues faced in nation-building.

Succeeding the indigenous Chinese and older migrants in the 20th century, the discourse of Chinese migration to Singapore has been updated in the 21st century with regards to the new migrants arriving on the shores of Singapore. At the start of the normalisation of relations between Singapore and China at the non-governmental Track II level, the Singapore China Friendship Association (SCFA) was started by Ambassador Zhang Qing, the first Chinese envoy of the People's Republic of China (PRC) to Singapore in 1992, "to provide an alternative platform for communication and networking between the people of Singapore and China through various forms of economic cooperation as well as cultural exchange programs" and "to play a part in promoting Singapore as a friendly and open society, one that welcomes talents and makes our [SCFA] friends from China to feel right at home".[11] Associations like the SCFA and individuals from Singapore who reached out to their Chinese counterparts were representative of the visible and tangible Track II diplomatic contributions of the Chinese community in Singapore in improving relations bilaterally.

Contemporary Chinese migration

Almost a decade later, according to Leo Suryadinata, Singapore instituted an "open door" policy inviting talented overseas migrants including Chinese to

---

[10] Chong Hui-Hui Rachael and Tan Ying-Ying, "Attitudes toward Accents of Mandarin in Singapore", in *Chinese Language and Discourse*, John Benjamins Publishing Company, 2013, p. 122, at <http://www3.ntu.edu.sg/home/yytan/Tan_Ying_Ying/Publications_files/04cho.pdf> (accessed 10 February 2015).

[11] Singapore China Friendship Association (SCFA), "About Singapore China Friendship Association", at <http://www.singapore-china.org/about_ssfa_eng> (accessed 11 February 2015).

the island city, and so in 2000, there were 290,118 permanent residents (PRs) and 76.1% of them were Chinese ethnic.[12] According to a 2010 *CNN* article quoting the 2010 Singapore Census report, mainland Chinese migrants made up 8.8% of the overall population.[13] *The Wall Street Journal* explained the attractiveness and powerful draw of Singapore for mainland Chinese:

> It is safe and orderly. Wages for basic jobs are higher. And it comes with a degree of familiarity: The majority of Singaporeans are ethnic Chinese, whose ancestors started arriving in large numbers in the 1830s.[14]

Supporting the narrative of Singapore's attractiveness, in 2012, a survey by Bank of China and the wealthy elite-ranking *Hurun Report* named Singapore as "the third most desirable immigration destination" for rich Chinese after North America.[15] Most of the incoming non-elite migrants served the important role of support to Singapore's labour supply needs. In 2013, Singapore's Finance Minister Tharman Shanmugaratnam stated publicly in the budget for 2013 that foreign workers and immigrants made up more than one-third (33.6%) of the total workforce.[16]

While the earlier arrivals may have served the demand for affordable labour, the current arrivals may be contributing in another manner — i.e. boosting the low birth-rate in Singapore — besides parking wealth. The Singapore government noted in its white paper: "If we do too little to address the demographic challenge, we risk becoming a steadily graying society, losing vitality and verve,

---

[12] Leo Suryadinata, "Chinese Migration in the Globalizing World: A Brief Comparison between Developed and Developing Countries", Singapore, Nanyang Technological University (NTU) and Chinese Heritage Centre (CHC), 2009.

[13] Eddie Tee, "China Comes to Chinatown in Singapore", *CNN* website, 7 October 2010, at <http://travel.cnn.com/singapore/visit/bringing-back-china-chinatown-782334> (accessed 10 February 2015).

[14] "The Chinese Migrants Who Shocked Singapore: A WSJ Investigation", *The Wall Street Journal*, 26 August 2013, at <http://blogs.wsj.com/chinarealtime/2013/08/26/the-chinese-migrants-who-shocked-singapore-a-wsj-investigation/> (accessed 5 February 2015).

[15] Andrew Jacobs, "In Singapore, Vitriol against Chinese Newcomers", *The New York Times*, 26 July 2012, at <http://www.nytimes.com/2012/07/27/world/asia/in-singapore-vitriol-against-newcomers-from-mainland-china.html?pagewanted=all&_r=0> (accessed 5 February 2015).

[16] Palash Ghosh, "Singapore Seeks to Cut Quota on Foreign Workers amid Worries over Immigration, Rising Labor Costs", the *International Business Times* (Ibtimes) website, 26 February 2013, at <http://www.ibtimes.com/singapore-seeks-cut-quota-foreign-workers-amid-worries-over-immigration-rising-labor-costs-1103229> (accessed 12 February 2015).

with our young people leaving for opportunities elsewhere."[17] Brenda Yeoh and Lin Weiqiang's important article indicated that, for the Singapore government, migrants include new arrivals who contribute to the nation's economic growth and they could help mitigate declining birth rates that are likely to have long-term impact.[18]

To welcome the new migrants and let them settle in, Singapore has come up with innovative policies to ensure better integration. At the point of Yeoh and Lin's writing in 2013, the Singapore government set up a National Integration Council to encourage closer bonds between Singaporeans and new migrants and launched a Community Integration Fund to sponsor pro-integration projects up to S$200,000 (US$156,250).[19] There are also clubs initiated by PRC nationals such as Tian Fu Club (a Sichuanese social club) for integrating new migrants into Singapore's social fabric.[20] The presence of these clubs serve to integrate migrants better into mainstream Singaporean society while acting as a bridge between the newer arrivals and older generations of Singaporean Chinese. Describing the importance of migrants to a migrant society, Deputy Prime Minister Teo Chee Hean said:

> "Quite naturally, we expect that our new immigrants should adopt to our values and norms, and we get upset if they have not yet done so," he said, speaking in English, Singapore's lingua franca. "However, I do agree that we should not let recent reactions towards new immigrants and foreigners undo the good job that we have done in building a strong and cohesive society out of people from many lands."[21]

Investment guru Jim Rogers was also in favour of Singapore welcoming migrants: "… nearly everyone in Singapore is an immigrant or family of an immigrant … Lee Kuan Yew [Singapore's founding Prime Minister] is a

---

[17] Palash Ghosh, "Singapore Seeks to Cut Quota on Foreign Workers amid Worries over Immigration, Rising Labor Costs".

[18] Brenda SA Yeoh and Lin Weiqiang, "Chinese Migration to Singapore: Discourses and Discontents in a Globalizing Nation-State", *Asian and Pacific Migration Journal*, vol. 22, no. 1, 2013, p. 32, at <http://profile.nus.edu.sg/fass/geolinw/apmj2013v22n1art2.pdf> (accessed 30 January 2015).

[19] Brenda SA Yeoh and Lin Weiqiang, "Chinese Migration to Singapore", pp. 31–54.

[20] Brenda SA Yeoh and Lin Weiqiang, "Chinese Migration to Singapore", pp. 31–54.

[21] Andrew Jacobs, "In Singapore, Vitriol against Chinese Newcomers".

second-generation immigrant."[22] The same report noted that Chinese celebrity elites like Jet Li and Gong Li have also moved to Singapore.[23]

Besides attracting foreign talents and celebrity elites, intermarriages also form another avenue for the entry of new migrants. According to a report in *The New York Times*, many Chinese "successfully assimilate" and the Singapore government's figure in 2012 indicated that 30% of Singaporean marriages are between a native-born Singaporean and a foreigner, an increase of 23% over 2002.[24] Given the right opportunities, pro-integrationist associations and other forms of community help, economic incentives as well as the willingness on the part of new migrants to assimilate, the current influx of mainland Chinese migrants may resemble previous batches of former migrants integrating into the fabric of post-65 (post-independence) generations of Singaporeans. In other words, the current generation of Chinese migrants becomes less exceptional in their integration efforts into the main fabric of Singapore society and more normative in following the integration efforts of earlier generations of migrant Chinese detailed earlier.

The thematic sections below will examine five selected aspects of Chinese community's contributions to Singapore over the years, in the field of education, afterlife traditions, arts and culture, food culture and the economy. These five aspects are by no means comprehensive but serve to highlight sectors in Singapore where contributions to the main fabric of Singaporean society can be discerned easily. The five areas are part of the public sphere of the social and community life that resonates with the Singaporean identity.

Education

The author developed the content on education based on his fieldwork research conducted in the Chinese Heritage Centre (CHC) at Nanyang Technological University (NTU) on 28 January 2015. The information in this section is derived from an exhibition, entitled "Nantah Pictorial Exhibition", held at the auditorium of the Chinese Heritage Centre. An achievement by

---

[22] David Yin, "Singapore Needs Immigrants, Says Jim Rogers", *Forbes Asia*, 6 June 2013, at <http://www.forbes.com/sites/davidyin/2013/06/06/singapore-needs-immigrants-says-jim-rogers/> (accessed 12 February 2015).

[23] David Yin, "Singapore Needs Immigrants, Says Jim Rogers".

[24] Andrew Jacobs, "In Singapore, Vitriol against Chinese Newcomers".

the Chinese community in Singapore is the setting up of Nanyang University (Nantah) which was the first Chinese-medium university in Singapore. After its establishment, Chinese-language education in Nantah reached a milestone in 1965 when the Nanyang University Curriculum Review Committee, chaired by Professor Wang Gungwu, released the committee report on the reorganisation of Nantah, restructuring of salaries, and new course syllabus and calendar. In the following year, Nantah welcomed the initial batch of students from non-Chinese language streams and English became the dominant medium of instruction in the university. The spirit of volunteerism was strong on campus when Nantah undergraduates assisted with road construction at Lorong Dorao on 9 April 1967. Nineteen sixty-eight was an eventful year. The Department of Malay Studies was set up in 1968, drawing in Malay students in addition to Chinese undergraduates. In 1968, Minister for Education Ong Pang Boon publicly declared at the ninth convocation that the government would recognise the degrees issued by Nantah, another important milestone.

Perhaps the most important visitor received on campus was Prime Minister Lee Kuan Yew, who was invited by the History Society of Nantah on 21 July 1967 to give a talk to the staff and students of the university. On 11 August 1970, Prime Minister Lee Kuan Yew was invited for a second time by the History Society to present a lecture on "Nantah and Our Future" to the students. The campus also received other foreign dignitaries and distinguished scholars in the 1960s and 1970s. Nobel Laureate Professor Yang Chen Ning also visited the campus in 1967 and he was appointed as the University External Examiner for the 1970–1973 period.

On 19 February 1972, Queen Elizabeth II toured Nantah, escorted by Wee Cho Yaw, chairperson of the University Council. The Minister for Culture, Jek Yuen Thong, officiated the Nanyang University Art Museum on 21 July 1972. In the same eventful year, the campus was caught up in a pioneering feminist movement when, in late September 1972, some female Nantah undergraduates publicly threw *University Life*, a campus publication, into trash bins. One of the articles allegedly had content that was contradictory to women's progress. In 1978, Nantah developed a joint campus in Bukit Timah adopting a bilingual medium (English and Chinese) in order to measure up to the quality of graduates from the University of Singapore. Eventually, Nanyang University merged with University of Singapore in 1980 to become the National University of Singapore (NUS). The alumni rolls of Nantah graduates were eventually moved to Nanyang Technological University (NTU) in 1996. By then, the institution had fully matured and is now an internationally ranked varsity.

The Yunnan Garden of the Nanyang Technological University today. Photo credit: Lim Tai Wei, 28 January 2015.

Economy

In his fieldwork at the CHC exhibition, the author noticed a photograph of Singapore-based Oversea-Chinese Banking Corporation located in Xiamen, Fujian, one of the many enterprises that tapped into economic opportunities made possible by Deng Xiaoping's "reform and opening-up" policy. Since then, this has led to bilateral flow of investments. Wealthy investors from China also contributed to Singapore's property sector in 2013, topping the number of non-Singaporean purchasers of private property in Singapore from January to October 2013, and they have diversified their investment into industrial and commercial properties turning away from residential properties, despite the Singapore government's cooling-off measures.[25] Besides property investments, Chinese visitors and migrants also contribute to gentrification, revival, museumification and conservation of heritage and cultural sites related to the Chinese community. A case in point is Chinatown which has been widely featured in the international media.

---

[25] Channel Newsasia, "Foreign Buyers of Private Homes Mostly Mainland Chinese: Study", *Today*, 5 November 2013, at <http://www.todayonline.com/singapore/foreign-buyers-private-homes-mostly-mainland-chinese-study> (5 February 2015).

Chinatown — a platform for tourism and settlement

According to the Urban Redevelopment Authority (URA) of Singapore, a small Chinese community had already resided in the Chinatown's Maxwell Road and Neil Road area before the British colonial authorities marked it out for Chinese residential use. Chinatown has now become the largest conserved historic district in Singapore that is made up of Telok Ayer (1820s), Kreta Ayer (1830s), Tanjong Pagar (late 1880s) and Bukit Pasoh (early 1920s).[26] As part of Singapore's heritage legacy, Chinatown is another major promising site in attracting Chinese tourists. The commodification of Chinese heritage itself can be a source of tourism revenues and public intellectual interest. Chinatown, which is traditionally a stopover place of interest for Chinese tourists and locals alike, reflects changes in successive Chinese newcomers to Singapore. Some Singaporeans highlighted the mainland Chinese newcomers' contributions to local businesses and the small and medium-sized enterprises (SMEs) sector.

A *CNN* article dated 2010 on Singapore's Chinatown quoted a Singaporean's response to new shops and stalls in Chinatown run by newcomer migrants from China: "They go the extra mile for service," says Zedy Ng, a Singaporean designer who patronises a mainland Chinese-operated restaurant along New Bridge Road, "When I go to their restaurant during closing hours, they will wait for you instead of switching off some lights as a hint for you to leave."[27] *CNN.com* published this interesting article in 2010 to detail changes in contemporary Chinese migration and describe how southern dialects in Singapore's Chinatown like Cantonese, Hokkien, Teochew and local pidgin Mandarin have given way to mainland Chinese Mandarin,[28] adding to the diversity of previous generations of settled immigrants who mainly came from the southern part of China. Agreeing with this assessment, *CNN* quoted another Singaporean respondent, Tony Tan based in Joo Chiat Road: "In my opinion, the Singapore Chinatown of the future will take on a wider representation of what makes Chinese people Chinese. This will extend beyond the Singapore story of the early Chinese migrants."[29]

---

[26] Urban Redevelopment Authority (URA), "About Chinatown (includes Maxwell No. 38 and 89 Neil Road)", at <http://www.ura.gov.sg/uol/conservation/conservation-xml.aspx?id=CNTWN> (12 February 2015).

[27] Eddie Tee, "China Comes to Chinatown in Singapore".

[28] Eddie Tee, "China Comes to Chinatown in Singapore".

[29] Eddie Tee, "China Comes to Chinatown in Singapore".

(Left) Given the rich cultural tapestry of the Chinese community in Singapore, Chinese heritage has been showcased in institutions like Chinatown Heritage Centre for visitors and tourists visiting the location. Photo credit: Photo collection of Lim Tai Wei.

(Middle) Similarly the former Tao Nan School was converted into a Peranakan museum to preserve important artefacts and memories of the early Straits Chinese community. Photo credit: Lim Tai Wei.

(Right) The National University of Singapore's private Peranakan museum. The magnificently restored shophouse is a pristine showcase of Peranakan-style architecture and fixtures. Photo credit: Lim Tai Wei.

The Chinese Garden in Jurong which contains elements of local interpretation of Chinese landscaping traditions. But there are features of Singaporean innovations that include situating a Japanese Garden next to it and the ground in front of the Chinese Garden now being used by South Asian workers for cricket games. At the time of writing, the garden is undergoing a makeover that may introduce more Singaporean innovations into the garden space. Photo credit: Lim Tai Wei, 31 January 2014.

Other tourism sites in Singapore with Chinese cultural themes but indigenised with local features include the Chinese Garden.

Traditions related to ancestral worship

Besides educational achievements and heritage preservation, another major feature of the Chinese community in Singapore are traditional customs related to the afterlife rituals and ceremonies that are still in practice. In some ways, the traditional practice represents continuity in how Chinese community members religiously and ritually sent off deceased members of the family and then continue to pay their respects to the deceased in annual tomb-sweeping pilgrimage to the cemeteries or columbaria. For older generations of Singaporeans, it also represents the ties that bind as elderly Singaporeans visit their hometown for the symbolic act of ancestral worship. This practice, however, is becoming less ubiquitous with younger generations of Singaporeans who have firmer roots in Singapore and less attachment to ancestral or hometown native place. For most Chinese Singaporeans who still practise traditional rites of paying respects to their ancestors, the rituals are conducted mainly in Singapore itself. The local cemeteries, burial grounds and columbaria are important features of community life in this aspect.

Chinese burial grounds evolved from collective cemetery spaces in Singapore organised according to hometown ties. But the lack of space and issues of hygiene have motivated the authorities to rely on multiracial multistorey columbarium spaces as final resting spaces for the deceased in Singapore. A picture of a collective epitaph dated 1919 in the Pek San Teng cemetery can be found at the Chinese Heritage Centre exhibition on overseas Chinese coordinated by renowned overseas Chinese expert and journalist Lynn Pan. According to the explanatory caption, those who passed away without children may be buried in these collective graves. In the CHC exhibition, there are even maps of this cemetery printed for Cantonese immigrants with individual graves and places of burial marked out according to clan, ancestry, surname and native birthplace.

Tiong Bahru, where the author had done extensive fieldwork, used to be a cemetery for the Chinese Hokkien community in Singapore. "Tiong" in Hokkien dialect refers to "terminal end", or to "pass away". When the graves were removed in the first half of the 20th century, the Singapore Improvement Trust (SIT), a public housing agency administered by the British colonial government, built art deco-style (specifically a form of late art deco movement known as "streamline moderne") public housing in the Tiong Bahru area, which still survives to this day as one of the world's largest intact and well-preserved art deco-design public housing heritage. This area embodies the cosmopolitanism

(Left) Ancestral worship continues to be a point of continuity for Chinese Singaporeans as the Taoists and Buddhists among them make offerings to the deceased on special occasions. A piece of Cantonese sponge cake (*fa-gao*) as well as mandarin oranges are used as offerings. Photo credit: Photo collection of Lim Tai Wei.

(Right) Offerings to the deities of *Fu* (prosperity), *Lu* (status) and *Shou* (longevity) are placed alongside ancestral tablets in some Chinese Singaporean families. The ancestral tablet is not shown in the picture. Photo credit: Photo collection of Lim Tai Wei.

(Left) Traditional ancestral worship and Taoist offerings made outside the home of a Chinese Singaporean family in an art deco-inspired (streamline moderne) housing estate. The fusion of traditions and a modernist design movement here exemplifies the hybridised metropolitan Singaporean culture. Photo credit: Photo collection of Lim Tai Wei.

(Right) A typical Taoist funeral arrangement set up at the void deck of a Housing Development Board (HDB) block of flats. This funeral setup was completed before the arrival of the family, priests and the coffin. Photo credit: Photo collection of Lim Tai Wei.

of Singaporean Chinese social history that witnessed how an early Chinese community burial ground was transformed into a colonial-era estate that encapsulates elements of Western architectural design and eventually into a nostalgic retro bohemian neighbourhood which still contains elements of indigenised and hybridised East-West fusion cultures (an art deco movement-inspired architectural style integrated with objects of worship related to Taoist deities and ancestral tablets).

Arts and culture

The sustainability of traditional Chinese cultural practices in Singapore is also reinforced by successive waves of Chinese migrants. That the celebratory atmosphere of the Chinese Lunar New Year festivities, observed as a public holiday in Singapore, continues to be kept alive is a good example. It is also during the Lunar New Year period when Chinese cultural traditions are most visible with lion dances, light-ups in the Marina Bay and Chinatown areas. Many households and public spaces display Lunar New Year decorations. The consumption of certain foods and fruits, such as pomelos and the indigenous dish of *lo hei*, becomes a common experience. These are all hallmarks of the Singaporean Chinese community life and experiences that greet both established and new migrants alike. The Chinatown light-up for the year of goat began on 31 January 2015 and featured goat-shaped lanterns displayed extensively along the main thoroughfare of the Chinatown. The festive atmosphere is further enhanced by elements of Singapore's old established indigenous foodstuffs on sale like the iconic Lim Chee Guan and Bee Cheng Hiang barbequed pork jerky and restaurants serving the indigenous Chinese New Year dish *lo hei*, alongside confectionery sold by Koi Kee (a well-known Macanese bakery) and new migrant food cultures such as north-eastern Chinese dishes (*dongbei cai*) and Shaanxi noodles and buns.

(Left) Traditional lion dance is performed during the Chinese Lunar New Year festivities. Photo credit: Photo collection of Lim Tai Wei.

(Right) The Chinese Lunar New Year light-up in Singapore's Chinatown in the year of the horse in 2014. Photo credit: Photo collection of Lim Tai Wei.

(Left) The pineapple décor, a Nanyang-style Lunar New Year decoration that is a play on homophones. "*Wong lai*" in Cantonese means "pineapples" or "the arrival of prosperity". Sometimes, the pineapple is turned topsy-turvy to literally mean "the arrival of prosperity" given that the homophone "*dao*" can mean "arrival" or "turned upside down". Photo credit: Photo collection of Lim Tai Wei.

(Right) There are foodstuff commonly consumed by all dialect groups in Singapore. For example, mandarin oranges and pomelos are popular fruits consumed during the Lunar New Year regardless of dialect groups. Photo credit: Photo collection of Lim Tai Wei.

From traditional culture to cosmopolitanism

Besides traditional practices, Chinese arts and cultural contributions in Singapore are visible in the form of hybridised fusion of modern and contemporary art works. The influx of Chinese cosmopolitan culture from other Chinese-speaking societies such as Hong Kong, Taiwan and Macau is also visible in Singapore. Singapore becomes a melting pot of cultural influences combining those of Greater China with local Singaporean cultural traits as well as new incoming cultural practices by new Chinese migrants to create a hybridised cosmopolitan atmosphere. Cross-pollination process between these three sources of Chinese culture is in the arena of popular culture. Chong and Tan's paper on Chinese accents (including Taiwanese Mandarin or TM) highlights the soft cultural influence of Taiwanese-accented Mandarin on Singaporeans through Taiwanese popular culture (*Tai liu*):

> The Chinese pop culture in Singapore is heavily reliant on the pop culture in Taiwan. Taiwanese variety shows and dramas are constant features in the local free-to-air Chinese TV channels. In addition, foreign shows (e.g. Korean, Japanese and Hong Kong) which require Mandarin dubbing are acquired from Taiwan, which means that they would have been dubbed over in TM. TM is a

variety that is not only familiar to Singaporeans, but can be said to be one that is heard most frequently.[30]

Besides linguistic influence through Singaporean youths' consumption of Taiwanese popular cultural products, Singaporeans are also exposed to internationally renowned works of art by Taiwanese artists. In other words, Singaporean acceptance of Chinese culture is all-inclusive (mainland or Greater China) of migrants who can contribute to the country's cultural scene and not exclusive only to certain class, creed, ethnic group of Chinese migrants.

In January 2015, a public space exhibition of sculptures by Taiwanese rock sculptor Ju Ming was on display at the Singapore Botanic Gardens. Photo credit: Photo collection of Lim Tai Wei.

Food

Perhaps one of the most long-lasting and strongest Chinese cultural influences on Singapore's social fabric is the culinary cuisine that the Chinese community has brought to the dining tables of Singaporeans. The Singaporean Chinese food identity is reinforced by local eating habits, lifestyles and customs. Singaporeans are increasingly delighted by the growing choices of Chinese dishes. The original southern cuisines familiar to older migrants are commonplace in Singapore,

---

[30] Chong Hui-Hui Rachael and Tan Ying-Ying, "Attitudes toward Accents of Mandarin in Singapore", p. 123.

particularly the Cantonese (*Yue*), Teochew (*Chaozhou*) and Hokkien (*Minnan-Fujian*) dishes. Singapore has been an innovation centre of Chinese-originated food even from the days of early migrants. Hainanese chicken rice, *lo hei*, Hainanese curry rice are some examples of the early indigenous Singaporean Chinese dishes with strong Nanyang flavour. This is how National Library Board's Singapore Infopedia characterised the *yusheng* dish which is central to the ritualistic act of *lo hei* (the action of tossing the salad vegetables high while uttering "Huat Ah!" to herald prosperity and luck for all at the dining table):

> Today's colourful version of *yusheng* and the practice of eating it on the seventh day of Chinese New Year appear to be unique to Malaysia and Singapore. Four local chefs are credited for developing *yusheng* as we know it today. They named the dish "Lucky Raw Fish" and popularised it as a new-year delicacy. The chefs are Lau Yeok Pui and Tham Yui Kai, master chefs at Lai Wah Restaurant along Jalan Besar, and their good friends Sin Leong and Hooi Kok Wai.[31]

(Left) Another local innovation — Hainanese toasted bread with *kaya* (coconut and egg jam) spreads. Although normally associated with the Hainanese community in Singapore, this is a Nanyang Southeast Asian food innovation, probably not originated from or found on Hainan Island but developed in Singapore and Malaysia through the *kopitiam* (coffee-shop) culture that was associated with the Hainanese community in Singapore. These photos were taken by the author in different settings. The photo was taken in a Singaporean coffee shop or *kopitiam*.

(Middle) Hainanese curry rice, a dish in Singapore that may not be found in this exact form on Hainan Island, China. It is a good example of Nanyang-style Chinese food. Photo taken at the author's residence featuring a Hainanese curry takeaway.

(Right) Hainanese chicken rice, an indigenous Singapore dish that was developed by Hainanese settlers to Singapore and attributed to Hainan Island in name only, based on their adaptation and imagination of culinary culture in China. Photo taken at the author's residence with the dishes made by his family member. Photo credit: Photo collection of Lim Tai Wei.

---

[31] National Library Board, Singapore Infopedia, "Yusheng", 2015, at <http://eresources.nlb.gov.sg/infopedia/articles/SIP_177__2009-01-08.html> (accessed 12 February 2015).

(Left) *Zhui kueh*, a type of rice cake with pickled vegetables normally associated with the Hokkien culinary culture in Singapore. Photo credit: Photo collection of Lim Tai Wei.

(Right) *Kuay chup*, another Hokkien-inspired rice noodle usually consumed with stewed bean curds, egg and pig intestines. Photo credit: Photo collection of Lim Tai Wei.

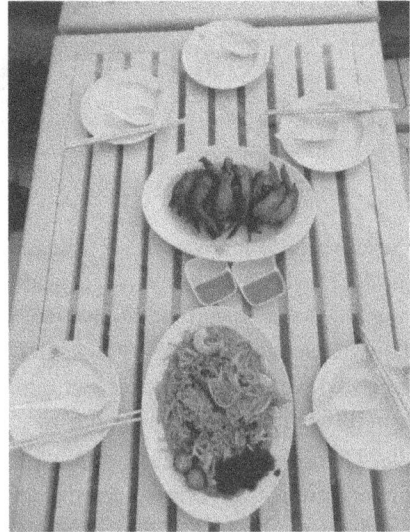

(Left) *Chai tow kueh*, a Hokkien-style fried carrot cake that has become the mainstay of Singaporean Chinese dishes in hawker centres and food courts. Photo credit: Photo collection of Lim Tai Wei.

(Right) This photo was taken at an outdoor alfresco dining place popular with Singaporeans at the Marina Bay area. Hokkien *mee* has become a mainstay of Chinese-originated noodle dish in Singapore with a local Southeast Asian Nanyang innovation of *belacan* chilli commonly used in Malay or Peranakan cooking. This exemplifies cosmopolitanism of the Chinese in Singapore. Photo credit: Photo collection of Lim Tai Wei.

(Left) Teochew *bak chor mee*, a noodle dish popular with Singaporeans. Photo credit: Photo collection of Lim Tai Wei.

(Middle) A Teochew seafood fish maw dish in claypot. Photo credit: Photo collection of Lim Tai Wei.

(Right) *Soon kueh*, a popular breakfast and snack item. Photo credit: Photo collection of Lim Tai Wei.

(Left) Cantonese egg tarts — a popular item that is the quintessential Singapore dim sum experience.

(Right) Cantonese *chee cheong fun* rice rolls — a popular breakfast food in Singapore.

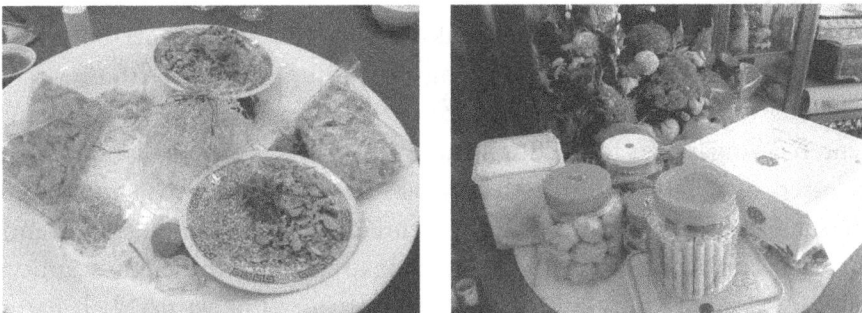

(Left) *Lo hei*, a salad-like dish eaten in Singapore and Malaysia during the Lunar New Year. Added into the mixture of vegetable-based ingredients are smoked salmon or raw fish slices.

(Right) The tradition of eating Lunar New Year titbits and snacks, such as spicy prawn rolls and other local confectionery, is kept alive in Singapore.

(Left) *Tudousi* or potato strips, a characteristic north-eastern Chinese dish, has appeared in menus of eateries run by new Chinese migrants and also gained gradual acceptance by Singaporeans willing to try new cuisines and delight their palates.

(Right) *Shouzhua yangrou* or hand-held grilled lamb ribs is characteristically a Sichuanese cuisine but has found its way into *dongbei* (north-eastern Chinese) dining menus. This is a relatively new dish introduced by chefs and restauranteurs who are among the new Chinese migrants making inroads into the culinary culture of Singaporeans. Their businesses are patronised by new Chinese migrant customers as well as Singaporeans alike.

Besides local innovations of Chinese dishes, Hong Kong and Taiwanese culinary trends have also added to the existing choices, offering the likes of the *chacaanteng* culture (local neighbourhood Cantonese-style restaurants and cafes) from Hong Kong and the snack culture from Taiwanese Shilin night market which can be found in Singapore's mall spaces. The diversity of choices is further reinforced by dishes introduced by new migrants from north-eastern China such as *dongbei cai* and Shaanxi noodles and bun. Food culture has therefore become a barometer of cultural cosmopolitanism in the melting pot of Singapore.

Different groups of Chinese-speaking societies have contributed to the wide variety of Chinese cuisines on Singapore dining tables. With the arrival of Hong Kong immigrants before and after 1997, Hong Kong's popular cuisines also entered Singapore's food courts and eating spots. The popular Hong Kong-style dessert or *tongshui* culture that has infiltrated Singapore's shopping malls is one such example. Besides local interpretations of Chinese foods and the imported Hong Kong street food, the Singaporean Chinese community also developed its own indigenous culinary culture. The *lo hei* dish eaten by Singaporeans to herald the Chinese New Year with shouts of "Huat Ah!" (to prosper) festive greeting exemplifies a Chinese cuisine with local Singaporean identity.

Conclusion

Singaporeans have expressed a spectrum of views in the mass media about migrants in general — ranging from critical and negative views to positive and sympathetic opinions. But, arising from a cacophony of diverse views, moderate and rationale voices appear to be more dominant. Singaporeans have reacted against anti-foreignism emanating from certain segments of society over the past few years since 2011. Michael D Barr, who authored a book on Singapore's ruling elite, makes the following argument at the *East Asia Forum*:

> … it is a credit to Singaporeans that their reactions to foreigners have not been more uniformly hostile: there does at least appear to be an emerging level of sympathy both at the elite and grassroots levels for the plight of temporary low-paid foreign workers.[32]

Singapore has always been a migrant society. A media narrative in *The International Business Times* pointed out that in multicultural Singapore, definitions like "natives" and "immigrants" are "rather fluid" since the majority Chinese are "… themselves the descendants of immigrants from China".[33] Historically, migrants have contributed to the workforce of large multinational companies, providing affordable and hardworking labour supply for an FDI-dependent (foreign direct investment) economy. The *Voice of America* quotes the response of an anonymous Singaporean living overseas about contemporary Chinese migration: "Singapore has always been a migrant society, and its economy is built on meritocracy of opportunities. The influx of expatriates or migrant workers is not a negative development."[34] It will take some more efforts of the older generations of Chinese Singaporeans, whose forefathers came from China, to work with new Chinese migrants and find a point of compromise and equilibrium for optimal integration.

---

[32] Michael D Barr, "Singapore's Impotent Immigration Policy", East Asia Forum, 2 April 2014, at <http://www.eastasiaforum.org/2014/04/02/singapores-impotent-immigration-policy/> (accessed 12 February 2015).

[33] Palash Ghosh, "Singapore Seeks To Cut Quota On Foreign Workers Amid Worries Over Immigration, Rising Labor Costs".

[34] Yong Nie, "Mainland Chinese Drawn to Singapore, Tensions Follow", Voice of America, 10 October 2011, at <http://www.voanews.com/content/mainland-chinese-drawn-to-singapore-tensions-follow-131562633/168095.html> (10 February 2015).

Chapter 10

Singapore's Media Image in China

HUANG Yanjie and ZHAO Lingmin

In official and popular media in China, Singapore has a presence much larger than its territorial size. The official media is most interested in what lessons China could draw from Singapore in a variety of policy-related domains, such as providing public housing, managing social stability, maintaining clean government and effective governance, and party-building of the ruling People's Action Party. Official reports and analyses have become more focused in content and rational in tune. The locus of popular media has shifted to travel writings, pop music and more recently, encounters of tourists and sojourners. Singapore's image in popular media has become more diverse and more realistic than in the past.

Singapore's media image in China: two diverging views

China's media can be divided into two spheres: the official media which is tightly controlled by the state and reflecting its views, and the highly regulated popular media which reflects more closely the prevailing social consciousness. The former covers China's news agencies, major magazines, most state television programmes and a larger part of social science literature; the latter includes movies, songs, TV dramas, popular literature and the internet. In order to understand Singapore's media image in China, we need to make a distinction between these two spheres since they often work on different principles and thus produce different images of Singapore.

The image of Singapore on the official media is relatively stable. Since Deng Xiaoping's official trip to Singapore in late 1978, the official media has focused on the Singapore model and its usefulness for China in the reform era.[1] Certain aspects of Singapore, which are of policy interest to the Chinese government such as public housing, social management, political system and clean government become the most common and recurrent themes for the state newspapers, magazines and most scholarly works on Singapore. While the reports and analyses have kept pace with Singapore's development and China's growing knowledge about Singapore, the themes and some basic judgements have remained unchanged over decades.

On the other hand, the popular media displayed changing perspectives of Singapore. From the earliest interest in Singapore's TV dramas to the proliferation of numerous travelogues and migrant writings on the internet, the image of Singapore in Chinese popular media has become far more complex, realistic and divergent over the last two decades. The changing vantage points and resultant views also tend to reflect a more comprehensive, albeit shifting focus on Singapore in the popular media. Currently, Chinese popular knowledge and perception of Singapore has moved far beyond policy domains such as public housing and clean government, to encompass areas like Singaporean culture and life experiences.

The clear division between the two spheres has made the characterisation of Singapore's image in China a rather difficult task since neither the official nor the popular media has provided the full picture. The official view has so far proved to be more stable, clearer but limited in scope, whereas the popular view, though covering more diverse themes, tends to register a motley collection of changing images and impressions. The two spheres, though structurally and functionally divided, could interact with and impact each other. This paper will thus delve into both spheres before making a synthesis of Singapore's overall image in China over the years.

In the discussion that follows, we will sketch the ways Singapore has been represented in Chinese media, either through the lens of official reports or the transmission of popular culture and personal experiences. In general, the overall media image of Singapore in China is positive. Over the years, it has gradually transformed from a rigid, simplistic and sometimes idealised image to a more complex, detailed, nuanced and realistic one.

---

[1] Before Deng's visit, the official media portrayed Singapore as lackeys of the Americans. Only after Deng's visit in 1978 did Singapore's media image become more positive. The year 1978 is a watershed since it marks the shift in China's domestic and international priorities from ideological-based political struggles to more pragmatic doctrines of reform and opening door.

Singapore in China's official media

Under China's current media regulation and news system, reports on Singapore fall under international news. Major sources of reports in this category include The *Reference News* (*Cankao Xiaoxi*) under *Xinhua News Agency*, *International Herald News, Global Times* under the *People's Daily,* and current affair magazines *The Globe* and *World Knowledge* under the Ministry of Foreign Affairs.

Most Chinese newspapers and magazines focus on domestic events, with international news reports occupying only a secondary position. Within the international news coverage, most space is given to major world powers like the United States, Europe, Russia and Japan. In terms of the number and frequency of reports, Singapore is not featured prominently in China's media reports.

However, Singapore could be said to be one of the most frequently reported countries in mainland Chinese media among the smaller countries. There has been a tradition of over-reporting on Singapore relative to its size in the Chinese news media since the early 1990s.

During the reform period, Singapore made its first appearance in the Chinese official media in the late 1970s, particularly after Deng Xiaoping made his historical trip to Singapore in November 1978.[2] In the following year, the *People's Daily* published a few short pieces on Singapore. On 1 April 1979, it published an article titled, *The Beauty of Greening in Singapore.* The article praised Singapore as a beautiful garden city and urged China to model its city development on Singapore.[3] On 6 December 1979, another article briefly reviewed Singapore's housing development and again lauded it as one of the best in the developed world.[4]

In 1992, during Deng Xiaoping's historic Southern Tour, he famously commented that Singapore has a well-regulated and well-ordered economy and society and urged Chinese officials to learn from Singapore.[5] Since the Southern

---

[2] As noted earlier, the pre-reform image of Singapore was a running-dog of the imperialistic power of the United States. However, in this period, Singapore was not frequently reported in the official media. Only after 1978 did news reports on Singapore begin to increase dramatically.

[3] "The Beauty of Greening in Singapore", *People's Daily* (Online Version), 1 April 1979.

[4] "Singapore's HDB Development", *People's Daily* (Online Version), 6 December 1979.

[5] Deng Xiaoping, Speech at the Southern Tour, *Selected Works of Deng Xiaoping*, Beijing, Central Literature Press, vol. 3, 1997.

Tour, Singapore has become a brand name in China, attracting the attention of Chinese government officials at both central and local levels.

In the two decades of reform since 1992, Singapore has been the only country which the Chinese government has consistently looked up to as a role model for China's development.

Singapore's experience is particularly pertinent to China because the People's Action Party (PAP), as the single ruling party in Singapore for five decades, has always been successful in running an efficient and clean government and achieving a harmonious and well-managed society. Chinese social elites, especially the intellectuals and government officials, are particularly interested in Singapore's development experience.

Although the number and frequency of reports on Singapore are limited, the attention it attracts and the influences it has on the Chinese media and society are enormous. Furthermore, the internet-based media eagerly circulate and reproduce news reports on Singapore from printed sources.

Based on these news reports, Chinese intellectuals and officials are eager to find in Singapore's image, China's own shortcomings and ways to rectify these shortcomings through relevant policy measures.

In China's print media, five areas on Singapore have particularly attracted media attention and provided most themes and topics of discussion, namely, Singapore's social management and social policy, the Housing and Development Board (HDB) system, the administrative system with efficiency and probity of public officials as its core values, the PAP and finally, China–Singapore relations.

Singapore's social management system

Singapore has been featured most prominently in China's policy discourse on social management in recent years. The policy agenda of strengthening social construction and perfecting the social management system was first brought up at the Fifth Plenary Session of the 16th Party Congress of the Chinese Communist Party (CCP). Since then social management has become one of the most frequently mentioned terms in China's policy discourse. In the view of the Chinese print media, Singapore is synonymous with a harmonious society; reports and discussions on Singapore's social management system has thus become a hot topic in the Chinese media.

On 26 February 2008, *Shenzhen Special Zone Daily* (*Shenzhen Tequbao*), one of the most influential policy-oriented newspapers in China, published an article by Lü Yuanli, China's leading expert on Singapore, titled, *How Singapore Manages Society*. This article made a scholarly discussion of Singapore's social management model. In his arguments, Lü subdivided the Singapore model into four dimensions: political, economic, cultural management and measures. Politically, the Singapore model is a democracy plus *minben* policy (care for people's livelihood) or a trusteeship model of democracy. Economically, it is a mix of Confucian and Adam Smith, namely, free market coupled with Confucianist work ethics, robust strategic planning and active interventions. In terms of cultural management, the Singapore model embraces both the principles of responsibilities and spirit of freedom. In terms of measures, the Singapore government is a strong government and its leadership is often referred to as strongman leadership. However, in terms of work style, Singapore's management is guided by pragmatic rationalism.[6]

Lü's article is widely read and circulated in China. In many ways, the article is representative of the consensual perception of Singapore's management model in China's senior official and intellectual circles.

While Lü's article outlined some of the fundamental concepts of Singapore's social management and development model in Chinese public policy discourse, more recent reports focused on the specific cases and implementation details in Singapore's social policies and even Singapore's current challenges. On 12 June 2012, the official *Xinhua News Agency* published a report on Singapore's experience in forging social solidarity. In this article, the author laid out the many social problems that the Singapore government faced around the time of its independence, such as ethnic conflicts, neighbourhood estrangement and the waning of family values.

The article argues that Singapore's success in dealing with these problems is based on a range of effective policy measures, such as the designing of the family-based HDB system, educational programmes based on the principles of equality and nation-building and grass-roots community-building projects among many others. In this report as in many others, the Singapore model tends to be portrayed and perceived as a set of concrete measures rather than a general strategy.[7]

Compared with other Chinese provinces, Guangdong is perhaps one of the earliest and best students of the Singapore model. As one of China's industrial

---

[6]Lü Yuanli, "How Singapore Manages Society", *Shenzhen Special Zone Daily*, 26 February 2008.

[7]Zeng Peng, "How Does Singapore Promote Social Solidarity and Its Lessons for China", *Xinhua News Agency*, 12 June 2012.

hubs, Guangdong is particularly keen on borrowing Singapore's experience in labour management. As such, Guangdong's provincial official media are among the most attentive to developments in Singapore and its potential exemplary effect on China.

In June 2012, the then Guangdong party secretary and now Vice Premier Wang Yang made a trip to Singapore with the specific objective of studying Singapore's social management. This trip received high-profile coverage in *Guangzhou Evening*, the official newspaper of the Guangdong Provincial Party Committee. The report cited Lim Swee Say, Singapore's minister in the Prime Minister's Office and secretary-general of the National Trade Union Congress, as saying that the majority of the 1,600 labour disputes arising each year in Singapore were resolved without resorting to third-party arbitrage. Due to efficient mechanisms for resolving labour dispute, strikes have been a rare occurrence in Singapore since the 1970s. The report also argued that the uniquely harmonious labour-capital relations are core to Singapore's competitiveness. Echoing Wang Yang's policy directives, the article urged Chinese officials to learn from the Singapore experience in protecting the legal rights of employees and establishing tri-party mechanisms among the government, trade union and enterprises, thus creating an institutional environment for harmonious labour relations.[8]

More recent reports on Singapore's social management have also focused on Singapore's legal and institutional environment that is conducive to good social management. On 17 September 2011, *Xiaoshan Daily*, official paper of the Xiaoshan city government which has substantial economic cooperation with Singapore, published an extensive investigative article on Singapore's social management titled, *Singapore: Model of Efficient Social Management*.[9] The author highlights that a small country like Singapore owns the world's best airline, second largest harbour and third largest petrol refining hub. The author provides a comprehensive view of China's perception of Singapore's social management. The article sought to uncover the reasons behind the success, singling out four principal institutions, namely, the "Meet-The-People-Session for all Members of Parliament", recruitment of social elites into civil service, zero-tolerance for corruption and the principle of the rule of law. [10]

Social management has become the prime focus of Chinese reports on Singapore and its influence is not limited to the print media. Singapore's social

---

[8] "Learning from Singapore's Social Management", *Guangzhou Evening*, 7 June 2012.
[9] Peh Shing Huei and Kok Kian Beng, "Revelation of the Lion City: China Documentary Find What Makes Singapore Tick", *The Straits Times*, 28 October 2012.
[10] "Singapore: Model of Efficient Social Management," *Xiaoshan Daily*, 17 September 2012.

management has always been a favourite topic among China's reform-minded elites, such as senior officials and intellectuals.

Singapore's housing development

Since the commercialisation of housing in mid-1994, rising housing price has always been a central locus of China's social conflicts. Following the global financial crisis of 2008, rapidly rising housing prices in large cities have become one of the most contentious issues in Chinese society, especially among the younger generation.

The government's visible hand in pushing up housing price and the laggard supply of welfare housing are particularly attracting public censure. In comparison, Singapore's HDB system has drawn much attention and applause from the Chinese media.

On 17 September 2010, *Eastern Guardian*, a local newspaper under the official Party paper *Nanjing Daily* published an extensive report on Singapore's HDB system titled, *Singapore's HDBs: Price Comparison Makes Me Cry*. The article uses examples of Singaporean households to make its point. For a couple family with a monthly household salary of S$2,500, a three-room flat of about S$200,000–300,000 is quite a bargain. This is especially true when a Chinese couple have to pay a similar if not higher price for a flat of similar size in Shanghai or Beijing while they earn less than half the income of an average Singaporean. The article also praises the Build-to-Order system as a mechanism of efficient allocation. The Chinese system, which offers subsidised housing to a few socially privileged, was regarded as exploitative and unequal.[11]

On 26 September 2011, *Hainan Daily*, the official party newspaper of Hainan province, published a substantial article on the HDB system. The long article laid out many aspects of the HDB system, ranging from inception, related government regulations, criteria and method of purchase to the repair and renovation of the flat. The article commends the HDB system as a project for both national development and social solidarity and in accordance with the Confucius social vision of homeownership for all residents.[12]

On 13 November 2011, China's official *Xinhua News Agency* published on its website another thought-provoking piece article on the HDB system. Like all previous Chinese reports, this article highlights the extremely high rate of

---

[11] "Singapore's HDBs: Price Comparison Makes Me Cry", *Eastern Guardian*, 17 September 2012.
[12] "The Housing Utopian Comes to True", *Hainan Daily*, 17 September 2011.

homeownership in Singapore and the various aspects of the HDB system. In the light of the Chinese real estate bubble, this article highly appraises the HDB system as an effective social policy for putting social considerations before pure economic reasoning.[13]

Singapore's clean government in the Chinese media

That the Singapore government is clean and efficient is one of the most salient aspects of Chinese perception of Singapore. However, what makes it even more relevant for the Chinese central government is the fact that this high level of efficiency and cleanness has been achieved even though the PAP has been Singapore's ruling party since 1959. This is highly relevant for the CCP, which has been in power for 60 years but is unable to run a similarly clean government since its economic reform.

Guangdong is again at the forefront of Chinese media report on the Singaporean experience in clean government. On 14 December 2004, a *Guangzhou Evening* article praised Singapore as the exemplary model of clean government in Asia. In this article, a detailed account of Singapore's anti-corruption campaign was provided and the gist of Singapore's strategy in fighting corruption was summarised as a combination of the rule of law and high salaried officials, a system that has evolved over many years.

A year later, *China Youth Daily*, the official paper of the Communist Youth League, published a scholarly article by Cai Dingjian on Singapore's anti-corruption system. Cai was a visiting scholar at the East Asian Institute of the National University of Singapore for three months. A legal scholar by training, Cai made extensive field studies on Singapore's political and civil service system during his three-month stay. In an article based on empirical evidence, Cai argued against the conventional view that attributed Singapore's clean government to high salary for top officials. In his view, high salary for its senior officials is primarily a strategy to attract talents from the private sector and not a strategy to control corruption. Singapore's clean government is rooted in the fact that no country in the world has held clean government in higher regard than in Singapore.[14]

---

[13] "Singapore's HDB System as Social Policy", *Xinhua News Agency*, 13 November 2011.

[14] Cai Dingjian, "What Can China Learn from Singapore", *China Youth Daily*, 9 November 2005.

A few years later, in October 2008, one of China's top experts on Singapore, Lü of Shenzhen University contributed an article, *Learn from Singapore's Experience in Building Corruption-free Government*, in *Shenzhen Special Zone Daily*. This article outlines Singapore's formula for clean government as having four pillars, namely, the core value of clean government, policy of high salary, rule of law and anti-corruption regulations.[15]

The scholarly views of Lü and Cai found resonance in a reflective article by Zhu Mingguo, deputy party secretary of Guangdong, written after his trip to Singapore and published in the *Study Times*, official paper of the Party School of the Communist Party of China. In this article, Zhu sang praises of Singapore's independent anti-corruption agency, rule of law and core value of clean government, while conceding that high salary is a policy for recruiting top talents rather than preventing corruption.[16]

Following official reports on Singapore's clean government, more and more detailed accounts of Singapore's anti-corruption experiences began to appear in China's mainstream print media. In an article published by *Huaxia Times*, a renowned financial paper based in Beijing, the author focuses on analysing the details of the laws and regulations on corruption, and their effectiveness. The article especially contrasted the '55-year Phenomenon' in China, namely, pre-retirement officials' high propensity for corruption, with the extreme low corruption rate of Singaporean officials at pre-retirement age. The article points to the strict application of laws and regulations, especially the forfeiture of CPF for corrupt officials, as the most effective weapon against pre-retirement corruption.[17]

Debates on democracy in Singapore in the Chinese media

Singapore's democratic system has always been a topic of heated debate in the Chinese media. Unlike many western reports, Chinese reports on Singapore's political system always have a strictly pragmatic orientation. In general, the Chinese media seldom examine Singapore's democratic system against standard abstract theories of liberty and democracy. Instead, the Chinese media tend to

---

[15] Lü Yuanli, "Learn from Singapore's Experience in Building Corruption-free Government", *Shenzhen Special Zone Daily*, 27 October 2012.

[16] Zhu Mingguo, "Why Singapore Can Be Clean and Efficient", *Study Times*, 1 December 2010.

[17] Li Aiming, "How Singapore Keeps Officials Clean", *Huaxia Times*, 5 August 2011.

explain and interpret the Singapore's political system against the background of Singapore's history and economic development, and people's livelihood.

Despite the pragmatic tendency, most Chinese reports on Singapore's democracy still borrowed many ideas and vocabularies from Western counterparts in stressing the authoritarian element in Singapore's political system. It was in May 2011 after Singapore's watershed general election that most Chinese reports regarded it as a milestone for Singapore's democracy; some media even considered Singapore's democracy as 'high-quality democracy' in contrast to democracy in some other Asian countries.

In January 2003, *Strategy and Governance*, China's most influential political journal on national development, published a paper on Singapore's democracy by Xiao Gongqin, who is long regarded as an intellectual father of China's authoritarianism. In this article, Xiao characterises the Singapore state as a successful one-party authoritarian state with a democratic facade in which the PAP carefully maintains its powers and secures electoral majority through its control of political, economic and social resources.[18]

Although Xiao, an advocate of authoritarianism, is by no means critical of Singapore, his article has provided the stereotypical Chinese understanding of the Singaporean political system, especially for the more liberal-minded intellectuals in China who are critical of the Singapore model. For example, on 21 October 2009, Shanghai's leading newspaper *Eastern Morning* published an article titled, *Singapore: One-Party Rule under Democracy*. Echoing Xiao's characterisation but in a negative tone, this article claims that Singapore is authoritarian, undemocratic and not free.[19]

However, this rigid view of the Singapore state has begun to change since May 2011. This change is reflected in an article, *The Singapore We Misread*, published by *Nanfengchuang*, one of China's leading political magazines in June 2011. After giving a first-hand account of Singapore's general election in May 2011, the author refutes the conventional Chinese view that Singapore is merely authoritarian, arguing that this false view among Chinese intellectuals grows from a misunderstanding of the real Singapore.

In reality, the one-party rule belies the fact that Singapore has an effective democratic system of government and the ruling party has extensive grass-roots organisations that directly answer to the people. China should learn from

---

[18] Xiao Gongqin, "Lessons from Singapore's New Authoritarianism", *Strategy and Governance*, 2003, no. 1.

[19] Liang Jie, "Singapore: One-Party Rule under Democracy", *Eastern Morning*, 18 October 2009.

Singapore's democracy, the article argues, not by duplicating the institutions, but by learning from the core values of the Singapore government.[20] This revisionist view in *Nanfengchuang* was echoed by *China News Weekly*, a leading official current affairs magazine under the *Xinhua News Agency*, which argues that Singapore is a genuine democracy and will move towards a more perfect model of democracy after the 2011 general election. [21]

According to the *People's Tribune*, a current affairs magazine affiliated with the *People's Daily*, there have been three different views on Singapore's political system in China's mainstream media since Singapore's 2011 general election. The first view is the affirmative view, which regards the Singapore democracy as the model for Asia and an improvement of the European model. According to this view, the increasing pressure from the people in Singapore serves as a positive force for the government to provide better services.

The second view takes a neutral standpoint. According to this view, Singapore is a well-functioning democracy sui generis and the general election has not made any significant changes to Singapore politics. The third view regards Singapore's democracy negatively and as imperfect and incomplete, especially the lack of freedom of speech.[22]

China–Singapore relations in the Chinese media

Although China–Singapore relations ought to be a major area of interest for Chinese media reports on Singapore, in reality, there are relatively few reports since China–Singapore relations have been generally smooth and free of controversies. However, there are several periods when China's reports on China–Singapore relations visibly increased, in particular during Deputy Prime Minister Lee Hsien Loong's visits to Taiwan in July 2004 and to Beijing in September 2012 as prime minister.

In July 2004, most Chinese print media were critical of Lee's visit to Taiwan. However the criticisms were considered mild and restrained when compared to the harsh opinions of netizens in various online platform. On 23 July 2004, the official *Xinhua News Agency* published in its affiliated paper *International Herald* an article titled, *Lee Hsien Loong is Now Paying for His Visit to Taiwan*, in which it lists both governmental and societal responses to

---

[20] Zhao Lingmin, "The Singapore We Misread", *Nanfengchuang*, 2011, no. 11.
[21] Ji Bin, "China Misread Singapore's Political Systems", *China News Weekly*, 2013, no. 6.
[22] Li Wen, "Changing Face of the Singapore Model", *People's Tribune*, 2012, no. 16.

the events alongside Lee's official explanation of the visit.[23] Like most other articles in mainstream media, this article only mildly criticised the visit as indiscreet and hurtful to the Chinese people, without airing any antagonistic sentiments.

One month thereafter, Shanghai's *Bund Pictorial* published an article by Cai Yunhua, director of the Institute of Southeast Asian Studies of Jinan University, which analysed the deeper causes and backgrounds of Lee's visit to Taiwan. In this article, the author tries to put the Chinese readers in the shoes of Singapore's leadership on the Taiwan issue.

Reflecting on the realpolitk of Singapore's survival and development strategy vis-à-vis its international environment, the article seeks to downplay and justify Lee's visit as an ordinary trip to maintain Singapore's history-bound friendship with Taiwan, rather than as a challenge to China's sovereignty over Taiwan.[24]

Similar views were voiced in an article titled, *A Word to PM Lee: Please Wisely Cut the Taiwan Complex*, published in the *People's Tribune* under *People's Daily*. Although the article title suggests that the Singapore government should sever ties with Taiwan, the content is in fact an optimistic outlook of Lee's China policy spelt out in his inaugural speech. [25]

During Lee's visit to China in September 2012, the media's focus was his speech at the Central Party School of the CCP. In a report on *Study Times*, Lee's visit to the Central Party School was described as the second time this well-known politician of the Asia-Pacific region stepped into the highest academy of the CCP.[26]

In another incident, the *Global Times* under the *People's Daily* published an article titled, *Lee Hsien Loong Warns China Not to Underestimate the United States*, which highlights Lee's high regard for the United States' flexibility and immense creative power despite the current economic problems it faces.[27] By then, both the traditional print media and the internet-based new media have grown much more attuned to Singapore's pragmatic international strategies.

---

[23] "Lee Hsien Loong is Now Paying for His Visit to Taiwan", *International Herald*, 23 July 2004.

[24] Cai Yunhua, *Bund Pictorial*, 16 September 2004.

[25] Wu Yingchun, "A Word to PM Lee: Please Wisely Cut the Taiwan Complex", *People's Tribune*, September 2004.

[26] Cheng Guanjun, "Prime Minister Lee Hsien Loong on Internet Politics and Sino-American Relations", *Study Times*, 17 September 2012.

[27] "Lee Hsien Loong Warns China not to Underestimate the United States", *People's Daily*, 18 September 2012.

A more recent contention in Chinese media rose in response to the remarks made by the late Lee Kuan Yew, Singapore's former minister mentor on the need for US rebalancing in the light of China's geopolitical rise in 2009.[28] This time the official media has been relatively muted but the popular media responded rather vehemently, labelling Lee's view as apologetic for US hegemony or even unabashedly anti-China.[29] However, just like the earlier case with PM Lee, the public animosity subsided due to rather mild official response, which seems to reflect again China's increasingly rational and sophisticated global media strategy.

Singapore's general image in China's official media

In general, Chinese media reports on Singapore are highly focused on Singapore's social, legal and political institutions, and in particular, various social policies. The most frequently reported and discussed themes include the HDB system, clean government and social management. Almost all the reports highly appraise Singapore's success and recommend Singapore's experience to China.

Chinese reports on China–Singapore relations in the print media have always been more rational and balanced than those in the internet media. However, the internet media is also becoming more rational in recent years. Although voices of protest are always raised against policy moves or statements made by Singapore's leaders that are perceived as against Chinese interests, the Chinese media has begun to think of international issues from a bilateral, rather than unilateral perspective.

Although the Chinese media are largely controlled by the government, there is substantial space for topic, scheme and perspective selection when it comes to international news and events. This flexibility in turn exerts a powerful influence on the government's attitudes as it routinely gathers news reports and comments from major newspapers and magazines as part of its policy reference.[30]

---

[28] "MM Calls on US to Retain Key Role in East Asia", *The Straits Times*, 29 October 2009.

[29] "Li Guangyao de yanlun baolu Xinjiapo shi Meiguo weidu Zhongguo de qiaotoubao" (Lee Kuan Yew's Remarks Reveals that Singapore is America's Beachhead in Containing China), *Zhonghuawang luntan*, 4 November 2009, available at <http://military.china.com/zh_cn/critical3/27/20091104/15689477.html> (accessed 6 March 2015).

[30] Influential papers, such as *People's Daily, Guangming Daily* and *News of Shenzhen Special Areas*, are read and used as policy references for the leaders. Reports and commentaries from other papers are also routinely compiled as policy reference materials.

As mentioned earlier, Chinese media reports on Singapore tend to focus on Singapore's public institutions. They rarely touch on other softer features of Singapore, such as arts, education, health care, historical heritage, geographical landscape and cultural diversity.

The tendency has made Singapore a very salient model for the Chinese government, but not for the ordinary Chinese. To the ordinary folks, Singapore's image is often formulistic and even lacklustre. In this sense, more reports on Singapore's attractions other than its social and political institutions will enhance Singapore's appeal to the ordinary Chinese. Media is an important channel of soft power. Singapore can extend its soft power to China through active use of the Chinese media such as engaging in more intensive networking with Chinese media and providing them with opportunities to closely observe and report on Singapore. The reports on Singapore's society will serve to enrich Singapore's media image and enhance the Chinese people's understanding of Singapore.

Singapore in China's popular media

To reiterate, Singapore's image in China's official media is routinely portrayed as a development model for China. The official media displays little interest in China–Singapore relations and in aspects of Singapore that are not centrally concerned with China's development. Compared with this rather rigid view, Singapore's image in China's popular media tend to romanticise Singapore's cultural convergence with and divergence from China, rather than focusing on its development model. They have a more diverse and changing view of Singapore, with themes and focuses varying widely over time.

In general, Singapore's image in the popular media evolved from being a part of the Sinosphere to being one of a distinctive multicultural domain. In the 1980s and 1990s, the dominant view of Singapore is as a part of the Sinosphere that largely shares Chinese cultural and social views. This was more of a fantasised image largely created by the circulation of Singapore's TV dramas, movies and popular songs in China. Since the late 1990s, the Chinese have begun to perceive Singapore as culturally more distinctive and fundamentally 'foreign'. Meanwhile, the Chinese audience has also begun to develop a more sophisticated view of Singapore's culture as comprising a more traditional and familiar component, as well as a more modern and foreign component. The more intensive cultural exchanges between tourists, students and workers of the two countries and the development of an internet-based new media, which drastically changed the way people report and share information, have made a major impact on the popular image of Singapore.

Singapore and Chinese popular culture until the mid-1990s

In the 1980s and early 1990s, direct cultural contact between Singapore and China was limited. The image of Singapore in Chinese popular media was thus mainly shaped by various forms of indirect contact, and most importantly, through the circulation of popular culture in the Chinese language. Meanwhile, Chinese communities in Singapore as part of the Sinosphere also tended to produce works that appealed to the cultural taste of mainland Chinese.

One of the most popular Singapore cultural exports to China in the 1980s and early 1990s was TV drama. Based on anecdotal tallying, from 1984 to 1993, China imported 26 Singaporean TV dramas. From 1994 to 1999, the number was about 22. Among the almost 50 TV dramas, several had made an enduring impression on the Chinese audience. Thereafter, the number plummeted and so has its impact on the Chinese audience.[31] In recent years, however, there seems to be a resurgence of Singapore-made Chinese TV dramas in China, especially historical dramas like *Little Nyonya* (*Xiao Niangre*) and *From China to Singapore* (*Cong Tangshan Dao Nanyang*), which carried critical reflection of the formation of Singaporean Chinese identities.

Singapore's TV dramas and the image they created conform to the perception of the developed peripherals of the Sinosphere in the 1980s and early 1990s, including those produced in Taiwan and Hong Kong. During this period, China was relatively underdeveloped vis-à-vis the Four Tigers, both economically and culturally. The TV dramas that depicted the contemporary scene in Hong Kong, Taiwan and Singapore thus provided not only a source of entertainment, but also a vision of China's prospective future. While these Chinese dramas mostly told stories of love, family and career of a young generation in a rapidly developing world, they also portrayed a large canvas of vibrant Chinese communities under rapid economic growth and social transformation; they certainly struck a chord with contemporary Chinese who were just embarking on a similar historical experience.

Of the many Singaporean TV dramas popular in China, *On the Journey* (*Renzai lutu*), which was broadcast in Singapore in 1985 and in China in the late 1980s, has a special place. Like many other contemporary Singaporean

---

[31] <http://www.redotnews.com/society/show/1031.html> (accessed 21 March 2015).

dramas, the drama told the stories of two young couples who work in an international hotel based in Singapore. The story was a *Bildungsroman* of youths living under conflicting social values: traditional values of loyalty and sacrifice versus modern values of love and individual freedom in an interests-oriented world of competition for success. In particular, it underlined the difficult choice between love and career success, often resulting in the sacrifice of love for career advancement.[32] Such storyline, though not necessarily innovative, appeals to Chinese youths who have similar aspirations and clashes of values.

The immediate popularity and natural familiarity of *On the Journey* and its likes in China of the late 1980s were not without a reason. The director of the drama was Liang Liren, an active legendary figure in the cultural scene of Sinosphere. A Chinese national, Liang joined the Red Guards in the 1960s and became an illegal immigrant to Hong Kong in the early 1970s. In Hong Kong, he underwent basic training in TV drama and became a top scriptwriter. In the early 1980s, Liang served shortly as a director of TV dramas (1983–1986) in the Singapore Broadcasting Corporation (1980–1994).[33] While Liang's personal story was certainly legendary, it was by no means singular. In the 1980s, such cultural circulation between Singapore, Hong Kong and other parts of Greater China was typical and representative of the cultural production in the Sinosphere.

The only historical drama with comparable popularity was *The Awakening*, more popularly known in Chinese as *Nanyang Shrouded in the Mist (Wusuo Nanyang)*. The drama depicted the struggle of first-generation Chinese migrants and workers in rubber plantations of the British Strait Settlements in the early 20th century. In this drama, the migrants had to cope with not only the harsh natural environment and living conditions but also a repressive and exploitative British colonial authority and its local allies in their struggle for survival. This depiction immediately appealed to the lingering Maoist ideological heritage and the nascent nationalist sentiment in mainland China.

Another important channel of cultural exchange between Singapore and China in the 1980s and early 1990s was popular literature. Like the Chinese literature in Taiwan and Hong Kong, Singapore's Chinese literature also

---

[32] For a summary of the story, refer to the following online source: <http://baike.baidu.com/subview/40526/8182190.htm> (accessed 21 March 2015).

[33] <http://zh.wikipedia.org/wiki/%E6%A2%81%E7%AB%8B%E4%BA%BA> (accessed 21 March 2015).

enjoyed a wide audience in the first decades of China's opening up. During this period, Singapore's Chinese writers attained a wide urban readership through novels, plays and most importantly, essays. Among the most popular works were poetry by Zhou Can and travel essays by Tan Youjin, or You Jin to her Chinese readers. You was particularly popular in China in the early 1990s. Born and raised in Ipoh, Malaysia in 1950, You Jin belonged to an older generation of Singaporeans who were still well-versed in Chinese literature and classics. She became famous in China for her travel literature, often in the format of essays, which tended to integrate nostalgia, rumination and travel experience in simple language and short paragraphs. At the height of her fame, she was often compared to the late Taiwanese writer San Mao (Chen Maoping) and Hong Kong essayists like Dong Qiao who wrote similar travelogues albeit in a more emotive and poignant style.

The image of Singapore as viewed through the popular media in China before the mid-1990s was not very different from that of Hong Kong and Taiwan. Like Hong Kong and Taiwan, Singapore was imagined as another rapidly developing overseas Chinese settlement with a repressive colonial past. The Chinese audience tended to think of Singapore as sharing a similar history and likely the same future as other parts of the Sinosphere. As discussed earlier, this distorted image was largely due to the dominant roles of the peripheral, such as Taiwan, Hong Kong and Singapore in cultural production, in the Sinosphere. This singular dominance of the peripheral would change as the Chinese economy grew further and mainland Chinese media entered a phase of rapid growth and transformation, which ironically, would result in the dissolution of the imagined unity of such a cultural sphere.

Contemporary Singapore culture in China

Since the mid-1990s, the image of Singapore in China started to change gradually. Singapore's dramas declined in Chinese popular media as mainland Chinese dramas became the mainstay of cultural consumption. Similarly, Singapore's Chinese literature also declined in status as the new generation of Singaporean writers failed to reach a wide audience in the Chinese literary scene. The locus of Singapore's representation in the Chinese popular media shifted from TV dramas to popular music by Singaporean singers, a development which no longer portrayed Singapore's society and landscape.

Meanwhile, more and more mainland Chinese began to study and work in Singapore, some even becoming first-generation migrants in Singapore. This growing body of transnational population constantly on the move between China and Singapore tended to bring home a new and more realistic image of Singapore. In our view, they have made the most important impact on Chinese imagination through their numerous travelogues, which have been increasingly circulated in a decentralised fashion outside the official print media via the vast world of Chinese social media in the Age of the Internet.

The popularity of Singapore's TV dramas in China declined around the mid-1990s. However, they did not disappear from Chinese popular media. Singapore continued to be portrayed via a number of popular Singaporean TV dramas as cultural imports to China. A good example is the Singaporean TV series *Little Nyonya* (2008), which was broadcast in Chinese television in 2009–2010 and became widely popular among Chinese viewers. Like other epic dramas like *Nanyang Shrouded in the Mist*, it addresses the important historical transformation of Chinese identity and traditional culture in the Straits communities in the face of sweeping modernisation in the early 20th century. However, instead of focusing on Singapore, this highly acclaimed Singapore-made historical drama centred on *peranakan* culture in Malaysia. Its impacts on the Chinese imagination were restricted to minor themes like food, music and clothing. [34]

Singaporean movies, now gaining some popularity in the global film market, provide mainland Chinese with a glimpse of contemporary Singaporean society. *I Not Stupid* is perhaps the most well-known Singaporean movie in China. It tells of the ordeals of Singaporean schoolboys under a highly competitive meritocratic education system, with a family and social system underpinned by values and expectations that their Chinese counterparts can easily identify with. Such shared values and systems make Singaporean movies appealing to a Chinese audience. However, like contemporary TV dramas, the movie simply reminds the Chinese of a shared social value and cultural system, and does not provoke a more in-depth view of Singapore's particular social and cultural background among the Chinese.

From the mid-1990s, a few Singaporean singers emerged on the popular music scene in China. These singers were mostly born in the 1970s and early 1980s, including Kit Chan, Mavis Hee, Tanya Chua, Stephanie Sun, JJ Lim and Do Cheng Yi. The most prominent of these Singaporean singers is Stephanie Sun (Sun Yanzi), who gained widespread popularity in China in the 2000s. Her debut was an instantaneous success in Taiwan, followed by more

---

[34] For instance, reviews often focused on nyonya food, see "A Chinese View on Little Nyanya: The Nyanya Cousin", <http://www.nanyang.com/node/376160> (accessed 23 March 2015).

popular albums in China and other part of the Sinosphere. At her zenith of popularity, she was chosen to sing four featured songs for the Beijing Olympiad in 2008, the highest honour for Chinese female singers including those from mainland China.[35]

Most of the Singaporean singers were popular in China for their nostalgic and romantic songs with beautiful lyrics and soft rhythms. Unlike their Chinese counterparts, Singaporean singers tended to have a better grounding in both classical Western training and popular East Asian music, as in the case of Stephanie Sun. They generally have sound financial backing, good tertiary education, and further training and grooming in countries such as Taiwan, Japan and the West before they made their debut. Ironically, however, this kind of background also made Singaporean singers less distinctive as a cultural group as compared with singers from Hong Kong and Taiwan. Thus while there were millions of Chinese audience for Singaporean singers, few were aware of where they come from. Unlike movies and TV dramas, these songs convey little of Singapore itself in the Chinese cultural imagination.

Apart from TV dramas, films and songs, Chinese website *Lianhe Zaobao* probably commands a more salient presence for ordinary Chinese. According to Beidu Baike, 75% of *Zaobao's* eight to 10 million daily readership comes from mainland China.[36] While *Zaobao* certainly provides a way for Chinese to learn more about Singapore, it is more of a mirror than a window: unsubscribed Chinese viewers can only access its sections on China news, which only covers overseas views on China, including Singapore's views, rather than Singapore's report on itself. This is quite rational economically as the majority of the viewers from China are only interested in an objective report of the Chinese story. This however deprives the Chinese of the opportunity to learn more about Singapore. In this regard, *Zaobao* does little to enhance the mainland Chinese's understanding of Singapore despite its huge readership.

Tourism and migration as emerging windows to Singapore

In the 1980s and mid-1990s, most Chinese learned about Singapore through the official media and the handful of Singaporean dramas, songs and movies available to the Chinese audience. While these channels, especially official media, are still churning out stories and images of Singapore, they have become

---

[35] "Chudao shinian: Stephanie Sun" (Ten Years after Debut: Sun Yanzi), *Southern Weekly*, no. 21, 2010.

[36] <http://baike.baidu.com/view/1065754.htm> (accessed 21 March 2015).

less important since the mid-1990s. With the boom in tourism between the two countries, travelogues and travel guides became available to ordinary Chinese and especially tourists. While there was no tourist guide on Singapore before the late 1990s, there were more than six guides on Singapore published in 2014 alone, with one specifically focused on *How to Go Around in Singapore by MRTs.*

With internet and global migration, the community that most eagerly provides and disseminates news and knowledge about Singapore in China now is not professional journalists, but the new Chinese migrant community in Singapore. There are several major web portals that broadcast all kinds of news stories and personal anecdotes on life in Singapore. While the immediate audience is the migrant community in Singapore, they also reach a wider audience in Chinese society through family and friendship networks.

In 2014, a book titled, *Everything about Singapore,* was published by the Zhejiang Provincial Publishing Group. This book offers a most comprehensive and contemporary Chinese view of Singapore. In contrast to earlier works on Singapore, which were mostly by professional scholars, this work is a compilation of blog articles by an ordinary Chinese migrant in Singapore known only by his pen name. The obscurity of the author and his simple narrative distinguish the book as a bona fide account of Singapore by an ordinary folk who has lived in the two countries.

Among the things that the book highlights are Singapore's basic national policies, social customs, and Singaporeans' basic patterns of life and values. The basic tone is affirmative. For example, it compares the mannerism of mainland Chinese and Singaporeans and concludes that the Singaporean way is more civilised:

> "Singaporeans speak more softly than Chinese. Speaking loudly on phone in buses or subways is considered very impolite. Singaporeans regard personal privacy highly: if someone is working on the computer and some colleagues and superiors look at the screen from behind, they will be deemed as lacking in manners. Many Chinese will however regard it as natural".[37]

Moreover, the author remarks approvingly that the social world of Singapore is also closer to a typical Western society, rather than the more complicated

---

[37] Zui Baotun, *Xinjiapo naxieshi* (Everything about Singapore), Hangzhou, Zhejiang Publishing Group, 2014, p. 99.

Chinese way:

> "Singaporeans rarely force you to drink....Interpersonal relationships in Singapore are lighter and less intensive than that in China. There are less gift exchanges and little complex office politics. There is no such complicated relationship network as in China. Thus people accustomed to the Chinese way may regard Singaporean society as too cold". [38]

The author also highlights Singapore's school systems and their emphasis on character cultivation, especially the spirit of service, which is totally absent in the Chinese education system.[39] While this book, like the official view of Singapore, regards Singaporean society as more civilised and developed than Chinese society, there is a clear difference: the official view sees in Singapore a model for China to adapt and a mirror for China to correct itself, while the more personal assessments of Singapore from a migrant perspective depict Singapore as fundamentally different and in a sense not duplicable in China. In other words, despite its strengths, the Singaporean way may not necessarily be a model for China. Interestingly, the cultural distinctiveness of Singapore poses minimal problem for migrants who have already become part of Singaporean society.

Not every Chinese tourist or migrant loves Singaporean culture however. As mentioned earlier, Singaporean culture is often characterised by visitors from mainland China as lacking in interpersonal warmth. Some observers also point to a lack of creativity and cultural depth, and some even regarded it as a boring place without many unique features.[40] However, this is not the dominant view. The dominant view still holds Singaporean society and culture as more habitable and civilised than the Chinese way.

Conclusion: Singapore as a paragon of development and civilisation for china

Since the late 1970s, Singapore has been featured prominently in China's official and popular media. In both media spheres, Singapore has been portrayed as a small country with a Chinese majority and is more developed and civilised.

---

[38] Zui Baotun, *Xinjiapo naxieshi* (Everything about Singapore), Hangzhou, Zhejiang Publishing Group, 2014, p. 100.

[39] Zui Baotun, *Xinjiapo naxieshi* (Everything about Singapore), Hangzhou, Zhejiang Publishing Group, 2014, p. 101.

[40] <http://blog.sina.com.cn/s/blog_5048cdc30102dyqo.html> (accessed 23 March 2015).

Whereas the official media has focused more on the development aspect of the Singapore model, the popular media tend to focus on Singaporean culture, which has evolved from a part of the larger Chinese cultural imagination to a distinctive multi-cultural realm.

The official media is most interested in Singapore's lessons for China in a variety of policy-related domains. Singapore's experience in providing social housing, managing social stability, preventing corruption and enforcing effective rule with the PAP as the dominant political actor has unique relevance to the Chinese government and leadership. Over the last decades, official reports and analyses on these matters have become more detailed and focused. While there are dissenting voices and critical words, the mainstream official report on Singapore still holds it as a paragon of economic and social development that China could aspire to.

The popular media, on the other hand, exhibit different themes and visions across different periods of time. Initially, the Chinese look at Singapore as a distant cultural relative. This view gradually underwent a major revision when the Chinese had less Singaporean elements in their popular media and began to examine Singapore more closely through travel writings and even personal experiences. In the internet age, it is this more realistic and personal look on Singapore that dominates mainstream Chinese popular view of Singapore.

Singapore's rise to prominence has much to do with contemporary China's social and economic transformation through marketisation and urbanisation. Throughout the last three decades, Singapore has played a salient role in facilitating such a development. This was initially achieved by Singaporeans assuming roles as advisers, engineers and professionals in China; more recently, however, the overwhelming majority of those who cross the border are now Chinese. Each year, Singapore would host hundreds of thousands if not millions of tourists and hundreds of officials and students from China. Singapore's image as a developed and civilised country has been created by not just the media but also the expanding network of exchanges.

Last but not least is the impact of the late Lee Kuan Yew, founder of modern Singapore and an old friend of China. Lee was probably as well-known in China as the name of Singapore itself.[41] For many Chinese, Lee Kuan Yew is

---

[41] For example, almost all Chinese news media headlined Lee's passing. The typical characterisation of Lee was that of "the last Great Statesman and Strategist of Asia" of the last century and father of the Singapore model.

almost synonymous with Singapore. The image of Lee as a visionary, pragmatic and incorruptible leader has much to do with the dominant image of Singapore as a developed and civilised nation in China's official and popular media. Although Lee has passed away, his legacy and his prominent media presence in China are likely to continue to reinforce this image of Singapore in China.

Chapter 11

Chinese Studies in Singapore

JOHN Wong and LIM Tai Wei

The idea of 'Chinese studies in Singapore' can be conceptualised as an academic subject as well as contemporary China studies for think tanks in Singapore. Chinese studies in Singapore is shaped by factors such as domestic politics in Singapore and its impact on contemporary China research. For an institutional analysis of contemporary China studies in Singapore, the writing touches on the evolution of the Institute of East Asian Philosophies to the Institute of East Asian Political Economy and finally to the East Asian Institute.

Contemporary China studies and Chinese studies in the Singapore Context

For a country with a civilisation and culture as complex as China's, it warrants dedicated and specialised academic study. This has given rise to a number of disciplines on Chinese studies. 'Chinese studies in Singapore' can be conceptualised as an academic subject as well as contemporary China studies for think tanks in Singapore. In the former, it is a discipline that is shaped by factors such as (i) domestic politics in Singapore and its impact on contemporary China research; (ii) quality of immigrant stocks; and (iii) the government's attempt to reverse the 'de-sinification' trends of Singapore society by promoting the 'Speak Mandarin' movement and supporting contemporary China studies or China watching out of pragmatic and utilitarian policy considerations. These factors will be discussed at length in this chapter. In the publishing industry, it is also an academic subject that is divided into the following conventional academic publishing genres: Chinese studies (humanities, classics, language, linguistics, culture, history and civilisation) and contemporary China studies (economics, sociology, anthropology and political science of post-1949 China). There is also a popular conception of

'Chinese studies' that tends to see it in generic terms: the study of China and all things Chinese. Chinese studies in Singapore can also constitute language training, China watching and Sinology in Singapore, focusing on personalities, institution-building and policy-making (including the 'Speak Mandarin' Campaign, language teachers training and pre-tertiary and tertiary educational institution-building).

In terms of the prevailing political climate before 1989, to study contemporary China then involved political sensitivities in an ethnic Chinese-majority Singapore located in the non-socialist bloc of the world during the Cold War. Contemporary China studies in Singapore struggled with larger macro-environmental geopolitical factors such as the bipolar world during the Cold War where China was identified first with the socialist camp and then as a third independent socialist power. Despite Cold War factors, it took several generations of scholars to embark on a long path of instituting contemporary (post-1949) China studies in Singapore. The path was by no means easy, given the deep-seated suspicions and intellectual resistance against the discipline of contemporary China watching in the context of the Cold War.

The decline of the Chinese language schools

The development of China watching in Singapore bears more differences than similarities with the Western context. Though China watching in Singapore did not start off as a Cold War activity as in the West, it was also heavily influenced by political considerations having developed under strong government auspices. On the surface, Singapore looks very Chinese, with ethnic Chinese constituting over 70% of its population. In reality, for political reasons, Singapore did not provide a conducive intellectual climate for scholars to become interested in modern Chinese studies.

Before its independence, Singapore used to be a 'Chinese educational bastion' for Southeast Asia, developing a comprehensive Chinese-language education system without government support. Singapore also founded the first Chinese-speaking university outside of China — the Nanyang University (or Nantah in short) — entirely through private efforts. However, the Chinese education system quickly declined in the immediate period after independence as the young government of the newly independent Singapore government led by Lee Kuan Yew did not as yet develop or promote Mandarin Chinese education (the 'Speak Mandarin' Campaign started only in 1979) while the Chinese newspapers (*Nanyang Siang Pau* and *Sin Chew Jit Poh*) were both regarded as hotbeds for spreading Communism and Chinese chauvinism,[1] unsuitable for a multicultural environment like Singapore. Misleading or chauvinistic information would have a negative impact on the development of Singapore because most of its population received rudimentary levels of education in its early days of nationhood.

Though the left-wing Chinese groups facilitated his ascension to power, Lee quickly split up with them after he recognised the Communist threat and how it could endanger the survival of Singapore in the regional geo-political context of the anti-communist and Chinese-minority Southeast Asia. He also realised that Chinese chauvinism could breed communalism, which would threaten the stability of Singapore as a multi-racial society. Thus, the government cracked down on Chinese newspapers and introduced measures to integrate all schools by starting bilingual education at the primary educational level, with English as the major medium of instruction, leaving Chinese, Malay and Tamil to be taught as mother tongues.

As a result, the Chinese language ability (both reading and writing) of the young generation of Singaporean Chinese was severely weakened. As younger Singaporean Chinese started to speak English at home and to each other outside their immediate family, their Chinese language standard further deteriorated. Since books and newspapers from China were banned in Singapore and visits to China prohibited, young Singaporean Chinese grew up with very little background knowledge of the history and geography of China. All these had contributed, intentionally and unintentionally, to what may be called the 'de-sinification of Singapore society' in the sense that society as a whole is becoming less Chinese because of the racial mix and more importantly because of the demise of the Chinese education and the decline in the language ability (reading Chinese, not just speaking Mandarin) of the Chinese population in Singapore. 'De-sinification of Singapore society' was not the original intention of the government but a natural outcome of political and historical forces in Singapore.

Recognising the dangers of losing its cultural roots, the Singapore government encouraged its people to learn more about the Chinese language and culture and to speak more Mandarin with the annual 'Speak Mandarin Campaign'. The 'Speak Mandarin Campaign' was useful for social mobilisation since the Chinese community in Singapore was disunited and disparately divided into dialect groups. Speaking the common language of Mandarin allowed different

---

[1] For further information, please see Lim Mun Fah, "Chinese Education in Singapore: As You Sow, so Will You Reap", *Sin Chew Daily*, 26 November 2009; and Thum Pingtjin, "Chinese Language Political Mobilization in Singapore, 1953–63", PhD thesis for Oxford University, 2011.

dialect groups to communicate with each other. A discussion on Chinese studies or studies about China would not be complete without a brief introduction of state policies related to this area.

The founding father of modern Singapore Lee Kuan Yew entrenched the principle of picking up Chinese history, tradition and culture in the Singaporean cultural fabric. This is to ensure that the island state becomes the only ethnic Chinese society outside Greater China to serve as the intermediary and bridge between mainland China and the rest of the world while strengthening the community bonds between different dialect groups in Singapore. Lee argues:

> Learning the Chinese language means imbibing the core items of Chinese history, tradition and culture. The Confucianist values of loyalty, honour, discipline, filial piety, emphasis on family, respect for authority — all vital for nation-building and for cultivating citizens with honourable personal attributes. These values will provide cultural ballast to our people as we adjust to a fast-changing world.[2]

This single quotation captured the essence of Chinese studies from the viewpoint of language acquisition, study of the classics and Chinese studies in the cultural sense. The process is conceptualised as part of nation-building efforts in serving as a reference point for traditional core values. The civil servants in Singapore led the way by switching to the use of Mandarin instead of using Chinese dialects. The Promote Mandarin Council publication noted the following historical effort by the civil service:

> Internally, all the government ministries formed their own committees to promote Mandarin. Classes in conversation Mandarin were started for ethnic Chinese civil servants who were not proficient and wanted to learn the language. By 1989, over 4,000 civil servants had taken these classes. Passing Mandarin proficiency tests became a condition for promotion.[3]

The government through its bilingualism plans for the civil servants therefore led the way for the emergence of a Mandarin-speaking environment in Singapore.

---

[2] Promote Mandarin Council National Heritage Board, *A Mandarin Anchor in a Changing World*, Singapore, Focus Publishing Limited of the Singapore Press Holdings, 2014, pp. 12-13. First published in Lee Kuan Yew's book, *My Lifelong Challenge: Singapore's Bilingual Journey,* 2011.
[3] Promote Mandarin Council National Heritage Board, *A Mandarin Anchor in a Changing World*, p. 29.

Institutional development of contemporary China studies in Singapore

In terms of contemporary China studies, however, the 'Speak Mandarin Campaign' which focused on domestic priorities of community togetherness and business communications expediency did not directly help with fostering the emergence of more experts in this specialised field. The 'Speak Mandarin Campaign' was targeted more at the general populace and more accurately a functional or utilitarian policy approach to encouraging language use for pragmatic businesses and heritage purposes. This also partly explains why Singapore had to invite contemporary China experts from the PRC (People's Republic of China) to Singapore to carry out its 'China-watching' activities!

Hong Kong and Taiwan have benefited from the influx of Chinese intellectuals as emigres from the Communist regime. Most of them were the former elites of the Kuomintang (KMT) and hence they all tend to be anti-communist. If these people were to come to Singapore, Chinese studies here would have been tremendously boosted including in the field of culture. Hong Kong was basically a 'Chinese culture desert' before 1949. Hong Kong's newspapers, art and literature started to flourish after intellectual refugees went to Hong Kong. Hong Kong and Taiwan started China watching, but their approach was not neutral and basically anti-communist.

Singapore by contrast had more humble beginnings in its immigrant stocks, many of whom worked as coolies and in other manual jobs. It could not build a China-watching think tank from individuals who were distant from the intellectual and cultural elite centres of China or the newly formed China-watching clusters found in Taiwan or Hong Kong.[4]

Given the historical factors stated earlier, not surprisingly, Singapore's road to China watching had gone through a rather long evolutionary process comprising three phases: (i) the Institute of East Asian Philosophies (IEAP) was formed in 1983 and its original purpose was to work on the curriculum for schools in Singapore to teach Confucian values. This down-to-earth functional approach's major objective was to teach Confucian values to ensure that Singapore's younger generation has a strong moral compass or be imbued with a social ballast to guide them through life; (ii) the re-organisation of the IEAP in 1992 to become the Institute of East Asian Political Economy (IEAPE), an independent think tank specifically for China watching;

---

[4] Singapore attracted highly talented Chinese from the Mainland, Greater China and beyond after it became economically successful as one of the four tiger economies. By then, the pool of talents that Singapore drew from was effectively global.

and (iii) the dissolution of IEAPE in 1997 and renaming it as the East Asian Institute (EAI), an autonomous research organisation within the National University of Singapore. The main mission of EAI, as a member of the wider university community, has gone from the early days of 'China watching' to *watching China* and *studying China*.

The key person behind the whole process was the late Goh Keng Swee, Singapore's first deputy prime minister (Lee Kuan Yew's 'right-hand man' from the start), having held portfolios in finance, defence and education.[5] Goh was behind Singapore's Confucianism campaign when he was the minister of education (and he was also the then chairman of IEAP) which provided the intellectual support to this campaign. Confucian studies were promoted primarily as a practical policy in setting up the school curriculum for the teaching of Confucian values at school. After retiring from politics in 1984, Goh became an economic adviser to China's State Council's Office of Special Economic Zones under Vice Premier Gu Mu. Goh's China assignment ignited his interest in China's economic reform and development, which in turn made him see the need to start China watching in Singapore.[6]

The beginning of contemporary Chinese studies or China watching in Singapore was the outcome of the foresight of Goh, who appeared to have foreseen correctly the rise of China after the Tiananmen incident — the intensification of economic reforms after Deng's *Nanxun* or Southern Tours. Hence, the IEAPE was set up for China watching and policy-related research on modern China. China watching in Singapore is quite different from other societies in the free world such as the United States and Taiwan, which tend to be ideologically oriented against the backdrop of the Cold War. Singapore's China-watching tradition from the start was non-PRC-oriented and non-Western in approach; it was conceptualised to be more objective and pragmatically policy-relevant.

In 1990, John Wong was appointed by Goh as director of IEAP and later IEAPE. With constant guidance and advice from Goh, Wong's IEAPE started the business of China watching in Singapore. The subsequently renamed IEAPE, EAI, was helmed by Wang Gungwu as its director and John Wong as its research director. Currently, EAI is headed by the PRC-born Zheng Yongnian

---

[5] For Goh's contribution to Singapore's development, including China watching, see Emrys Chew and Kwa Chong Guan (eds), *Goh Keng Swee: A Legacy of Public Service*, Singapore, World Scientific, 2012.

[6] Zheng Yongnian and John Wong, *Goh Keng Swee on China: Selected Essays*, Singapore, World Scientific, 2013.

who succeeded Wang as director of EAI, after a brief one-year directorship held by Yang Dali in 2007. Zheng first joined IEAPE in 1996. He was the first PRC scholar with a PhD in political science (Princeton) that was recruited by IEAPE.

Watching China to understand China at IEAPE

Wong's immediate mission at IEAP was to change its research focus from classical studies to the study of contemporary China with special emphasis on China's economic reforms and political changes, or 'China watching' in short. The initial batch of China scholars at IEAP comprised a motley group of former officials associated with the deposed Zhao Ziyang regime. They were all happy to be out of China after the Tiananmen crackdown. Except for a few, they were not dissidents in the sense that they were banned from returning to China. Academically speaking, they were not really scholars with training in academic research. They were more like interpreters or decipherers of what was going on in China. EAI's management found them very useful and knowledgeable resources for research because they had previously lived and worked in China, and were capable of providing insider knowledge and first-hand experience on understanding developments in China.

For the first two years, 'China watching' was carried out virtually under the cloak of Confucian studies, for good political reasons. China watching was actually all about researching on 'Communist' China, which was still a politically sensitive subject in Singapore at the time, and more so in the region around Singapore because of its anti-communist legacies. Singapore established formal diplomatic relations with China only in October 1990, shortly after Indonesia had done so. Back in the early 1980s when Deng Xiaoping had already started economic reforms, publications and newspapers from China were still banned in Singapore. Indonesia did not even allow the importation of Chinese books and newspapers regardless of their origins and anything bearing Chinese characters, even from Taiwan. In Singapore, even by 1990, news about China seldom appeared on the front page of the local Chinese newspaper *Lianhe Zaobao* while the English *The Straits Times* used the term 'red' for things associated with the PRC.

These Cold War legacies led the IEAP management to conduct its sensitive research initially under the cover of classical studies, especially since most of its researchers at that time were from China, with some having complicated political backgrounds. In late 1992 when China opened up much more after Deng's *Nanxun*, IEAP was renamed IEAPE.

Recruitment of suitable researchers posed even greater challenges. Back in the early 1990s, it was extremely difficult to recruit suitably qualified PRC scholars with training in modern social sciences. John Wong made several recruitment trips to the United States, the United Kingdom and Australia without much success. China in the 1980s sent quite a number of students abroad for further studies, but only a small proportion of them were in the social sciences, with even fewer seeking to pursue a PhD. In 1991, one could virtually count with one's own fingers the number of PRC students who had obtained a PhD from a good university in economics, politics or sociology. Those who did so preferred to stay in America, even for a teaching job in a small college. Not all of them were suitable for the kind of empirical research at the institute: a PhD in Economics, for instance, was likely to be too narrow or too 'mathematical' for policy-related studies. In fact, IEAPE was dogged by this serious recruitment problem throughout.

In the spring of 1992, Deng Xiaoping in his celebrated *Nanxun* speech singled out Singapore as a country that achieved both rapid economic growth and good social order — something the Chinese called 'spiritual civilisation'. He urged China to 'learn from Singapore' and later to 'do better than Singapore'. Shortly afterwards, the Chinese Communist Party (CCP) dispatched a high-level delegation to Singapore, led by Vice Minister Xu Weicheng from its Propaganda Department, for a study trip.[7] Following Xu's visit, about 400 delegations from various PRC localities and organisations visited Singapore, and many of them came to IEAPE to hold discussions and exchange views.

Over the years, IEAPE had participated in many activities connected with high-level official visits from China and Taiwan, including Zhu Rongji's trip to promote the Pudong project and the 'Wang-Ku' meeting (or 'Wang-Koo' as it was known in Taiwan) to discuss the Cross-(Taiwan)-Strait issue. In fact, several members of China's Politburo came to the institute to hold discussions with Goh. Many of China's top technocrats today have also been to the institute for various activities, including Zhou Xiaochuan, governor of the People's Bank of China; Ma Kai, minister at the State Council; and Guo Shuqing, chairman of China Securities Regulatory Commission.

---

[7] The delegation returned to China and quickly put out a book, *Xing-jia-bo jing-shen wen-ming* or 'Singapore's Spiritual Civilisation', Beijing, Red Flag Publishers, 1992. The book highlights Singapore's social and cultural development in a very positive manner. It was made available to all Party branches in China, creating a good image of Singapore among the Party's grass-roots members throughout China.

China watching in action

As IEAP and later IEAPE were charged with the primary mission of conducting policy research, all new scholars with research experience in universities had to re-adapt from carrying out publication-based academic research to practical policy-oriented research. In reality, both require sound scholarship as foundation plus familiarity with basic methodology and modern social science tools. The major difference lies more in the approach as well as the attitude of the researcher. Unlike academic papers, a good piece of policy-related research usually needs to be well-focused and factual, and not meant to test any hypothesis or reach any preconceived conclusion. It also needs to be concise, informative and readable.

The IEAP management took the view that for useful policy-oriented China watching, domestic developments in China should be carefully monitored in order to understand what was actually happening there. Goh wanted EAI staff members to give low priority to international relations studies, a subject considered to be full of personal perceptions and opinions. In discussing US–China relations, for example, a China scholar in Beijing would take an entirely different view from an American scholar in Washington, and indeed different American scholars from the left or right would further hold different views. It would also be difficult for EAI scholars to come up with a very good paper on this subject to be able to 'impress Prime Minister [later Senior Minister] Lee Kuan Yew', as indeed many Western scholars and commentators had constantly come to Singapore to consult Lee on various issues.

Thus, the main research agenda for IEAP/IEAPE was to focus primarily on the domestic political, economic and social development of China, and issues that were directly related to economic reform and development. Such a research agenda still by and large constitutes the bulk of EAI's research activities today. For many decades, modern Chinese studies in the West, especially in the United States, came under the heavy influence of the Cold War, focusing largely on problems and negative aspects of developments in China. Accordingly, many Western commentaries on China tended to be highly opinionated and heavily biased.

IEAP/IEAPE made strong efforts to consciously follow a more 'objective' approach to China research, and as non-Western and non-PRC in perspective as possible. Such an objective and neutral approach served the IEAP management very well, rendering EAI's research reports more relevant and more useful to the Singapore government, the basic tenet of scholars at EAI now. This pragmatic approach to policy recommendations and suggestions as well as academic inputs can be attributed to the transition from IEAPE to EAI which was not just simply an institutional transition from a privately constituted think tank to a full-fledged member of the National University of Singapore (NUS) family; it was also the decision to combine policy-relevant China-watching writings with the academic component of modern Chinese studies — a feature that still characterises EAI today.

As Taiwan had the best 'China watching' facilities in Asia, EAI assigned a scholar to go through Taiwan's major research publications on China, including those put out by its military intelligence units (such as *Fei-qing yan-jiu* or 'bandit studies') through the decades. The conclusion was startling: there was no evidence to show that major events like the outbreak of the Cultural Revolution had been predicted or anticipated beforehand in all the publications. This reminded EAI management of the limits of China watching. Henceforth, EAI has come to adopt this as the cardinal principle for its China watching scholarship: 'No foreign China expert knows what is happening inside *Zhongnanhai* (the residence of China's top leaders)'.

The primary mission of IEAP/IEAPE was to update the Singapore government on what was going on in China. For this purpose, short, readable research reports were circulated to cabinet ministers, ministers of state and permanent secretaries of various ministries. Wong wrote the first report as *IEAP China News Analysis* No. 1, which went out on 3 January 1991. This was soon followed by other papers issued under different titles: *IEAP Background Brief, IEAP Commentaries, IEAP Discussion Paper* and *IEAP Internal Study Paper.* In the first two years, most of these papers were written by Eu Chooi Yip (former secretary of the outlawed Malayan Communist Party's Southern Branch who returned to Singapore from his exile in China) and John Wong while Eu also translated into English many papers originally written in Chinese by PRC scholars. In short, IEAP/IEAPE practically functioned as a closed-door government think tank on China, with its research findings kept away from the public domain.

Studying China to understand China at EAI

In March 1997, IEAPE was dissolved and renamed EAI to become an autonomous university-level research organisation within the National University of Singapore. EAI's mission would be to conduct both academic as well as policy-related research on China (including Taiwan and Hong Kong) and China's changing relations with its neighbours in East Asia. In a sense, this contemporary China studies organisation had undergone a double reincarnation, first from IEAP to IEAPE and then from IEAPE to EAI.

To fulfil its academic mission, EAI started to organise weekly seminars and regular public lectures. In the past 18 years, EAI has organised many international conferences and workshops on developments in China while EAI scholars have also produced numerous books (mainly English but also some Chinese) related to China and other East Asian countries, working papers (both English and Chinese) and journal articles. Besides, EAI has published two academic journals, *China: An International Journal*, an internationally refereed journal with citation indexes of Thomson Reuters, and *East Asian Policy.*

Meanwhile, its policy-related research has been expanded to meet its public service obligations by regularly circulating (now weekly) to the Singapore government informative and policy-related reports as *EAI Background Briefs* on developments in China and the rest of East Asia. As at 16 September 2015, EAI had circulated 1,061 issues. Some reacted to an event like the unrest in Tibet or riots in Xinjiang while many dealt with developments of topical interest concerning the 18th Party Congress, the National People's Congress, and leadership changes at both central and local levels. Many others dealt with topics like social protests, housing and health-care reform, pollution and the environment, China's growing relations with the region and with the United States. These *Background Briefs* are usually based on in-depth research and specialisation of the individual scholars. Towards the end of every year, the institute issues *Background Briefs* that review China's domestic political and social development throughout the year, its economic growth and major changes in its foreign relations. Among the regular readers of the *Background Briefs* in the Cabinet was the late Lee Kuan Yew.

Besides, EAI often conducts briefings to ministers and senior officials in the Ministry of Trade and Industry (MTI), Ministry of Foreign Affairs (MFA) and Ministry of National Development on developments in China and Japan. From time to time, it was often asked by the MFA to brief visiting foreign dignitaries. Over the years, EAI was also commissioned to undertake consultancy reports for various ministries, including a detailed evaluation of the Singapore–China Suzhou Industrial Park for MTI. EAI has developed into a foremost research institute on East Asian development, particularly on contemporary China, in Southeast Asia. Within Singapore, it is perhaps the only research institute out of many others that has successfully maintained a good balance between academic and policy-related research. Recently, an organisation at the University of Pennsylvania ranked EAI as one of the top five 'think tanks' in Asia.

Chinese studies outside contemporary China studies

Having discussed the origins of contemporary China studies, it is useful to survey other institutions of Chinese or China studies as well. These accounts are however reductionist and brief due to word limit but the writing will endeavour to selectively cover some of them as much as possible within the space allocated; therefore the list of institutions is not meant to be comprehensive. Chinese studies-related humanities, and cultural and linguistic courses at the varsity level originated respectively in 1953 and 1955 with the founding of the Department of Chinese Studies in the Faculty of Arts and Social Sciences, University of Singapore and the Department of Chinese Language and Literature, Faculty of Arts in Nantah. They merged in 1980 to form the current department at the National University of Singapore. Five major areas are now designated as priority focuses of this department.[8] Studying Chinese humanities and civilisation is different from EAI's contemporary focus as the classics, literature and language provide the tools to understand the nuances of Chinese culture and are not at once translatable to policy recommendations. Both aspects are equally important for Singapore to understand developments in China. Classroom learning is supplemented by cultural activities external to the campus including Chinese calligraphy classes, seal carving, Chinese painting and lion dancing.[9] Within this cultural approach to Chinese studies, there is an indigenous strain known as the *Mahua* cultural movement. The Nanyang (South Seas) regions in Malaysia and Singapore developed their own strain of culture that became known as *Mahua* culture which included literature and other cultural forms. These authors saw an opportunity to publish and write a new genre of Chinese literature arising from the independence of the Federation of Malaya in 1957 which brought about a climate of political freedom.[10] Those who went to Singapore were known as *Xinhua* writers after Singapore became independent in 1965, breaking away from Malaya. *Xinhua* or even Indonesian Chinese literature (*Yinhua*) are all manifestations of the complexities of overseas identities, ideas of nationalities and ethnicities evolving over a long period of time. Discussions about Chinese studies would not be complete without a brief

---

[8] Faculty of Arts and Social Sciences Chinese Studies, "Introduction", 26 March 2014, available at http://www.fas.nus.edu.sg/chs/eng/aboutus/introduction.html> (accessed 28 February 2015).

[9] Faculty of Arts and Social Sciences Chinese Studies, "Introduction", 26 March 2014.

[10] Wan Lei, "Yao Tuo: A First Generation Malaysian Chinese Writer", *Malaysian Journal of Chinese Studies*, 2012, 1: 119-135, available at p. 122, <http://www.newera.edu.my/files/mces/MalaysianJournal/MJ1_p7.pdf> (accessed 3 March 2015).

mention of the extremely important ideas of the leading scholar in this field, historian Wang Gungwu. Jing Tsu and David Der-wei in Wang's introductory chapter to their edited volume argue:

> Historian Wang Gungwu cautions against the conceptual trap of presupposing a single Chinese diaspora, an idea that easily slides into the same register as other historically and politically laden terms: *huaqiao, huayi, haiwai huaren*. Designations of "sojourners," "Chinese descendents," and "overseas Chinese," respectively, were invented and privileged at different historical junctures to subsume the diverse phenomenon of diaspora under the dominant imaginary of the Chinese nation.[11]

Wang is credited with pioneering overseas Chinese studies with his seminal work on the Nanhai trade. This by itself is a sub-genre of both diasporic studies as well as a topic related to the study of China. However, it is his work on contemporary China, which he has at times confessed to be his first preference when it comes to academic pursuits, that has defined the intellectual character of EAI. It is also his academic standing and credential as the top administrator in the University of Hong Kong (HKU) that gave him the authority, legitimacy and network to invite other top scholars to EAI either as visitors or longstanding research fellows.

Wang's approach to observing China arises from an academically distant vantage point as an overseas Chinese, born and raised in Southeast Asia and educated in Singapore and the West, and then resided and worked in Hong Kong which is sufficiently proximate to mainland China. This is how the Minister of Education Heng Swee Keat described Wang Gungwu's multicultural and bilingual credentials:

> He was born in Indonesia and grew up in Malaysia and Singapore, and later moved to Hong Kong. Professor Wang has a deep understanding of Chinese history and culture. And when he analyses issues pertaining to China, he would include Western and Southeast Asian perspectives. His knowledge is therefore deeper as well as broader than many historians.[12]

---

[11] Tsu Jing and David Der-wei Wang, "Introduction: Global Chinese Literature", in *Global Chinese Literature Critical Essays*, ed. by Tsu Jing and David Der-wei Wang, The Netherlands, Brill, 2010, pp. 1–2.

[12] Promote Mandarin Council National Heritage Board, *A Mandarin Anchor in a Changing World*, p. 29.

Besides the cosmopolitan outlook and rich intellectual insights arising from it, Wang embodied the historical narrative himself, having witnessed or gone through milestone events that shaped China and the East Asian region, including but not exclusive to the Pacific War, the postwar period, decolonisation era, independence of Malaya and Singapore, China's monumental economic reforms, paramount leader Deng Xiaoping's *Nanxun* tour, handover of Hong Kong to China and the rise of China.

Wang's academic contribution was to centripetally pull Chinese diasporic studies from the fringes of studies on Chinese societies outside China to a more proximate relationship with contemporary China studies. Topics such as premodern overseas Chinese migration, contemporary motivations for migration and the reception of migrants by host societies are elegantly weaved into the tapestry of a larger Chinese studies fabric.

Wang's sophisticated conceptualisations of *huagong, huaren* and *huaqiao* in describing different categories of ethnic Chinese people have almost become Linnean-like in studying overseas Chinese. His core debate of the terms 'overseas Chinese' and 'Chinese overseas' have also become key concepts in defining identities of ethnic Chinese in all parts of the world, including what is known as 'Greater China'. Wang uses this powerful knowledge and system of epistemology to contribute to his core interest of studying mainland China itself, navigating issues of binding ties, hometown identification and sojourning experiences, and then applying them to define the Chinese self-identity and contemporary developments from the periphery and from a historical standpoint.

Chinese Studies. Other than historical and diasporic studies, the discipline of Chinese Studies is probably the most dedicated subject in learning about Chinese language and culture. According to a powerpoint presentation at the Department of Chinese Studies, the research activities of the department included (i) conducting regular meetings between teachers and students, research meetings, presentations, report on fieldwork, etc; (ii) hosting of foreign visiting scholars who have come to Singapore to conduct interviews, carry out fieldwork and collect information and facilitate the reporting of their fieldwork findings thereafter; (iii) working with local educational and civil groups to co-organise academic activities; and (iv) organising international academic conferences.[13]

---

[13] Department of Chinese Studies Faculty of Arts and Social Sciences, "Department of Chinese Studies Faculty of Arts and Social Sciences National University of Singapore", undated, available at <http://www.slideserve.com/ruth-johnston/department-of-chinese-studies-faculty-of-arts-social-sciences> (accessed 2 March 2015).

The department is divided into four clusters: 'The Chinese in Southeast Asia' cluster that researches on Southeast Asian Chinese society, history, literature, Chinese language, dialects, religions and beliefs, dialect groups and biographies; the 'Chinese Linguistics' cluster looks at linguistics; the 'Ming-Qing' cluster takes care of Ming-Qing period history and culture; the 'Print Culture and Popular Culture' cluster covers print media, newspapers in public spaces, cinema and cinematic culture, audio media, education and cultural dissemination, cultural productions, models of cultural consumption, trans-regional dissemination and inter-exchanges of cultural products and thoughts; and finally the 'Chinese Religions' cluster which concentrates on research related to the promotion of Chinese religions by China's research institutions (including Buddhism, Taoism, religions circulating amongst its population and the religious factions that have existed since pre-modern times).[14]

In November 2014, a fluent Mandarin speaker American Kenneth Dean broke new ground when he left McGill University to become the first non-Chinese Caucasian head of the Department of Chinese Studies at the National University of Singapore.[15] An expert on Chinese religions and temples who grew up in Taiwan where he first acquired the Hokkien dialect, he publicly professed his admiration for Singapore's efforts to preserve religious artefacts despite its modernisation drive.[16] Dean reflected an important development in this field, a global trend:

> "Chinese studies has become a more international field. Many foreigners have had big achievements in the past, so it's a field that's not limited by boundaries," he said.[17]

Dean expressed the important point that Chinese studies is no longer within the purview of ethnic Chinese but has become an academic field in which all stakeholders, irrespective of ethnicity, can participate and make contributions. Just as Wang, Wong and Zheng had contributed to contemporary China studies in Singapore as ethnic Chinese or mainland-born Chinese, Dean as an American was equally competent in teaching Chinese studies to Singaporean students,

---

[14] Department of Chinese Studies Faculty of Arts and Social Sciences, "Department of Chinese Studies Faculty of Arts and Social Sciences National University of Singapore".

[15] MyPaper, "Caucasian bags role as NUS Chinese Studies head", 3 November 2014, available at <http://mypaper.sg/top-stories/caucasian-bags-role-nus-chinese-studies-head-20141103> (accessed 28 February 2015).

[16] MyPaper, "Caucasian bags role as NUS Chinese Studies head".

[17] MyPaper, "Caucasian bags role as NUS Chinese Studies head".

having acquired the knowledge, academic qualifications and even understand Chinese cultural nuances from his stay in Taiwan.

Nanyang Technological University (NTU) courses. Outside of the comprehensive Chinese studies department at the NUS is the case of Nanyang Technological University (NTU); some of its faculty leaders also created courses related to the Chinese language and Chinese studies for special needs. For example, Cham Tao Soon's (former president of NTU) autobiographical account (a new 2014 book at the time of this writing) revealed that Eddie Kuo who became the dean of NTU's mass communications department was keen to include Chinese language journalism courses in his department to boost a shrinking group of individuals arising from the 'decline of Chinese-language standards'.[18] According to the same biographical account, NTU also had a scholarly exchange arrangement with China whereby the Chinese state dispatched students to NTU's Master of Science in Managerial Economics (conducted in Chinese) paid for by Singapore and Singapore in turn would send scholars to China funded by the Chinese state.[19]

The Polytechnics. Aside from the varsities, an important institution in Singapore's higher education sector is the polytechnics. Ngee Ann Polytechnic, one of the first few polytechnics founded in Singapore, will be briefly discussed here. The polytechnic's programme website advertising slogan reads:

> Intrigued by all things Chinese? Why not take it further and inspire a love for Chinese language and culture in the next generation? That's where our Diploma in Chinese Studies (CHS), the first and only such course offered at the polytechnic level, can come in to help![20]

This slogan is useful for understanding the significance of Chinese studies. First, the phrase 'all things Chinese' refers to the study of all aspects of China including not only the classics, cultural and linguistic subjects, but also its civilisation and thoughts as well, which are the conventional humanities-based understanding of Chinese studies beyond a social scientific approach to contemporary China studies. Second, the idea of 'a love for Chinese language and culture' is mentioned and this corresponds with the linguistic and cultural core of Sinology discussed in the introductory section of this chapter.

---

[18] Cham Tao Soon, "The Making of NTU — My Story", Singapore, Straits Times Press, 2014, p. 98.
[19] Cham Tao Soon, "The Making of NTU — My Story", pp. 114–115.
[20] Ngee Ann Polytechnic, "Diploma in Chinese Studies (N70)", 15 January 2015, available at <http://www.np.edu.sg/hms/courses/CHS/Pages/chs_en.aspx> (accessed 28 February 2015).

The polytechnic system which is designed to provide practical hands-on learning experiences and skills for its students offers Chinese studies for career enhancement methodology. To acquire cultural nuances and absorbing knowledge in its primary language, the Chinese studies department in Ngee Ann Polytechnic even teaches 70% of its courses in Chinese (Mandarin).[21]

Initiatives to teach the Chinese (Mandarin) language. Discussion on Chinese studies or studies about China would not be complete without a brief introduction of recent training programmes in this area. Recent initiatives of training centres continue to indicate that Lee and his successors did not relent on efforts to augment Mandarin use in Singapore. In the first decade of the 21st century, the Singapore Centre for Chinese Language was ceremoniously opened by then Minister Mentor Lee Kuan Yew on 17 November 2009 to teach Chinese as a second language subject to individuals who may not have been exposed to the language in their homes. The objective is to promote Chinese culture as well, training more than 2,500 Chinese teachers in this aspect from 2009 to February 2015.[22]

Training the teachers was an important assignment because the teachers in Singapore were in turn tasked to teach their students Chinese language and culture. Amongst the schools involved, the most important institution was probably the Nanyang Girls' High School. A glimpse of the training pro-gramme that Nanyang Girls' High School utilised can also be found in the latest publication by the Promote Mandarin Council at the point of writing:

> In its teaching the school emphasizes on listening, speaking, reading and writing as well as critical thinking. For instance, the teacher might present a Chinese newspaper article and ask the students how they would perceive the article from different points of view.[23]

This quotation from the publication is a valuable glimpse of how Singapore's top high schools in terms of Chinese language and culture teaching impart its knowledge to students who are probably at the front line of pre-tertiary Chinese studies or Chinese-related education. Besides Nanyang Girls' High School,

---

[21] Ngee Ann Polytechnic, "Diploma in Chinese Studies (N70)".

[22] Singapore Centre for Chinese Language (SCCL) Nanyang Technological University, "About SCCL", undated, available at <http://en.sccl.sg/cos/o.x?c=/wbn/pagetree&func=view&rid=70604> (accessed 28 February 2015).

[23] Promote Mandarin Council National Heritage Board, *A Mandarin Anchor in a Changing World*, Singapore, Focus Publishing Limited of the Singapore Press Holdings, 2014, p. 80.

Singapore's Ministry of Education also instituted important plans for another top-ranking high school in Singapore:

> Hwa Chong Institution has set up a satellite campus in Beijing. We want our students to go to China, Taiwan and Hong Kong for immersion. We also have special learning camps for Chinese language and culture, and these are all very good activities.[24]

At Nanyang Girls' High School and Hwa Chong Institution, Singaporean students have the opportunity to pick up Chinese studies, Chinese language and Chinese cultural subjects at a comparatively advanced level. The two institutions aim to create a core group of students who are well-versed in Chinese studies/language subjects, grounded in Singapore, have a strong Singaporean identity but forming a bridge with China through either exposure to expatriate teachers from China, or have participated in immersion programmes to China.

Other than the combined approach by the state's pre-tertiary schools and varsities in training Chinese language teachers, trade federations that deal with businesses in China or with China such as the Singapore Chinese Chamber Institute of Business (SCCIOB) also founded educational entities like its language studies centre to promote language and cultural courses. The SCCIOB has been performing this function since the 1990s, catering to individual language students at various levels of fluency and providing professional training for translation, teaching and presentation skills.[25] While these specialised centres are for professionals and teachers, Singapore's approach towards language acquisition is comprehensive with the Promote Mandarin Council involving community leaders and parents in the process to encourage youngsters in the practical and frequent use of the language from an early age.[26] Of note is the fact that Mandarin acquisition not only enables Singaporeans to partake in the discussions of cosmopolitan ideas about Chinese studies and contemporary

---

[24] Promote Mandarin Council National Heritage Board, *A Mandarin Anchor in a Changing World*, p. 120.

[25] Singapore Chinese Chamber Institute of Business, "Language Studies Centre", 2012, available at <http://www.scciob.edu.sg/index.cfm?GPID=436> (accessed 28 February 2015).

[26] Promote Mandarin Council National Heritage Board, *A Mandarin Anchor in a Changing World*, p. 6.

China with other foreigners and native Chinese speakers, but also serves a domestic social function. This is well-articulated by the Minister for Culture, Community and Youth Lawrence Wong:

> Our language reflects our belief systems, our thoughts and the spirit of our community. Understanding its nuances and cultural connotations allows us to express ourselves, identify with one another, and build emotion connections with one another.[27]

A popular understanding of Chinese studies thus serves the dual function of interacting with native Chinese speakers and foreigners who speak Chinese as well as facilitating social mobilisation of the local community. Chinese studies, Chinese language acquisition and understanding Chinese culture are therefore intertwined in both external and domestic community-building aspects.

Concluding remarks

Chinese studies in a broader general sense therefore serves the dual purpose of domestic retention of what has been described as a cultural 'ballast' by Singapore's founding father Lee Kuan Yew and an external outreach to China and Chinese-speaking foreigners outside Singapore. The foresight of Lee Kuan Yew and Goh Keng Swee correctly anticipated the rise of China today. Due to their initiatives, Singapore today has built up a viable intellectual and scholarly base for modern and contemporary Chinese studies, which is not traditionally and culturally oriented, but social science-based and therefore relevant and useful to interpreting China as a potential global power. Singapore's comparative advantage is reflected in the scholarly and research activities in EAI which has emerged as a foremost centre for China watching in the region and one that is well-recognised by China and in the West. In fact, 'Chinese studies' in concrete terms at EAI and in Singapore in general is evidenced by the institute's numerous published edited volumes and monographs as well as over 1,000 *Background Briefs* and reports on China. That is in essence a manifestation of contemporary Chinese studies in Singapore.

---

[27] Promote Mandarin Council National Heritage Board, *A Mandarin Anchor in a Changing World*, p. 7.

Index

www.ingramcontent.com/pod-product-compliance
Lightning Source LLC
Chambersburg PA
CBHW080643270326
41928CB00017B/3173